D1188920

AMERICA'S FILM LEGACY, 2009-2010

AMERICA'S FILM LEGACY, 2009-2010

A VIEWER'S GUIDE TO THE 50 LANDMARK
MOVIES ADDED TO THE NATIONAL FILM
REGISTRY IN 2009/2010

BY DANIEL EAGAN

continuum

The Continuum International Publishing Group
80 Maiden Lane, New York, NY 10038
The Tower Building, 11 York Road, London SE1 7NX

www.continuumbooks.com

© Daniel Eagan, 2012

All rights reserved. No part of this book may be reproduced, stored in a retrieval
system, or transmitted, in any form or by any means, electronic, mechanical,
photocopying, recording, or otherwise, without the written permission of the
publishers.

Library of Congress Cataloging-in-Publication Data
A catalog record for this book is available from the Library of Congress.

ISBN: PB: 978-1-4411-5869-7

Typeset by Fakenham Prepress Solutions, Fakenham, Norfolk NR21 8NN
Printed and bound in the United States of America

City of London Libraries	
AA	
CL 1203766 4	
Askews & Holts	Jan-2012
791.430973 EAG	£11.99

Contents

Introduction to the 2009–2010 edition

Each December twenty-five films are added to the National Film Registry, which was established by Congress to preserve the significant films in our motion picture history. The first five hundred films are covered in an earlier edition of *America's Film Legacy*. This volume includes entries from 2009 and 2010.

As did the previous edition, this book gives a general description of each film, along with relevant credits and awards. I am not trying to tell you what to think about the films, but to place them in context—show how they may have been inspired by earlier films, how they compare to other movies of their time, and how they may have affected movies to come. To that end I avoid when possible explaining plot lines or revealing surprises. My goal is to make you want to see the films themselves, either by discussing who made them and how, or by showing how they relate to other movies and to our culture at large.

On the other hand, this book is not going to hand-hold you through the process of why one film and not another was selected to the Registry. You can assume that simply by being on the Registry, a film has reached a certain level of recognition. If you feel strongly enough about a film that has not been recognized, please consider nominating it to the Registry yourself. You can do so at http://www.loc.gov/film/vote.html.

This edition includes a limited index of titles and filmmakers. We received many complaints about the lack of an index in the previous volume. However, a comprehensive index for five hundred titles would have contained thousands of entries. For the first edition, we felt that an alphabetical list of titles would function in the place of an index. With only fifty titles in this volume, the size of the index is not as critical.

In the five years since I first began working on this project, I have been struck by unexpected developments in the film industry. The collapse of the DVD market has made it more difficult to find and see specific older movies. Film buffs are at the mercy of studios that may or may not be interested in making obscure films available. The surviving big-box electronic stores no longer carry as large a selection of movies. Blu-Ray releases, an expensive alternative to DVDs, have not yet developed a rich library of back titles. That library may never come about due to the growing market for streaming video.

Paradoxically, while films have become available through more avenues of distribution, it has become much more difficult to actually view film.

Consumers have clearly chosen the convenience of watching movies at home, on television screens, computers, and other digital viewing devices. By doing so they sacrifice the most seductive aspects of film. Watching a movie on a television screen, you are essentially in control of the content. You can start, pause, rewind, and stop whenever you want. In fact, you never have to watch your DVD at all.

In a theater you surrender to film. Its images are larger than life, and they do not stop if you want to make a phone call or tie a shoelace. With silent film, you don't even have the luxury of dialogue to tide you over while fumbling with your popcorn or soda—you have to keep watching, keep concentrating, forgo control and let the film manipulate your emotions. When I first went to repertory theaters, I would watch movies with the fear that they might not ever be available again. I burned them into my memory, afraid to miss any details. It's hard to work up the same feeling for a stack of DVDs piled next to a TV.

Even within the community of movie archivists and historians, film is becoming an expensive luxury. Restrictions have been placed on viewing 35mm prints at the Library of Congress Motion Picture & Television Reading Room. A new generation of artists has turned to digital media, which is undeniably cheaper and easier to use than film. "Filmmakers! How will you survive the new century?" asked Helen Hill, the animator of the Registry title *Scratch and Crow*. It is an increasingly relevant question.

By watching the titles in the National Film Registry, we can learn once again of the power and beauty of film, and how important it is that we preserve it.

Introduction to the Original Edition

Developed in the late 1880s, motion pictures evolved from a sideshow novelty to the twentieth century's dominant art form. Today they still wield an overwhelming influence over both high and low culture. Identifying the most significant movies among the thousands of features, shorts, cartoons, experimental, and institutional titles was one of the reasons behind the National Film Registry. Established in 1988, the Registry singles out twenty-five movies a year; its total is now up to five hundred.

To gain an understanding of film, you could take a course in school, read histories, or consult other lists, perhaps Academy Award Best Picture winners, or any one of a number of AFI 100 Greatest compilations. But if you only paid attention to awards, you might never find out about *The House in the Middle*, or *Sky High*, or the Marx Brothers or Fred Astaire. And many lists are weighted toward recent releases from major studios. The National Film Registry acts as a corrective to commercially driven surveys. It includes independent, experimental, and animated films, the movies that helped establish the medium and then turned it into art. The Registry has no commercial ties, no angles to exploit, no axes to grind. It's compiled by filmmakers and historians, but also by the public. It is the definitive list of the American movies you need to know, whether blockbusters or flops, those made with hundred-million-dollar budgets or filmed in somebody's kitchen.

Why start another list? Because the movies that have been such an important part of our lives turned out to be a lot more fragile than anyone thought they would be.

One reason for that fragility is film itself. Film used to be made of celluloid, a synthetic material invented in 1868. When treated with camphor and nitric and sulfuric acids, the cellulose from cotton turned into a lightweight, flexible plastic that could fill in as a replacement for ivory and tortoiseshell. Celluloid became shirt collars, piano keys, Christmas ornaments, and, in 1889, chemists started to use it as a backing for photographic emulsion.

Transparent, strong even when thin, celluloid is an excellent medium for holding emulsion, a layer of silver oxide about .001 inch thick that contains the photographic record. Unfortunately, celluloid is also volatile. It's brittle when dry, moldy when wet. It burns, explosively in the case of nitrate, but dramatically enough even when safety stock. And if it doesn't catch fire, it will break down to its original elements. It mildews, rots, and given the chance reverts to a toxic pile of powdery ash or a bubbling, vinegary goo.

That's not all. Film tears. It rips. It scratches, folds, and creases. It stretches and shrinks, warps and flattens. Its sprocket holes enlarge, pull apart, and eventually shred. The emulsion flakes, chips, and peels. Then it fades away entirely.

Film is bulky and expensive to keep. It's stored on shelves, in file cabinets, under beds, in attics and garages, in bank vaults and self-storage centers and under ice-skating rinks. It's even more expensive to project than to store. And before, during, and after it's wound through projectors, film gets snipped, hole-punched, chopped, scraped, spliced, and yanked through rewinders.

Film is cut, censored, stolen, lost at sea, lost in the mail, lost off trucks, even lost in projection booths. It's bombed to oblivion during wars, burned in great smoking piles by studios, looted and hidden by collectors. It's banned from exhibition, withdrawn from circulation, used as fill by editors, melted for its silver.

The result? Half of all films made before 1950 are presumed lost. Up to 80 percent of all silent features no longer exist. Many of the films that do survive from the silent and early sound eras are in unstable condition, and could easily be considered lost as well.

Only a few years ago, many filmmakers doubted that our country's most important movies would survive the millennium. Even as markets for movies, both old and new, mushroomed in the late 1980s, it became increasingly apparent to film scholars and archivists that our film heritage was in dire condition.

In its early days, film was considered as disposable as newspapers. Producers would process prints until negatives wore out, and then simply shoot their movie over again. When sound arrived, some studios discarded their libraries of silent films. Storage reels were mislabeled or lost. Originals were mistakenly discarded as duplicates. Studios dissolved or went bankrupt, with the rights of film libraries lost in a haze of lawsuits. Copyrights were mishandled, and films fell into the public domain, with poor quality bootlegs flooding the market. Many executives simply couldn't foresee the economic windfall that video outlets and cable channels would bring, and allowed their B-movies, shorts, and newsreels to decay.

Paradoxically, advances in technologies—new film formats, computer special effects, digital sound—have made it even more difficult to preserve films. Every new technology threatens an older one. Once popular color and sound processes, widescreen formats, 3–D films, and even video formats have been made obsolete, or are becoming so.

Today, movies aren't just cans on shelves anymore. They are made up of many elements: stereo soundtracks, camera negatives, mattes, computer programs, and more. Preservationists as well as engineers trying to transfer movies to video are stymied by missing elements. Soundtracks are gone, reference negatives have faded or shrunk, and often the only prints that still exist have been cut. Right now it's almost impossible to reassemble the materials needed to reproduce the special effects in recent science fiction films. Some directors don't even know where the elements to their films are.

Preservationists have to deal with issues beyond the mere survival of films. They have to protect the actual content and structure of movies from commercial interests. In the 1980s, these included colorizing black-and-white films and cropping wide-screen films. Even classics could be edited to fit television time slots, or onto videocassettes. And films that seemed to have no commercial value could disappear from simple neglect.

In the 1980s, angry filmmakers denounced studios that refused to protect their works, or else diluted their power through colorization, panning and scanning, and editing. Industry icons John Huston, Frank Capra, and James Stewart joined contemporary filmmakers like Martin Scorsese and Sydney Pollack in lobbying Congress for a film preservation bill. In hearings before legislators, they pointed out how films as important as *It's a Wonderful Life* and *Citizen Kane* were in danger of being ruined.

In an effort to stop colorization, in particular, Representatives Robert J. Mrazek (D-NY) and Sidney Yates (D-Ill) introduced the National Film Preservation Act in 1988. The bill authorized the Library of Congress to select twenty-five American films each year that were "culturally, historically, or esthetically significant." The Library of Congress holds an archival print of each film selected; furthermore, the films must be labeled if they are altered from their original formats. Part publicity stunt, part a genuine effort to shape the direction of preservation, the list is updated annually, with new additions announced each December.

Anyone can nominate a film, by mail or on the Internet, but the actual selections are made by members of the National Film Preservation Board. To be nominated, a film must be at least ten years old. Details about the legislative history of the Registry can be found at http://www.loc.gov/film/filmabou. html. You can vote for specific titles by e-mail by checking http://www.loc. gov/film/vote.html.

Unlike lists compiled by magazines or organizations, the National Film Registry has no agenda other than quality. And the titles don't depend on individual fads or whims. These are the most important, and in many cases the best films ever made in this country. They cover the gamut of motion picture styles: actualities from the nineteenth century, documentaries, travelogues, propaganda films, cartoons, experimental shorts, and every type of feature film imaginable, from Oscar-winning Hollywood epics to obscure independent pieces.

Viewing these films has given me the chance to see remarkable artists like Duke Ellington and Lydia Mendoza performing in their prime. It has brought historical events like the Tacoma Narrows Bridge collapse and the Hindenburg disaster to life. The films form a record of wars, labor struggles, generational conflicts, and crime, but also of romance, humor, and inspiration. Themes and patterns emerge over the years. Farmers fare poorly, seduced by city sirens, ruined by fires, floods and drought, run off the land by financiers, attacked by Indians, crooks, and soldiers. Miners have it worse: jailed for complaining about wages, drowned in cave-ins and floods, bludgeoned to death and shot in the back by police. Strikes, marches, and demonstrations occur repeatedly, even in a musical like *Swing Time*.

The Registry films cover the extremes of human existence, from chain gangs and concentration camps to parties and honeymoons. Suicide is the driving force in a half-dozen titles. Executions are common as well, in both comedies and dramas. On the other hand, meals, kisses, and weddings are too numerous to count. Several films focus on children, and three feature childbirth. "Three" defines one of the many coincidences and convergences in the Registry. Three films have "duck" in the title. There are three "nights," three "wilds," three "littles." Three deal with the Gullah dialect, and three end with nuclear explosions.

While many titles in the National Film Registry are indisputable classics, some will be obscure to most filmgoers. Only a dozen have come out since 1990; more than twice that number were released before 1916. No print or online movie guide contains entries for all of the National Film Registry titles. Yet they form the history of movies in the United States. *America's Film Legacy* is your opportunity to learn why these films are judged to be among our country's most important works of art.

Acknowledgments

In addition to all those who helped with the original volume, I have several more filmmakers, archivists, curators, and historians to thank. I apologize if I have omitted anyone. Charles Silver at the Museum of Modern Art helped me screen many of the Registry titles, and provided access to the museum's extensive files. Mike Mashon, head of the Library of Congress Moving Image Section at the Packard Campus for Audio Visual Conservation in Culpeper, made several prints available. Josie L. Walters-Johnson at the Library of Congress arranged access to the Library of Congress Motion Picture & Television Reading Room. Gary Palmucci and Rodrigo Brandão at Kino International provided help with several titles, as did Brian Carmody and Brett Sharlow at Criterion. Dennis Doros at Milestone Film & Video supplied prints, photographs, and background materials. Author and editor Kevin Lally supplied titles and helped rearrange my assignments at *Film Journal International*. Bruce Goldstein, head of repertory at New York City's Film Forum, scheduled several Registry titles. Ivan Zimmerman offered legal advice. Rob Potter again copy edited my text, correcting my many mistakes and adding valuable insights into the works of several filmmakers. Joshua Kurp provided proofreading help. Ursula Jaroszewicz and Sarah Farmer-Castiglioni improved the quality of the frame enlargements. I have also relied on the research, expertise, and advice of Annette Melville and Ihsan Amanatullah of the National Film Preservation Board, Dwight Swanson of the Center for Home Movies, Dan Streible at NYU's Department of Cinema Studies, Andrew Lambert at the Anthology Film Archives, and the many authors and historians whose work I have shamelessly pilfered.

I'd like to thank the following for help with specific titles: *A Trip Down Market Street*: Rick Prelinger. *Preservation of the Sign Language*: Michael J. Olson, Archives Preservation Specialist, Gallaudet University; Patti Durr. *The Front Page*: Bruce Goldstein. *A Study in Reds*: Dorinda Hartmann, Assistant Archivist, Film and Photo Archive, Wisconsin Historical Society; Andy Kraushaar, Virginia Corvid. *The Cry of Jazz*: Edward Bland, Andrew Lambert. *I Am Joaquin*: Carmen Bautista. *The Jungle*: Harold Haskins, Jay Schwartz. *Hot Dogs for Gauguin*: Dan Streible, NYU Department of Cinema Studies. *Quasi at the Quackadero*: Sally Kruikshank. *The Red Book*: Janie Geiser. *Scratch and Crow*: Paul Gailiunas. *Study of a River*: Peter Hutton.

Finally, David Barker, Katie Gallof and the staff at Continuum displayed patience and guidance throughout the writing and editing process. My wife Melissa continues to provide more support than anyone could hope for.

How to Read the Entries

Individual film entries are listed in roughly chronological order, in part to avoid repeating facts about film techniques or biographical details about filmmakers. For each film I've tried to include all the pertinent information about how and when it was made. Each entry is structured as follows:

Title: In most cases, this is the title of the film as it appears on screen. Early movies did not have official titles. *Dickson Experimental Sound Film* (1894) was supplied later by historians, for example. Some films have more than one title. *The John C. Rice–May Irwin Kiss* (1896) is also known as *The Kiss, The May Irwin Kiss, The Picture of a Kiss,* and *Kiss Scene.* Where confusion may arise, I've listed alternate titles in the alphabetical index of titles.

The distributor, listed after the title, refers to the person or company responsible for getting a film into theaters. Most National Film Registry entries were distributed by the so-called major studios: Columbia, MGM, Paramount, RKO, Twentieth Century-Fox, Warner Brothers, Universal. Note that some distributors, like Edison and Thanhouser, are no longer in business. Distributors are distinct from production companies, which financed the filming process, although some shared duties. For some independent and experimental movies, especially those not released theatrically, the filmmaker is listed as the distributor.

Release date: Generally this is the earliest date a film was shown in theaters, although there are many exceptions. Some films were made in separate parts over several years, like the *Why We Fight* (1943–45) series. In these cases, the films are listed after the last portion was completed—1945, not 1943, for *Why We Fight.* Films that were not released theatrically, like *Marian Anderson: The Lincoln Memorial Concert* (1939), are usually listed by the year they were made.

Silent/Sound and **Color/B&W** are self-evident. I've noted silent films with musical scores only when the scores were recorded at the same time, such as *Sunrise* (1927).

Aspect ratio describes the shape of the frame. Early movies had widely varying aspect ratios, but by the turn of the twentieth century, 1.33 to

1 was the industry standard. This is roughly equivalent to the shape of pre-flat-panel television screens. When sound was introduced, the ratio was adjusted slightly to 1.37 to accommodate the soundtrack. With some exceptions this standard lasted until the 1950s, when widescreen processes became prevalent. Widescreen aspect ratios varied from 1.66 to 2.35, with 1.85—similar to a widescreen TV—the dominant choice in the last two decades.

Some films, like *Shane* (1953), were photographed in one format and projected in another. In these cases I've tried to list the filmmaker's preferred format.

Running time: basically how long it takes to project a film. Early films were sold by the foot, and until the 1920s running times were measured in lengths: actual feet at first, later by reels. A reel could hold 1,000 feet of film; two reels referred to a short that for convenience's sake I will estimate at about twenty minutes long.

But these films were photographed by hand-cranked cameras and exhibited by hand-cranked projectors. Both steps could either speed up or slow down a film's running time. The introduction of electric cameras and sound equipment standardized filmmaking speeds at 24 fps (frames per second). In many cases it's unclear what fps was for earlier films; estimates range from 14 to 20 fps.

Furthermore, many films exist only in battered, cut prints, minus intertitles, individual shots, and sometimes entire scenes. Determining a precise running time for some films is an impossible task, so the timings listed in this book should be treated as estimates.

MPAA ratings have been assigned by the Motion Picture Association of America (MPAA) since 1968. Originally these comprised G, M, R, and X; currently, they are G, PG, PG-13, R, and NC-17. Some films released prior to the implementation of the MPAA system were rated later; these are indicated under "Additional Credits." Explanations for ratings can be found at http://www.filmratings.com/.

Cast includes the performers who received screen credit, with the names of the characters they played in parentheses. Alternate names are included in brackets. Early films did not list actors; I've included those who could be verified under either "Cast" or "Additional Cast."

Credits are usually listed in this order: director, writer, producer, director of photography, production designer, music, sound, costume, make-up, casting. Credits have changed over the years: yesterday's art director is today's production designer, for example.

Additional cast: Many performers did not receive screen credit. Their names can be determined through studio payroll files or, in some cases, through visual identification. This category is by no means exhaustive.

Additional credits include personnel who contributed to a film without credit, or who were replaced during the production. It is also an opportunity to list alternate titles, production and release dates, and other pertinent information.

Awards are based on records from the Academy of Motion Picture Arts and Sciences (http://www.oscars.org/awardsdatabase).

Other versions include sequels, prequels, remakes, and other relevant titles. For example, *The Big T.N.T. Show* (1966) is not officially a sequel to *The T.A.M.I. Show* (1964), but is listed because it followed the same style and format and was made by many of the same filmmakers. For the most part I do not include foreign-language remakes, or films that include generic characters. It would be pointless to list every vampire movie under *Dracula* (1931), for example.

Availability: One of the goals of the National Film Registry legislation is to store an archival copy of each title at the Library of Congress. Technically, every film can be screened there. On a more practical level, a number of Registry films can be seen in libraries, museums, and archives across the country. Most are available for the home market as well. When possible, I've listed the distributor, release date, and ISBN and UPC numbers, and, if applicable, websites for these titles. I have not included older home-market formats like 8mm, or newer ones like Blu-Ray. An increasing number of films can be viewed online, through the Library of Congress American Memory site (http://www.loc.gov/rr/mopic/ndlmps.html), the Internet Archive (www.archive.org), and other sites.

List of 2009–2010 Selections in Chronological Order

List of 2009–2010 Selections in Alphabetical Order

Newark Athlete

A frame from one of the earliest extant films.

Thomas Edison, 1891. Silent, B&W, 1.33. 19mm. 1 second fragment.

Credits: Filmmakers: W.K.L. Dickson, William Heise.

Additional credits: Title supplied later. Also known as *Club Swinger, no. 1*; *Indian club swinger*; *Newark Athlete (with Indian Clubs)*. Filmed in May or June, 1891.

Other versions: Gordon Hendricks, author of *The Edison Motion Picture Myth*, prepared a twelve-second copy of the film by rephotographing the original frames.

Available: Library of Congress American Memory site, memory.loc.gov

The earliest film on the Registry, *Newark Athlete* marked an important step in the evolution of Thomas Edison's idea for a Kinetoscope "Moving View," which he wrote down in October, 1888. With laboratories in Menlo Park, New Jersey, and then in West Orange, Edison developed several lines of business based on his inventions. He also cultivated a public persona as an inventor, earning sobriquets like "the Wizard of West Orange."

By 1888, Edison, who received his first patent in 1869, had already developed a cylinder phonograph, the first practical means of recording sound. He had improved telegraph transmissions, developed the light bulb, and had opened the first electric power plant in New York City. The Kinetoscope

1

would draw from his previous inventions and also from the work of several other innovators.

Many nineteenth-century toys operated on the principle that under proper conditions we see sequential images as a single moving image. These conditions include displaying the images at an adequate speed (usually more than ten per second) and using some form of shutter system to prevent them from blurring together. The thaumatrope, the phenakistoscope, the strobo-scope, and the zoetrope are just some of the examples that had been popular since the 1830s.

Edison had met with Eadweard Muybridge and had seen the photog-rapher's "zoopraxiscope," essentially a version of a phenakistoscope, but one which projected images painted onto glass disks through a lens. Edison thought he could combine the results of a zoopraxiscope with those from his phonograph, perhaps by arranging small photographs on a cylinder and then viewing them through a lens. He assigned his assistant, William Kennedy Laurie Dickson, and Charles A. Brown to the project.

Dickson and Brown did not make much progress until Edison returned from a European trip during which he met French inventor Etienne-Jules Marey, who was also working on a motion picture machine. Marey placed images, or photographs, on a strip of film which was then pulled in front of a lens—more like a ticker tape machine than a phonograph. Edison hired William Heise, who had experience with similar machines, to assist Dickson. They built a horizontal-feed camera that exposed images on a 3/4–inch film strip. Small perforations helped move the film through the mechanism.

The first examples were viewed through a peephole device Edison would market as the "Kinetoscope." Edison showed what later became known as *Dickson Greeting* to members of the Federation of Women's Club on May 20, 1891. In the film, Dickson smiled and bowed. As reported in *Phonogram* magazine: "Every motion was perfect, without a hitch or a jerk."

Several films were made at the time, including one of lab worker James Duncan smoking a pipe and another of various athletes from the Newark area. These were filmed in a building Dickson had commissioned in 1889 for photographic experiments.

Newark Athlete, also *Club Swinger no. 1* and *Indian Club Swinger*, exists in two fragments. The first version shows a youth holding two clubs which he starts to swing to his left. The shot lasts for one second, or about 30 frames. A second fragment loops, or repeats, this image six more times.

In *The Emergence of Cinema*, film historian Charles Musser points out several important features about these experiments. First, Dickson filmed his subjects against a black background, which made them easy to see. Second, he framed them differently, sometimes using full-body shots, sometimes moving in for close-ups. As Musser put it, "Variety in camera framing and the focal plane were assumed from the outset." Third, Dickson seemed to be drawing from Muybridge for his subject matter.

Just as it had been for Muybridge's zoopraxiscope, photographing athletes—in this case someone exercising with clubs, later muscleman Eugen Sandow posing, and soon boxers re-enacting matches—was a natural fit for the new process. Athletes moved, which is what suited the medium best. Films of a lab worker smoking a pipe, or Dickson shaking hands with Heise, offered little that couldn't be accomplished with still photography.

Sports in fact would drive motion pictures, make them economically viable, teach an audience to value them. The same would happen when television and then cable were introduced to consumers. Sports and athletes were big reasons why viewers purchased television sets, and why networks covered athletic events so diligently.

Edison told reporters how excited he was about the films, which he claimed solved earlier problems in taking photographs fast enough to reproduce smooth motion. "Now I've got it," he said, adding, "That is, I've got the germ or base principle. When you get your base principle right, then it's only a question of time and a matter of details about completing the machine."

On August 24, 1891, Edison filed patents for his motion picture camera (the "Kinetograph") and the Kinetoscope. It would take him several years before he could market a machine for projecting movies.

Dickson, meanwhile, set out to improve the process. One of his first steps was to switch from a horizontal feed to a vertical one. He also replaced film that was three-quarters of an inch wide with stock that was twice as wide, similar to today's standard 35mm. He bought both negative stock for exposing and positive stock to make prints. Dickson also ordered two lenses, including a telescopic lens for shooting distant objects.

Edison planned to introduce his invention to the public at the 1893 World's Columbian Exposition in Chicago. That meant Dickson would have to come up with more product. In December, 1892, he began construction of the Black Maria, the world's first motion picture studio. (For more information about Dickson and the Black Maria, see *Dickson Experimental Sound Film*, 1894.)

A Trip Down Market Street Before the Fire

License plates provided clues to dating *A Trip Down Market Street*. Courtesy Rick Prelinger.

Miles Brothers, 1906. Silent, B&W, 1.33. 35mm. 13 minutes.

Credits: Filmed for Miles Brothers Moving Pictures. Supervised by Earl Miles.

Additional credits: Filmed on April 14, 1906.

Available: Internet Archive, www.archive.org

The film industry in the United States first centered around New York City, with companies like Thomas Edison, Vitagraph, and American Mutoscope located in or around Manhattan. Movies spread as cameramen sought new subjects for travel pictures, as promoters went on tour with packages of films, and then as theaters opened in towns and cities. Production companies followed: William Selig opened Selig Polyscope in Chicago in 1896; Siegmund Lubin, the Lubin Manufacturing Company in Philadelphia in 1902.

In San Francisco, the Cineograph Theatre, one of the first in the country devoted exclusively to movies, opened on Market Street in 1897. The four Miles Brothers—Harry, Herbert, Joseph, Earl[e] C.—became involved in the industry soon after, first by touring with films in Alaska, then opening a storefront theater in Seattle in November, 1901. It cost a dime to watch a program, and according to film historian Charles Musser, the brothers could make as much as $160 a day. However, they had trouble securing enough titles to satisfy customers, who soon abandoned the theater for other entertainment.

The brothers tried making their own films, like *Dog Baiting and Fighting* and *Blasting in Treadwell Gold Mine*, which they sold to American Mutoscope, better known as Biograph, in New York City. They were working out of a New York office in 1903 when they hit upon a new strategy. Production companies like Edison or Biograph generally sold their titles outright to theaters. In December, 1903, Biograph began to switch its moviemaking efforts from "actualities," which is how the industry referred to nonfiction films, to "story" films. To get rid of its backlog of actualities, Biograph sold them on the cheap at eight cents a foot.

The Miles Brothers bought up as many Biograph titles as they could, then headed for San Francisco. Along the way they offered the titles to small-town theater-owners on an exchange, or rental, basis. Renting instead of selling films quickly became the industry norm.

The brothers retained their office in New York, and marketed their own titles through the Miles Brothers Moving Pictures. They also distributed foreign films. In 1906, they decided to concentrate more on making films than distributing them, and built a large, state-of-the-art studio in San Francisco. Years later *The Moving Picture World* was still writing about the all-electric facility that Harry Miles designed.

According to film historian Geoffrey Bell, the Miles Brothers gained a reputation for innovative movies, like *A Trip Down Mt. Tamalpais*, which placed a camera on the front of a train to show Marin County views. For *A Trip Down Market Street*, Harry Miles equipped a camera with a special magazine that could hold a thousand feet of film, enough for roughly ten minutes. Miles had it mounted on the front of a cable car and then filmed, in one continuous take, the entire Market Street run, from 8th Street to the Ferry Building. (The film actually begins at the site of the Miles Brothers studio at 1139 Market Street.)

A Trip Down Market Street was originally made for Hale's Tours and Scenes of the World, an amusement park novelty in which movies were shown in a small theater that was outfitted like a railroad car. George C. Hale, a former fire chief, opened the first in Kansas City in 1905, and soon licensed similar theaters throughout the country. Customers paid a dime to watch movies shot from trains, accompanied by "a slight rocking to the car as it takes the curves" and the occasional "shrill whistle" and "ringing bell," as Hale's promotional materials promised. Soon entrepreneurs were offering Trolley Car Tours or a simulated flight in a hot-air balloon.

For years it was assumed that *A Trip Down Market Street* was filmed in 1904 or 1905; the Library of Congress set the date as September or October of 1905. But David Kiehn, a film historian and archivist at the Niles Essanay Silent Film Museum at Fremont, California, had second thoughts. He checked the five San Francisco newspapers of the time, but could find nothing about the production. He had noticed rain puddles in the film, but weather reports for fall of 1905 spoke of "bone dry" conditions.

From the angle of the sun and construction records, Kiehn dated the film to late March or April, 1906. He confirmed from a license plate that one Jay Anway registered his car in early 1906. Kiehn discovered a Miles Brothers ad for *A Trip Down Market Street* in the April 28th edition of the *New York Clipper*, a trade magazine.

When his research was done, Kiehn had pinpointed the shooting of *A Trip Down Market Street* to April 14, just four days before an earthquake devastated the city. After processing the footage in their lab, the brothers sent a print by train back to their New York office on April 17.

Seen today, *A Trip Down Market Street* is a film of hypnotic beauty and wrenching poignancy. The camerawork is exceptional, pulling viewers in as the cable car moves forward inexorably. Details of the past emerge with startling clarity: stiff-looking clothes, boxy trucks, reckless pedestrians. Some cars seem to circle the block to pull back in front of the camera. Horses seem to outnumber automobiles. The tower of the Ferry Building, at first almost obscured by mist, looms in the frame.

In a matter of days, all would be lost. As Kiehn put it, "It is very possible that the people who are staring right at the camera, and if you look at it, right at you, those people would be gone in just a few days."

The Miles Brothers lost their studio to fire, but still rushed to cover the disaster. A newspaper reporter wrote, "The Miles boys began taking the pictures while the houses were crumbling from the first earthquakes and did not stop until after the fire had swept over the city." However, they had to drop their plans of making story films. Instead, they returned to actualities. They also began to film prizefights with some success. After the death of Harry Miles on January 1, 1908, the company went into a decline.

Little Nemo

The Princess and Little Nemo in Winsor McCay's groundbreaking animation.
Courtesy of Milestone Film & Video.

Vitagraph, 1911. Silent, B&W with hand-coloring, 1.33. 35mm. 11 minutes.
Credits: Supervised by J. Stuart Blackton. Animation by Winsor McCay.
Additional credits: Title on screen: *Winsor McCay, the Famous Cartoonist of the* N.Y. Herald *and His Moving Comics.* Released April 8, 1911.
Available: Milestone Collection DVD *Winsor McCay: The Master Edition* (2003). UPC: 0–14381–1982–2–5.

Winsor McCay was not only the most advanced animator of his time, he was also a canny marketer who knew how to promote himself and his products in newspapers, vaudeville, and on film. (For more about McCay's background, see *Gertie the Dinosaur*, 1914). McCay didn't invent comic strips, but he was the first to realize their full potential, both artistically and economically. He brought the medium to a level that illustrators today are still trying to match. Similarly, McCay wasn't the first to perform a "quick sketch" stage act. In 1894, as part of a vaudeville trio, illustrator and future film director J. Stuart Blackton drew what he called "Lightning Sketches," accompanying them with patter. But it was McCay who developed the idea into a viable touring act, working up a narrative framework that could be inserted into vaudeville programs.

Finally, McCay wasn't the first to use animation in films, but he was the first to show the world the form's artistic and narrative possibilities. In a sense, animation had been an important technique almost since the invention of motion pictures. Stop-motion animation allowed filmmakers to move objects at will. They could replace a live actor with a dummy, for example, in order to simulate a beheading, or pretend that a character had been thrown from a train. They could move furniture, make objects appear or disappear, even transform a toadstool into a chorus girl.

For his stage act, Blackton offered jokes and comments while he drew caricatures on a sketchpad. He performed part of his act in three short pieces filmed for the Edison company in July or August, 1896. The films necessarily had to dispense with his stage patter, reducing his act to the equivalent of a sidewalk portrait artist whose main talent is speed. Still, *Edison Drawn by "World" Artist* (Blackton was a cartoonist at the time for the *New York World* newspaper) became enough of a hit for the artist to bring it to Keith's Union Square Theater, a top vaudeville stage. It was after showing the film that Blackton and his partner Albert E. Smith purchased their own camera and projector—the beginnings of what would evolve into the Vitagraph studio.

French illustrator Emile Cohl used animation somewhat differently. An admirer of the famous caricaturist André Gill, Cohl participated in various art movements, like the "Incoherents," that made fun of traditional art, often transforming it with new, irreverent elements. In *Fantasmagorie*, finished in 1908, Cohl took line drawings based on stick figures and geometric shapes and transformed them from one object to another—from a head to a toy, for example. In his drawings, he could imply depth through the use of perspective, but like Blackton he characteristically worked on one plane. Cohl's drawings were "flat" in the sense that he didn't tried to move them forward or backward in space.

When Cohl and Blackton were making their films, McCay was experimenting with animating objects in a different medium, the comic strip. McCay's first successful strip was *Little Sammy Sneeze*. In this and its follow-up, *Dreams of a Rarebit Fiend*, McCay toyed with sequential action, distorted shapes, and even altered the frame of the panels holding his drawings. *Dreams of a Rarebit Fiend* was so popular that Edwin S. Porter directed a live-action version for Edison in 1906.

McCay's masterpiece was *Little Nemo in Slumberland*, an all-color, full-page strip that debuted in the New York *Herald* on October 15, 1905. In *Nemo* episodes, McCay drew fabulously intricate worlds that bordered on surrealism: buildings that could walk, a cavernous dragon's mouth used as a carriage, people flipped out of proportion as if by fun-house mirrors. The strip featured recurring characters, including Nemo, who dressed like Little Lord Fauntleroy; the Princess; Impie, a politically incorrect jungle savage; Flip, a green-faced, cigar-smoking clown who started out as Nemo's enemy but later became his friend; Dr. Pill; and others.

On top of his work for the *Herald*, McCay began performing a "lightning sketch" act in vaudeville in 1906. (Earning $500 a week, he performed on a bill with W.C. Fields.) In 1907, Klaw & Erlanger announced that they were mounting a musical adaptation of *Little Nemo* on Broadway, with a book by Harry B. Smith and music by Victor Herbert. Little Nemo was played by Gabriel Wiegel, a midget who had previously starred as *Buster Brown*. A critical success but not a financial one when it opened in 1908, the play toured for two years. When McCay was prevented from taking his vaudeville act to London, he left the *Herald* to work for William Randolph Hearst.

At some point in 1909, McCay also began to think about animated films. He later said that he was inspired by his son Robert's flip books, but it's probable he had seen films by Cohl and Blackton. He ended up working with Blackton, and befriended Cohl when the French animator worked in the Eclair studio's New York office. In his study of McCay, animator John Canemaker suggests that McCay may have turned to film as a way to spruce up his vaudeville act.

McCay signed a contract with Vitagraph, and had Blackton direct his first film, which was modeled after Blackton's *Humorous Phases of Funny Faces* (1906). In the live action portion of his film, McCay is enjoying drinks at a club when he bets disbelieving visitors that he can finish the 4,000 drawings needed for an animated film in one month. (The onlookers include cartoonist George McManus, who created *Bringing Up Father*, and the florid John Bunny, perhaps Vitagraph's biggest star at the time.)

Animation takes up only four minutes of the eleven-minute film, but it is animation of an originality and vigor that had never been seen on the screen before. McCay first featured three of his *Little Nemo in Slumberland* characters: Nemo, Impie, and Flip. They stand in a row and proceed to tumble, gyrate, somersault, and stretch with lifelike precision. Suddenly animation has depth, and operates on more than one plane. Canemaker notes the work's "naturalistic movements, realistic timing, and a feeling of weight in the line drawings." Nemo later "draws" the Princess, who comes to life; they depart in the mouth of a dragon.

Vitagraph released the film on April 8, 1911, and by April 12, McCay was screening it in his vaudeville act. Reviews were glowing. *Motion Picture World* called it "an admirable piece of work," adding, "It should be popular everywhere." McCay was so happy with the public response that he paid to have his prints hand-colored.

In 1909, the *Little Nemo in Slumberland* strip was perhaps more popular with artists than the public, but its influence has been pervasive, in characters like Ojo the Unlucky from L. Frank Baum's *Oz* books; Maurice Sendak's *In the Night Kitchen*; references on *The Simpsons*; popular songs by groups like Genesis; and animation by Hiyao Miyazaki. McCay's next films, particularly *Gertie the Dinosaur*, contain further breakthroughs in animation.

Preservation of the Sign Language

George William Veditz's powerful personality is evident even in the shadowy dupe prints that remain of *Preservation of the Sign Language*.

National Association of the Deaf, 1913. Silent, B&W, 1.33. 35mm. 14 minutes.
Featuring: George William Veditz.
Credits: Produced by the National Association of the Deaf. Transferred to 16mm in 1934.
Available: Online at Gallaudet University website, http://videocatalog.gallaudet.edu/

The first permanent school for the deaf in the United States was formed in Hartford in 1817. Now called the American School for the Deaf, it was founded by Mason Cogswell, whose daughter Alice was deaf; Rev. Thomas Hopkins Gallaudet; and Laurent Clerc, a deaf teacher who brought a form of signed communication with him from Paris. At the time, sign language also developed in specific regions, urban centers like New York and Philadelphia, but also on Martha's Vineyard, home to a sizable deaf community.

Schools for the deaf were established in twenty states by the 1850s. In 1856, Amos Kendall donated land in northeast Washington, D.C., for the Columbia Institution for the Instruction of the Deaf and Dumb and Blind. Gallaudet's son Edward Miner became the first superintendent in 1857. On April 8, 1864, President Abraham Lincoln signed a bill that turned the Columbia Institution into a college authorized to confer degrees. What became the National Deaf-Mute College in 1865 was renamed Gallaudet College in 1894.

Along with instruction in fundamental courses, students in state schools received vocational training, in nutrition and shoemaking, for example. They were taught sign language and fingerspelling along with written English. After the Civil War, however, reformers campaigned for "oralism," which taught lipreading and spoken speech, and for an end to what they called "manualism," arguing that sign language impaired speech development and segregated the deaf community.

As the twentieth century approached, oralism grew in popularity, spurred on in large part by inventor Alexander Graham Bell. A follower of eugenics, Bell worried that by assembling in clubs, using sign language, and intermarrying, deaf people were forming a "deaf race." An 1880 conference in Milan, the International Congress on Education of the Deaf, voted to ban sign language. Nebraska passed a law in 1913 ordering schools to use oralism instead of manualism. Many deaf teachers who could not teach speech lost their jobs. Some schools punished students who signed, forcing them to wear gloves or fold their hands during class. This was the atmosphere George Veditz faced when he made this film.

Formed in 1880, the National Association of the Deaf took steps to protect sign language. That same year, George William Veditz entered Gallaudet College. Born in Baltimore in 1861, Veditz lost his hearing to scarlet fever at the age of eight. Graduating from Gallaudet as valedictorian in 1884, Veditz became a teacher as well as an outspoken defender of sign language. Through the Colorado State Association of the Deaf and later as president of the NAD, he campaigned to widen the use of sign language. First he had to make sure that it would survive for future generations.

"The only way in which this can be done is by means of moving picture films," he wrote. "The N.A.D., the National Association of the Deaf, has collected a fund of $5,000, called the Moving Picture Fund, for the purpose. We now have films of Gallaudet, of Fay, of Hotchkiss, of McGregor, and will have more until the five thousand dollars is spent. I am sorry that it is not $20,000."

The NAD formed the Motion Picture Committee in 1910 with a mandate to film "excellent examples" of sign language and distribute these movies throughout the country. According to historian Dr. Carol Padden, treasurer (and later chairman) Roy Stewart handled much of the administrative work of the Committee, including hiring filmmakers, obtaining extra copies of films, and reporting on the revenue they generated.

Between 1910 and 1921, 14 films were produced by the Committee. They included *The Lorna Doone Country of Devonshire, England* (1910) with

Dr. Edward M. Gallaudet; *Yankee Doodle* (1920), a "humorous recital" by W.E. Marshall; and *The Death of Minnehaha* (1913), a "dramatic recital" by Mary Williamson Erd, and the only film to feature a woman. (Veditz did not think much of the film, complaining about Erd's looks and her "gyrations.")

Most of the titles, including Veditz's, were filmed in 1913. Apart from *Minnehaha* and *Yankee Doodle*, the films are straightforward recordings of speeches delivered in sign language. (*An Address at the Tomb of Garfield*, 1913, shows Willis Hubbard speaking at the tomb with a crowd behind him. Two Gettysburg-themed films use footage from the battlefield.) Some entries use props like curtains and busts to approximate a stage backdrop. All were shot in 35mm and in daylight. Veditz's was apparently filmed in one take, although there appears to be an edit around the eight-minute mark, which may have been the result of damage to the original print or when it was reduced from 35mm to 16mm.

Whether you know sign language or not, Veditz is a forceful screen presence. As Padden notes, "His hair is parted neatly in the middle, so his face can be clearly seen, and he is careful to sign precisely and in large gestures." Veditz uses his body to add emphasis, tilting and swaying, sweeping his arms wide or pulling them in to his torso. When he fingerspells, he addresses his audience from his left to right.

The speech, translated over the years by Padden and others, opens with a reference to Abbe de l'Épée, an early advocate who founded the first free school for the deaf, and who helped formalize what is often referred to as Old Signed French. Veditz notes that sign language has been prohibited in France and Germany, and goes on to warn that oralism could destroy sign language in the United States. He refers to a "new race of Pharaohs," of the "worthless, cruel-hearted demands of people that think they know all about educating the deaf but know nothing about their thoughts and souls, their feelings, desires, and needs." He closes with a line that has become a rallying cry for defenders of sign language: "As long as we have deaf people on earth, we will have signs."

Along with the other films, Veditz's title was offered for rent by the NAD to individuals and organizations—the St. Louis Day School, for example, or a convention in South Carolina. The films were gradually transferred to 16mm, a process that diminished the quality of the imagery. At this point opening credits were added to some of the entries. Gallaudet College assembled 16mm copies of the films under its "George W. Veditz" collection, and donated these to the Library of Congress in 1947.

According to Padden, Veditz's film essentially dropped out of sight until it was screened at a 1977 conference on the research and teaching of American Sign Language. Since that time, some of Stewart's private correspondence has surfaced, including Veditz's transcription of *Preservation of the Sign Language* into written English, which he included in a 1915 letter.

In her article "Translating Veditz," Padden uses this transcription to show just how accomplished Veditz was, as both writer and orator. His use of repetition and rhythm, his turn of phrase, and his precision mark a formidable intellect. Among many examples, Padden takes this signed sentence: "But for thirty-three years their teachers have cast them aside and refused to listen to their pleas." "Cast aside" Veditz signs as "grab-hold-forcefully-push-down." His written English equivalent: "For thirty-three years their teachers have held them off with a hand of steel."

Veditz had an eventful life. An editor, translator, and expert chess player, he became a noted authority on poultry, pigeons, and Colorado floriculture. He died on March 12, 1937.

Battles over sign language continue to be fought today, although we have come to accept signing as a part of public discourse. "Fifty years from now these films will be priceless," Veditz wrote, and his prediction has come true. The Preservation films offer portraits of some of the most important figures in the deaf community, as well as an idea of how sign language has changed over the past hundred years, in some cases becoming less literal, more streamlined. *Preservation of the Sign Language* in particular allows us to see and judge Veditz, praised by Padden for "his intonation, phrasing, choice of vocabulary, and even his grammar."

Stewart prepared a list of the 14 films in the Preservation series. The Library of Congress list deviates from this slightly, as does the George W. Veditz collection at Gallaudet University. Following are Stewart's titles:

No. 1: *The Lorna Doone Country of Devonshire, England;* Dr. Edward M. Gallaudet, 1910.
No. 2: *Emperor Dom Pedro's Visit to Gallaudet College*; Dr. Edward A. Fay, 1913.
No. 3: *Memories of Old Hartford*; Dr. John B. Hotchkiss, 1913.
No. 4: *Signing of the Charter of Gallaudet College*; Dr. Amos G. Draper, 1915.
No. 5: *Lincoln's Gettysburg Address*; Dr. Thomas Francis Fox, 1915.
No. 6: *A Lay Sermon—The Universal Brotherhood of Man and Fatherhood of God*; Robert P. McGregor, 1913.
No. 7: *Preservation of the Sign Language*; George William Veditz, 1913.
No. 8: *The Death of Minnehaha*; Mary Williamson Erd, 1913.
No. 9: *An Address at the Tomb of Garfield*; Willis Hubbard, 1913.
No. 10: *Discovery of Chloroform*; Dr. George T. Dougherty, 1913.
No. 11: *A Plea for a Statue of D'l Epee in America*; Rev. Dr. James H. Cloud.
No. 12: *The Gallaudet Play*; 1913.
No. 13: *Yankee Doodle*; W.E. Marshall, 1920,
No. 14: *Convention of American Instructors of the Deaf at Staunton, Va. in June, 1914.*

Mabel's Blunder

Mabel Normand and Harry McCoy about to get into trouble in *Mabel's Blunder*.

Keystone, 1914. Silent, B&W, 1.33. 35mm. 14 minutes.

Cast: Mabel Normand (Mabel [office girl]), Charles Bennett (Boss), Harry McCoy (Harry [boss's son]), Eva Nelson (Harry's sister), Charlie Chase (Harry's friend), Al St. John (Mabel's brother).

Credits: Written and directed by Mabel Normand.

Additional credits: Produced by Mack Sennett. Released September 12, 1914.

Available: Library of Congress.

Born in rural Quebec in 1880, Michael Sinnott was encouraged to become an actor by fellow Canadian Marie Dressler. Touring in burlesque, toiling in chorus lines, he made little headway until he joined the Biograph studio in 1908, where he used his stage name Mack Sennett. At first an extra, within a year he was taking lead parts and selling scripts to his mentor, D.W. Griffith. "He was my day school, my adult education program, my university," Sennett said of the director. Soon he was assisting Griffith, and then producing and directing his own films.

Although his early writing efforts included such noteworthy dramas as *The Lonely Villa* (1909), as a director Sennett gravitated toward comedy, helping define a film style marked by broad stereotypes, relentless pacing, and plots that made fun of the very films moviegoers favored. "I stole my first ideas from the Pathés," Sennett admitted later, citing the French as the inventors of slapstick.

Writing, directing, and acting, Sennett churned out an enormous amount of film, often working with Fred Mace, an actor he had toured with years earlier, and Mabel Normand, an actress who sometimes performed under the name Muriel Fortescue. Years later, Sennett wrote about her: "Mabel was frisky, as skittery as a waterbug and oh, my Lord, how pretty!"

Normand was born on Staten Island, New York, in 1892. She attended a seminary school in Massachusetts until she was thirteen, then became a model in New York City. She posed for photographs and lantern slides, for artist Charles Dana Gibson, and, according to her biographer Betty Harper Fussell, for "hats, cold cream, hairbrushes, shoes, stockings, combs, hair tonics, veils, gloves, satchels, lingerie, umbrellas, necklaces, frocks, evening wraps, furs, [and] bracelets."

When she was seventeen, Normand started working for Biograph, acting in serious dramas for Griffith like *The Eternal Mother* (January 1912), but also in Sennett comedies like *Hot Stuff* (March 1912) and *Oh! Those Eyes* (April 1912). Here's how Sennett described her: "She was like a French-Irish girl, as gay as a wisp, and she was also Spanish-like and brooding. Mostly she was like a child who walks to the corner on a spring morning and meets Tom Sawyer with a scheme in his pocket."

Early in 1912, Sennett, with financial backing from Adam Kessel and Charles Baumann of the New York Motion Picture Company, left Biograph to form Keystone. He brought with him Mace and Normand, who by now had begun to write scenarios. Ford Sterling joined the studio by the fall.

In Keystone's early titles, Sennett worked and reworked the same themes and gags, primarily mistaken identity situations involving the pretty, lighthearted, and droll Normand. *The Flirting Husband, Mabel's Lovers, The Deacon's Troubles, A Temperamental Husband*—in film after film, Normand bested straying husbands, flirting clerks, drunken mashers, and moronic cops, sometimes the victim of dunkings and mud baths, but almost always ending up with both dignity and romance intact.

In June 1913, Roscoe "Fatty" Arbuckle joined the Keystone team. Moviegoers loved the screen chemistry between Normand and Arbuckle, which Sennett capitalized on by releasing a new film almost every week that summer. Some were just slapstick chases or brief travelogues, but others helped establish a romantic comedy template that is still in use today.

By the end of 1913, Normand had started directing her own films, albeit guided closely by Sennett. Keystone was releasing so much material that Sennett relied on what he called "subdirectors" to work on simultaneous productions. Sennett first oversaw a committee of writers who came up with story ideas, then blocked out individual scripts with cast and crew, a stenographer taking down his advice about camera placement, cutting, and other technical details. He had a precise vision of what Keystone films should look like, and tried to shape his various production units to achieve a uniform style. Sennett expected to use about a quarter of the footage that was shot, which gave directors a surprising amount of room for on-set improvisation.

But film historian Kevin Brownlow cites an incident on a Normand set that showed the limitations to Sennett's approach. Charlie Chaplin had joined Keystone early in 1914, and it is in one of Normand's films, *Mabel's Strange Predicament* (February 1914) that he developed his famous tramp costume. Normand was filming a gag involving spraying a hose. Chaplin wanted to elaborate on it by staging a joke from an early Lumière actuality. Normand refused, telling Chaplin they didn't have the time to work out more business.

Chaplin later complained about Normand, calling her too young—which was technically true, but she had been working in film four more years than Chaplin. And in the director's defense, Chaplin's style of filmmaking led to endless, expensive delays on his own projects, like *City Lights* (1931), which took over a year to shoot. But his point remained: Sennett's movies generally did not dawdle over niceties like characterization and atmosphere.

Mabel's Blunder, filmed in 1914, is a good example. On the one hand, it's a charming vehicle for the star, playing up her flirtatious nature, showing off her good looks, and letting her engage in some mild, genuinely funny slapstick. On the other hand, it was a genre product that placed stock characters into stock situations to play out familiar jokes with a minimum of logic or credibility.

Mabel's Blunder had three main locations: an office set on the Sennett lot, some nearby streets, and an outdoor cafe and restaurant. The office set figured into countless Sennett shorts, as did Mabel's character as a secretary who attracts the attention of the boss (played by Charles Bennett) and his son (Harry McCoy). Working at Vitagraph, comedian John Bunny made many similar movies with the same kinds of sets and characters, even one, *Troublesome Secretaries* (1911), with Mabel herself. Bunny's *Stenographers Wanted* (1912) plays out almost exactly like *Mabel's Blunder*, with the same sets and similar gags, albeit a different story line. Mabel had already made her share of office comedies for Sennett: *Mabel's Stratagem* (December 1912), for example, in which a wife gets jealous of her husband's secretary, or *Hubby's Job* (May 1913), in which the boss tries to woo his married stenographer.

What sets *Mabel's Blunder* apart is its optimistic tone and unhurried pace. Normand leaves the broader jokes to Al St. John (Arbuckle's nephew), giving her character more time to react to situations. Several mistaken identities, two involving cross dressing, move the plot along, but Norman makes it clear in her inserts and cutaways that nothing too drastic is at stake, and that everything will work out for the best. Viewers are in the hands of expert farceurs who are so comfortable with what they're doing that the film seems to be made up on the spot.

Normand was a popular star, but she never attained the status of an actress like Mary Pickford. Some authors have argued that she lacked ambition or drive, pointing to her prolonged absences from the Keystone lot. After Sennett moved Keystone into the Triangle studio, Normand limited her filmmaking even more. She continued to direct, and appeared in some wonderful domestic comedies like *Fatty and Mabel's Simple Life* (January 1915) and *Fatty and Mabel Adrift* (January 1916). Directed by Arbuckle, these were quite different from the usual Keystone chaos, offering an almost dreamy atmosphere and tempo, and allowing characters to develop in leisurely, digressive scenes.

It's difficult to judge how Normand's personal relationship with Sennett affected her work. It's clear that both relied on and benefited from each other, but Normand did not devote herself wholeheartedly to Keystone. Ultimately she broke with Sennett and signed a contract with producer Samuel Goldwyn, in part to move out of shorts and into features. Vehicles like *Mickey* (1918) proved popular enough, but entering the 1920s, Normand's style of tomboyish hijinks began to seem forced. In 1922, she and actress Mary Miles Minter were implicated in the murder of actor William Desmond Taylor, effectively ending her career.

The Bargain

A cornered William S. Hart.

Paramount Pictures Corp., 1914. Silent, B&W, 1.33. 35mm. Approximately 70 minutes.

Cast: William S. Hart (Jim Stokes, the Two-Gun Man), J. Frank Burke (Bud Walsh, the Sheriff), Clara Williams (Nell Brent), J. Barney Sherry (Phil Brent, Nell's father), James Dowling (Wilkes, the Minister).

Credits: Directed by Thos. [Thomas] H. Ince.

Additional credits: Directed by Reginald Barker. Produced by Thomas H. Ince, the New York Motion Picture Company. Scenario: William S. Hart, William H. Clifford. Cinematography attributed to Joseph H. August or Robert Newhard. Production dates: June 11–August 5, 1914. Released December 3, 1914. Digitally restored from the Paper Print Collection by The Library of Congress.

Other versions: Re-issued by Hart in 1920 as *The Two-Gun Man in the Bargain*.

Available: The Library of Congress; Alpha Home Entertainment DVD (2010), Sinister Cinema DVD-R (2008).

Around 1909, movie production began to shift from New York and Chicago to Los Angeles. In his memoir *One Reel a Week* (cowritten with Arthur C. Miller), Fred Balshofer explained why: "Los Angeles with its mild climate and sunshine beckoned as an escape from both the winter months of the East as well as the ever-present Patents Company detectives." Balshofer, one of the heads of the New York Motion Picture Company, was referring to attempts by the Motion Picture Patents Company to monopolize film production. Another factor was California's relatively low labor costs, about half that of New York's.

The Chicago-based Selig Polyscope had a studio in Edendale in 1910. That same year D.W. Griffith and a troupe from Biograph set up a temporary studio in Los Angeles. The Nestor Company built the first actual Hollywood studio in the winter of 1911–1912. The New York Motion Picture Company, founded by Balshofer, Adam Kessel and Charles Baumann in 1909, had a California studio by November, 1913. In charge was Thomas Ince (poached from the IMP studio), who was vice-president, manager of Western production, and chief producer.

One of Ince's first steps was to hire performers from the famous Miller Brothers "101" Ranch, a Wild West and rodeo outfit based in Oklahoma. Working in a combination studio and camp in the Santa Ynez canyon, they brought spectacle, expertise, and not incidentally props to Ince's Bison "101" Westerns. These one- and two-reel shorts were soon among the most admired Westerns in the industry.

Westerns, whether in the form of songs, dime novels, or Wild West shows, had been a dominant part of entertainment since the days of James Fenimore Cooper. They were popular in films as well, although many producers just swapped in familiar melodramatic formulas to Western settings. All studios relied on them, from Edison (whose *The Great Train Robbery*, 1903, is in the Registry) to Vitagraph (*"The Bad Man"—A Tale of the West*, 1907) and even Pathé Frères (*A Western Hero*, 1909). By 1911, studios like Vitagraph and Lubin were releasing one Western a week.

That may have been the year William S. Hart viewed his first. In his tight-lipped memoir *My Life East and West*, the actor began Chapter VIII: "While playing in Cleveland, I attended a picture show. I saw a Western picture. It was awful!" The actor, pushing fifty, was having trouble finding stage work. He had roomed with Ince years earlier, and sought him out in Los Angeles during a summer tour of *The Trail of the Lonesome Pine* with the idea of making more realistic Westerns—films with better costumes and props, and more believable characters. As Hart remembers, Ince discouraged him, saying that the Western fad had died out.

Hart returned to Los Angeles in 1914 and played villains in two-reel shorts for Ince. About his first, *His Hour of Manhood*, Hart wrote: "When I saw the rushes on the screen, I knew it was terrible." He took one of Ince's scripts, "and in four or five days I gave it back to him, doubled in length." After polishing by C. Gardner Sullivan (who called it "splendid"), the script became Hart's first feature, *The Bargain*. (Hart said he worked with Sullivan, Ince's chief screenwriter, but most sources credit William H. Clifford with cowriting the scenario.)

Hart knew the value of playing a villain—he was Messala in the first stage production of *Ben-Hur*—and in this film began developing a screen persona as a "good bad man." In truth he was simply elaborating on proven Western tropes. Stories that presented Jesse James and Billy the Kid as outlaws with noble motives entranced audiences. G.M. Anderson, often regarded as the first Western star in movies, forged a similar character in films like *Broncho Billy's Redemption* (July 1910).

What made Hart's work different was the actor's imposing looks. Grim, hard-bitten, solid, he stood in sharp contrast to the dandies who populated many of the films of the time. At this stage in his career he had not mastered acting for the screen, and especially in the latter portions of *The Bargain* he seems to be trying too hard, flinging his hands around and lifting his eyebrows as if painfully contemplating the cruelty of fate. But when called upon to act, and not just emote, Hart is efficient, direct, and utterly commanding. He rides excellently, handles guns with authority, and has no trouble executing stunts.

The Bargain has some serious plot flaws, including an incredibly reckless sheriff and too many coincidences around Cochise County's one apparent waterhole. Taking place in Arizona in 1889, it details the fall and rise of Jim Stokes, a clever criminal who is reformed by love after being nursed back to health by a prospector and his daughter. When the past arises in the form of a discarded moneybag, Stokes must choose between confessing his crimes or abandoning his fiancée.

It's easy to trace Hart's influence down through decades of Westerns. Clint Eastwood's Bill Munny in *Unforgiven* (1992, a Registry title) can be seen as a variation on the "good bad man," although one we meet long after his criminal career has ended. What may surprise viewers today is how literally, and enthusiastically, Hart establishes Two-Gun Stokes's bona fides. The opening reel of *The Bargain* doesn't just identify Stokes as a crook, it shows him carrying out a pretty ingenious stagecoach holdup, a crime committed without exculpatory excuses or remorse. In his future films, Hart would temper his characters' motives, inventing reasons why they turned outlaw.

Ince's films were renowned for their production values, and they are on full display here. *The Bargain* has wonderful landscapes, composed to show the height and depth of the California countryside, and exposed to capture light that can be stark or crystalline. As film historian Eileen Bowser wrote about filming in California, "The extreme long shot became an important element of the spectacle: there was no other way to do justice to the wide open spaces."

The combination of California's far horizons and Westerns' constantly moving action forced cinematographers to adapt looser, freer styles of shooting. The camera tilts, pans, and tracks in and out in *The Bargain*, at times using a "pull back" motion that may have been borrowed from Selig's *In the Days of the Thundering Herd* (November 1913). In one remarkable scene, the camera pans almost 360 degrees around a crowded, chaotic saloon and gambling hall. It's a shot filled with dozens of costumed extras who fight, drink, gamble, and carouse, all executed flawlessly on a three-level set.

As Hart wrote, "What an exquisite pleasure it was to work in *The Bargain*. I rode five horses in the picture, but the principal one was 'Midnight,' a superb, coal black animal that weighed about twelve hundred pounds....We did skyline rides along the tops of ridges so fast that the cameraman could not hold us, no matter how he placed his 'setup.'"

Hart also obtained funding to bring the cast and crew to the Grand Canyon to shoot some breathtaking if incongruent footage. "What a glorious trip it was! I wore spurs and rode a horse at a full gallop on the worst turns of the narrow Hermit Creek Trail, on the brink of a thousand-foot drop."

This account doesn't quite square with Hart's version of arguments with Ince over the film, as well as over money and credit. Hart wrote that he left California and returned in defeat to his sister back East after one more feature. In reality he continued working for Ince, finishing the feature-length *On the Midnight Stage* and six more shorts before the end of the year. What's more, Ince named Hart director of his pictures for Bison. The next year Hart appeared in a few more shorts, but was turning to features exclusively.

Hart devoted an entire chapter of *My Life East and West* to his celebrated falling out with Ince, and according to film historian Richard Koszarski was "sincerely shocked" when he learned that his producer had been paying him a "scandalously low" salary. But it's doubtful that anyone else in the industry would have given Hart a chance to write and star in a feature, or provide him with such extravagant backdrops as those found in *The Bargain*. (Both Hart's and Ince's careers are covered more fully in the entry for *Hell's Hinges*, 1916.)

Heroes All

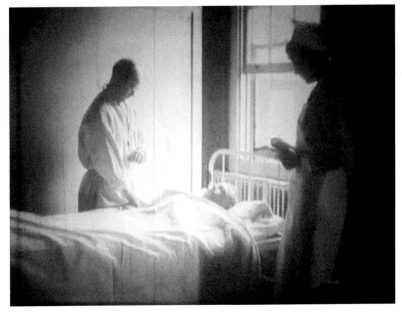

How the Red Cross tried to raise funds through film.

American Red Cross/General Film Company, 1919. Silent, B&W, 1.33. 35mm. 10 minutes.

Credits: Produced by the Bureau of the American Red Cross, distributed by General Film Company.

Additional credits: Produced by William Waddell. Released 1919.

Available: The Library of Congress.

Sponsored films exist from the dawn of cinema. On one level, the films by the Lumière Brothers can be seen as advertisements for their equipment. Some of the earliest theatrical films were commercials, like *Dewars Scotch Whisky* (1897). The Registry title *Westinghouse Works* (1904) functioned as public relations for Westinghouse, a way to explain the company's products and position it as a brand.

Heroes All was both a marketing film and a fund-raising one. It was produced by the Red Cross Bureau of Pictures, a sort of in-house movie studio. Formed during World War I, the Bureau released over 100 films before it was disbanded in 1921. Its movies ranged from instructional films about safety and first aid to vivid accounts of political upheaval in Europe. The Bureau provided important opportunities for cinematographers like Ernest Schoedsack, A. Farciot Edouart, and Merl LaVoy.

Seen today, the Red Cross films also show how newsreels and propaganda developed and evolved. They pushed the limits of what could be shown on screen, and directly engaged audiences in social problems that resisted easy solutions. Some titles staked out political positions that might make the current-day Red Cross uncomfortable.

The American Red Cross was founded by Clara Barton in 1881 as an outgrowth of the International Red Cross. At first it was a medical organization that offered assistance to battlefield casualties. By the turn of the twentieth century, it was known primarily as a first response to disasters, and also for its campaigns to educate the public in first aid and swimming.

In providing relief during World War I, the Red Cross incurred huge debts, threatening its existence. Films were seen as a potential source of income, and officials approached studios like the Triangle Film Corporation with the hopes of making a feature about the Red Cross. After two years covering the war, cinematographer Merl LaVoy returned from Europe in 1917 with *Heroic France*, a six-reel feature that was distributed by Mutual and later shown at Red Cross benefits. Material from LaVoy and from Paul Rainey, a self-professed "Official Photographer of the United States Army," made the idea of a Red Cross in-house movie studio seem plausible.

When the United States entered the war, President Woodrow Wilson ordered the formation of a War Council to take over Red Cross operations, chaired by banker Henry Davison. He was helped by public relations expert Ivy Lee, who set up fund-raising departments devoted to publicity, advertising, a Red Cross magazine, and the Bureau of Pictures under director Evan Evans.

Evans, a veteran of the Burton Holmes Travel Pictures, saw the Bureau of Pictures offering two types of movies: documentaries for general audiences that would be distributed to theaters, and specialized fund-raising films to be shown in churches, clubs, and schools. Evans was replaced by New York attorney Ralph Wolf, who signed contracts to sell Red Cross footage to four newsreel companies. By 1918, Wolf had managed to put together only five films, one of those produced by the French government.

In July, 1918, Lee named William Waddell head of the Picture Bureau (officially part of the Bureau of General Publicity). To get Red Cross product into theaters, Waddell signed a contract with the General Film Company. In return for 20% of the gross profits, General Film promised trade ads, a New York opening, and booking throughout the Keith circuit of vaudeville houses. The first release, in August 1918, was *The Historic Fourth of July in Paris*, a patriotic piece which documented a parade of American soldiers and Red Cross nurses. (When GFC went bankrupt, Waddell signed with the Educational Films Corporation in June 1919. But the Red Cross films did not make much headway in the theatrical market. A year later, Waddell signed a new agreement with the Society of Visual Education to market and distribute Bureau films.)

Waddell ramped up production quickly. By the fall of 1918, the Bureau was releasing a film every two weeks. Consciously or not, Waddell followed the strategy put forth by Evans: a set of general purpose films covering Europe; and a separate stream of more instructional documentaries shot in the US.

The former were produced by a Red Cross film unit stationed in Paris, part of the Publicity Department under Major Charles Morris. Along with Merl LaVoy, members included Ernest Schoedsack; Alexander Farciot Edouart, later a specialist in rear projection and special effects at Paramount, where he won three Oscars; Harold Wyckoff, who would become a noted still photographer at Paramount; and war photographer Donald Thompson. Largely unsupervised, the cameramen would spend up to six weeks at a time in various Eastern European countries, highlighting how the Red Cross was promoting American ideals through providing food and medical relief and by improving sanitation and hygiene. Concentrating on refugees, they also captured incidental ethnic culture: dress, folk dances, etc. Back home, ads promoted one-reel films that showed, for example, how the Red Cross "Aids 3000 Helpless Children and Old People Each Month at the Border Village of St. Evian."

With more footage than he could handle, Waddell introduced The Red Cross Travel Film Series, which would be distributed theatrically by The Educational Film Corporation. These served as general purpose travelogues, with Red Cross personnel shown almost in passing. According to Gary Veeder, who wrote an authoritative history of the Bureau, these films introduced a new style and strategy to sponsored documentaries: rather than group Red Cross workers in "official" poses, the cameramen showed them at work, in unstaged, realistic situations. Edouart's *Apple-blossom Time in Normandy* goes a step further by eliminating any mention of the Red Cross (apart from the opening credits).

LaVoy filmed primarily in the Balkans, photographing Queen Marie in Rumania and claiming to provide footage of the Sultan's harem in Turkey. Schoedsack, on the other hand, shot *The Fall of Kiev*, a moving, incisive look at a city under siege. His footage showed chaotic markets, the Russians attacking Polish positions, and, most effectively, an orphanage set up by the Red Cross. This was exactly the sort of fund-raising material the Red Cross needed, starting with picturesque travelogue footage and gradually narrowing down to heart-rending scenes of children in need. *To the Aid of Poland* (1919) took a similar approach, and was instrumental in introducing Schoedsack to his future *Grass* collaborator Merian C. Cooper, who was at the time fighting as an aviator for the Polish military. (*Grass*, 1925, is a Registry title.)

The press referred to these films as "propaganda" and "educationals." The Travel Film Project, which failed to earn profits, was discontinued in June, 1921, after fifteen films (some of the footage was reused in subsequent shorts). Waddell was ordered to concentrate on Red Cross issues at home: public health, first aid, water safety, and helping disabled soldiers.

Veeder singles out *Winning Her Way* and *Every Woman's Problem* as relevant examples. The latter is a staged film that shows how to properly bathe bedridden "Aunt Mary." Although professionally produced, these were utilitarian films, with little pretense to art. Unlike the travelogues, these were designed to be shown in schools, churches, and at benefits.

Heroes All was a fund-raising film in the tradition of *New Faces for Old* (1918), which showed the process of facial reconstruction practiced by the Mutilation Bureau in Paris, and *Helping Our Boys at Home* (1919), about how the Red Cross helped returning disabled servicemen in New York. These shorts had to balance a pessimistic present with an optimistic future. They had to show both a need and a solution—a reason to give money and proof that the money would help. And they had to do it in ten minutes or less.

Like *Helping Our Boys at Home*, the "plot" of *Heroes All* detailed how the Red Cross, and the government, rehabilitated wounded veterans. *Heroes All* had an additional purpose of showing off the new facilities at the Walter Reed Hospital (now the Walter Reed Army Medical Center of the U.S. Army Medical Department) in Washington, DC. Founded in 1909, the hospital enlarged from 80 patient beds to 2,500 during World War I. (The Center now has about 5,500 beds.) At the time of filming, it was a state-of-the-art faculty, with brand-new landscaping to boot.

After an introductory passage of soldiers arriving at Washington's Union Station, the film follows ambulances transporting them through the capital to Walter Reed. Viewers learn about the hospital as the soldiers do, with the camera visiting offices, laboratories, operating rooms, and wards. Rehabilitation includes physical therapy, exercise on playing fields and in swimming pools, vocational training, and recreation, including trips to theaters and ballparks.

The Red Cross is a subtle presence, with its first clearly identified personnel not appearing until well into the piece, on a patio ward where patients can recover in open air. You have to watch closely to see the veteran missing a leg in the background, a mark of the film's sophistication. The cinematographer uses the techniques of feature films—careful pans and tracking shots, traditional framing, reaction shots—putting viewers at ease while encouraging them to empathize with the veterans as characters in a story.

Heroes All wouldn't be a fund-raiser if it didn't include uncomfortable material. Just like *Let There Be Light* (1946, a Registry title), the filmmakers hold the more explicit shots for later in the film, when they would have the maximum impact. (Although made almost thirty years apart, the films have remarkable similarities, from scenes of soldiers arriving and departing hospital facilities to depictions of training and therapy.) It also closes on an especially upbeat note, with successfully rehabilitated soldiers departing by bus for bright futures.

Faced with media criticism and a largely uninterested audience, Red Cross directors could not justify maintaining an in-house film studio for long. Officials closed the Picture Bureau on December 30, 1921. An internal inventory of films prepared for the Society of Visual Education in 1922 recognized the value of *Heroes All*. Unlike *Helping Our Boys at Home*, which was "strictly a war picture," *Heroes All* was "good RC propaganda" about "post-war activities of the Red Cross at every Govt. hospital." Perhaps that's why it was one of the few Red Cross films to survive.

The Society for Visual Education continued to distribute some of the titles until 1940. The remaining prints and negatives were stored in government vaults before winding up at the Red Cross National Headquarters in Washington, DC. In 1941, G. Stewart Brown, head of the Public Information Service, tried to donate them to the National Archives, but was told there was no vault space available. According to Gerry Veeder, a majority of the films were lost. *Goodbye Brest* and *Heroes All* (both 1919) were found in an attic in 1980. The surviving reels were restored by Karl Malkames, and some footage was incorporated into the Red Cross Centennial film, *Growing Up Together*.

Heroes All is a good example of how difficult it is to track films through changes in ownership, distribution, and storage. Titles can disappear at any stage, before archives can make decisions about preservation. It may not even be clear what is important about a film until decades later. Today baseball fans would savor the film's candid shots of Cleveland Indians center fielder Tris Speaker and Washington Senators manager Clark Griffith, while others might be interested in the medical technology on display. How many more examples like these have been lost?

Stark Love

Helen Munday is eyewitness to an Oedipal struggle in *Stark Love*.

Paramount, 1927. Silent, B&W, 1.33. 35mm. 68 minutes.

Cast: Forrest James (Rob Warwick), Silas Miracle (Jason Warwick, his father), Helen Munday (Barbara Allen), Rob Grohan (Quill Allen, her father).

Credits: Written & directed by Karl Brown. Adaptation by Walter Woods. Photographed by James Murray. An Adolph Zukor & Jesse L. Lasky presentation of a Karl Brown production. Copyright 1927 by Paramount Famous Lasky Corp.

Additional cast: Roy, Ray, Quince Ghormley (Allen brothers); Wylie Underwood (Miller), Sim Hooper (Visiting preacher), George Rogers ("Widower from Black Creek"), Nathaniel ("Nathan") Burchfield (Old hunter who welcomes preacher); "Uncle" Grant Stewart, Dave Stewart (Musicians); Earl Wall (age 7), Kelly Wall (age 5) (Warwick siblings); Frank Forsyth, Ben Grant, Robert Elmer Rogers, Jim Carver, Della Davis, Jake Davis, Fay Davis, Carrie Davis, George and Mary Roberts, Posey Stewart, Martha Walters, Alice Patterson, Henry Stewart, Ollie Collins Crisp, Forrest Denton, Alma Stewart Buchanan, Alice Williams, Rena Blevins, Nate Blevins (extras).

Additional credits: Business manager: Captain Paul Wing. Assistant cameraman: Robert Pittack. Consultant: Horace Kephart. Released September 17, 1927. Current print: Acquired through the courtesy of the Czechoslovak Filmarchive. Restored in collaboration by The Museum of Modern Art Department of Film and The American Film Institute. Shot on location in North Carolina. (Some material reshot in New York City.) Helen Mundy is also cited in references as Munday and Monday.

Available: The Museum of Modern Art.

Filmed under trying circumstances in the mountains of North Carolina, *Stark Love* brought backwoods melodramas into the Jazz Age, adding a soupçon of Freud to a plot line that dated back well before the invention of cinema. Directed by veteran cinematographer and future screenwriter Karl Brown, the film was seen as a sort of experiment by the apprehensive Paramount executives who okayed its release. In later years Brown compared *Stark Love* to *Nanook of the North* (1922, a Registry title), but at the time it became another reason not to let directors off the studio lot.

Stark Love "had the handicap of being the first of its kind," Brown told film historian Kevin Brownlow many years later. "It was a stranger in town—nobody knew quite what to make of it." That was true only in the sense that no one had tried to shoot a feature film with amateur actors in North Carolina before. But what were once referred to as "hillbillies" had been a fixture in film since the early days of Edison and Biograph studios.

As J.W. Williamson points out in his book *Hillbillyland*, at least 476 movies about Southern mountain people were shot between 1904 and 1929. Biograph released *The Moonshiner* in 1904. *The Moonshiner's Daughter* (Kalem, 1908), *Mountaineer's Honor* (Biograph, 1909, directed by D.W. Griffith and starring Mary Pickford), and *Breed o' the Mountains* (Nestor, 1914) followed. Williamson cites over seventy movies about Southern mountaineers in 1914 alone, and notes that several stars of the time portrayed rural characters, including Pickford and her brother Jack, Mary Miles Minter, Richard Barthelmess, and Mabel Normand.

The story behind the filming of *Stark Love* is as interesting as the actual movie. Brown, the son of show people, assisted cinematographer Billy Bitzer on Griffith's *The Birth of a Nation* (1915) and *Intolerance* (1916, both Registry titles) before working as a cameraman for Famous Players/Lasky, a part of Paramount. It was while shooting *The Covered Wagon* in 1923 that Brown started reading *The Quare Women*, Lucy Furman's novel about Kentucky hillbillies. He came up with the idea for *The Log Cabin*, an Oedipal struggle based on "the awful steamy closeness of living and procreating in such crude quarters." Sample passage: "The girl looks wistfully, almost apologetically at the boy as she begins to unbutton the top of her bodice."

Jesse Lasky turned down Brown's proposal, but the director used office politics to obtain limited backing from Paramount head Adolph Zukor (perhaps encouraged by the studio's relative success with location films *Grass*, 1925, a Registry title, and *Chang*, 1927). Zukor's terms were strict: Brown got $50,000, a six-week schedule, and was supervised by "Captain" Paul Wing, credited as "business manager."

Brown oddly started his location scouting trip in New Orleans before traveling to Berea College in Kentucky. When the college turned down his request to film there, Brown wound up in Asheville by way of Nashville and Knoxville. There he found a 1913 volume, *Our Southern Highlanders*, reminiscences by Horace Kephart that were set in 1907. Brown was basing his "modern day" account on stories that were already twenty years old.

Kephart became a consultant on the film, and directed Brown to Robbinsville in Graham County. By December 1925, Brown had found his shooting locations there, mostly along Big Santeetlah Creek in the Snowbird Mountains. The remote Nantahala Gorge (in Williamson's words, "hardly representative of where actual mountain people lived") provided the striking opening shots of the film.

Brown built his story around the premise that mountain clans were so isolated from modern-day culture that they lived in an almost feudal society in which women were powerless chattel. He dutifully played out this premise in scenes of farming, cooking, and housekeeping, but shied away from what *Stark Love* was really about. Intertitles might refer to women in submission ("MAN IS THE ABSOLUTE RULER — WOMAN IS THE WORKING SLAVE."), but even in its very name, *Stark Love* was about sexual menace, Oedipal rivalry, and the heaving chests of countless purple plays and novels.

Brown could incorporate a Freudian sensibility that was beyond the abilities of someone like D.W. Griffith. And with relaxed standards, he could suggest more sexual scenes and themes than earlier filmmakers. But despite the addition of some psychological curlicues, Brown was simply substituting one set of stereotypes for another.

In Williamson's words, "Brown knew nothing of mountain people or of mountain living except what he had gleaned through the media (namely, Lucy Furman's fiction and a zillion other similar presentations, including, probably, many of those old nickelodeon movies.)" And as historians like Elijah Wald and David C. Hsiung have pointed out, mountaineers weren't nearly as isolated as we want to believe anyway. As Hsiung put it, "the remotest log cabin in darkest Tennessee" was always connected to a national economy by trails, tracks, roads, rivers. Brown's condescending take on hillbillies has continued through the years, much to the detriment of rural culture.

Perhaps because locals resented Brown's approach and ideas, casting proved challenging. He needed a "mountain girl," a son who hates mountain ways and wants to go to school in the city, and two patriarchs who drink moonshine and trade offspring for wives while working their women to death. The fathers were played by Kentuckians Reb Grogan and Silas Miracle, who agreed to portray such hateful men because they were identified as North Carolina, and not Kentucky, hicks. Forrest James, cast as the son, was found in a nightclub celebrating a football victory with his teammates. Wing discovered Helen Monday, a sixteen-year-old high school student, in Knoxville. She and James received $30 a week.

Brown relished telling stories about how difficult it was to film *Stark Love*, but what's really surprising in his interviews is his contempt for his cast, his subject, and indeed the people of the Smoky Mountains. About his star, he said, "Helen Mundy was the most difficult person I ever had anything to do with." Forrest James was an "Achilles" who spent his free time sulking in his tent. Brown told demonstrably false stories about local townspeople, depicting them in *Deliverance*-like terms.

Still, the decision to shoot on location paid off with stunning exteriors. Previous filmmakers had called California or even New Jersey "Kentucky" or "North Carolina." Here are the real Smoky Mountains, with distant horizons seen through ridge-line trees, boulder-strewn waterways, lush meadows and shadowy valleys. Despite the tawdriness of the script, Brown elicited excellent performances from the cast, in particular Mundy, a blazing screen presence. As might be expected given Brown's background, shots of the interiors are meticulously composed and lit, even when the unit had to film covering material at Paramount's studio in Astoria, Queens.

Stark Love is in the narrative tradition of the Registry title *Sunrise* (1927), even if Brown's directing technique is diametrically opposed to F. W. Murnau's. *Sunrise* used a romantic triangle to contrast the simple, even stark, morality of the country with an amoral city; *Stark Love* used its triangle to oppose modern civilization with an ancient and corrupt culture. Murnau built a new reality in a fortune's worth of sets on the Fox lot and near Lake Arrowhead; Brown imposed his version of reality in the hills of North Carolina. Both films reached essentially the same conclusions: the two lead stars belonged together no matter what.

Stark Love's influence did not extend much beyond Manhattan. It was covered in at least three articles in the *New York Times*, but when it proved a dud at the box office, interest quickly died down. (Did Mary Marvin Breckinridge see *Stark Love*? She filmed the Registry title *The Forgotten Frontier* a few years later, and the movies share similar shots and scenes, notably in how characters ride horses across rivers.) The change to sound movies by the end of the Twenties helped insure *Stark Love*'s neglect. In 1969, Kevin Brownlow discovered a 35mm print in Czechoslovakia, and persuaded archivist Myrtil Frida to allow the Museum of Modern Art to make a 16mm transfer. *Stark Love* was shown at the 1969 New York Film Festival. Brownlow, who received an honorary Oscar in 2010 for his decades of film preservation work, has always been a champion of the film.

According to Knoxville reporter Jack Neely, Helen Monday (the spelling she used) signed a contract with Paramount, but was dropped without another screen credit. She dated William Powell briefly before returning to Knoxville. After marrying, she moved to Michigan, where she died in 1987. Forrest James did not pursue an acting career.

Brown went on to a long but oddly undistinguished career, writing low-budget horror films and episodes of TV's *Death Valley Days* until well into the 1950s. When he was interviewed by Kevin Brownlow, he revealed the existence of his memoirs, portions of which were published as *Adventures with D. W. Griffith* in 1973. He died in 1990 at the age of ninety-three.

Lonesome

Universal, 1928. Silent with sound sequences, B&W with color sequences, 1.33. 35mm. 69 minutes.

Cast: Glenn Tryon (Jim), Barbara Kent (Mary), Fay Holderness (Overdressed woman), Gusztáz Pártos (Romantic gentleman), Eddie Phillips (The Sport).
Credits: Directed by Paul Fejos. Story: Carl Mann. Adaptation and scenario: Edward T. Lowe, Jr. Dialogue and titles: Tom Reed. Photography: Gilbert Warrington. Film editor: Frank Atkinson. Production designed by Charles D. Hall. A Carl Laemmle presentation of a Paul Fejos production.
Additional cast: Andy Devine (Jim's friend)
Additional credits: Produced by Carl Laemmle, Jr. Opened in New York City September 30, 1928.
Available: George Eastman House.

For his twenty-first birthday, Carl Laemmle, Jr., was given control of Universal by his father, Carl, Sr. The studio earned its bread and butter on shorts, Westerns and programmers, but the junior Laemmle had more ambitious plans. Like Irving Thalberg before him, he wanted Universal to concentrate on high quality, big-budget movies. And like rival studios MGM and Paramount, Laemmle turned to Europe for help. The elder Laemmle tried to merge Universal with UFA, a Berlin-based studio, and poached as much talent as he could. E.A. Dupont, Paul Leni, Edgar G. Ulmer, Conrad Veidt, and Paul Fejos all ended up at Universal.

In interviews, Paul Fejos described his life as a series of happy accidents. A man he met hitchhiking ended up financing one of his feature films, while another chance encounter led him to a job at the Rockefeller Institute for Medical Research. Fejos was born in Budapest, where he earned a medical degree in 1921. A year later he was in New York City, scuffling for odd jobs because he couldn't get his degree certified. After three years as a research technician at the Rockefeller Institute, he headed to Los Angeles with the vague idea of working in films.

With a $5000 stake from Edward M. Spitz, heir to a supermarket chain, Fejos set out to make a feature. He rented studio space by the hour and borrowed whatever sets he could find. He even "borrowed" his star, Georgia Hale, who was making another film at the time. When she wasn't available, Fejos used doubles, for close-up insert shots of her hands, for example. The finished film, *The Last Moment*, took its premise from Ambrose Bierce's "An Occurrence at Owl Creek Bridge." It impressed no less than Charlie Chaplin, who called Fejos a genius.

The film got Fejos a meeting with Laemmle, Sr., who wanted the director to make a big-budget "jewel" or "super-jewel" for Universal. "You should make for us an aviation adventure picture, or possibly a very sexy picture, but I mean a cleanly sexy picture," Fejos remembers Laemmle telling him. But the director had different demands: "I wanted absolute discretion on selection of story, absolute discretion on casting; only I and nobody else should see the rushes, and only I cut the picture."

Laemmle, Jr., agreed, signing Fejos to a five-year contract and suggesting that he find an idea for a movie in the Universal story department. "Most of them were stolen from classics and very badly adapted," Fejos said, but "I came across a title called *Lonesome*. It was a very small script, three pages, the outline of it. It was about a boy and girl in New York City who have no friends and who are utterly lonesome." Laemmle, Jr., told him that the studio had paid $25 for Carl Mann's treatment. Fejos cast Glenn Tryon, a relatively popular lead in Universal's light comedies, and Barbara Kent, a seventeen-year-old Canadian newcomer, as the two leads.

In *Lonesome*, Fejos followed the credo that filmmaking could be a means of personal expression, and not just a medium for communicating. His inspiration (as he was for most directors of the period) was F.W. Murnau, whose *Sunrise* (1927, a Registry title) employed every tool and device the Fox studio had to offer to fit his specific artistic scheme.

Like Murnau, Fejos was entranced by moving the camera, through panning and tilting, or with tracks or a crane. He felt that changing the frame, moving the image's boundaries, immersed viewers in the story. Fejos wrote that cinema's greatest asset was "that one can be, regardless of time and space, anywhere, and that [a] jump in time or in space can be made without pain for the audience."

Lonesome unfolds over the course of a day, Saturday, July 3rd. It follows two workers, Jim (played by Tryon), a machinist, and Mary (Kent), a switchboard operator, from the moment they wake up until they return to their apartments that night. Fejos had some sets built, but daringly shot much of the material on New York City locations, including streets, buses, and subways.

The camerawork is remarkably free and engaging for the time, evoking the work of Karl Freund and Carl Hoffmann in the German film *Variety* (1925) but also displaying Fejos's own preoccupation with time and movement. The director expands time to highlight his characters' loneliness, picking through each moment of their journey to work; and contracts it as the day ends and they are forced into decisions about their lives.

The latter half of the film takes place on Coney Island, a favorite location for filmmakers since Edison cameramen shot there in 1896. In fact cinematographer Gilbert Warrington shot in many of the same locations that earlier cameramen used, and achieved similar effects as those found in Edwin S. Porter's *Coney Island at Night* (Edison, 1905). Roscoe "Fatty" Arbuckle and Buster Keaton staged similar gags with arcade games in *Coney Island* (1917), and Keaton returned when he filmed *The Cameraman* (1929, a Registry title). King Vidor and cinematographer Henry Sharp also filmed on Coney Island for *The Crowd* (1928, a Registry title).

Fejos wanted to isolate his leads within the throngs crowding the beaches and boardwalks on a holiday weekend, and remembers going to great lengths with Warrington to make sure viewers could recognize Tryon and Kent quickly among dozens of extras. But Fejos didn't have the narrative discipline of a filmmaker like Keaton or Vidor. Shots of crowds and rides accumulate in *Lonesome*, but they don't always change or advance the plot. Keaton rigorously stripped away material that didn't apply to his story lines, even sacrificing gags if he had to. Vidor developed a film language in which one shot led to another like sentences in a paragraph, each shot making a specific point.

But the story line in *Lonesome* often seems to sputter, stand in place, even repeat itself. In one example, Tryon and Kent return to a ticket stall a half-dozen times with the same negative narrative result. Keaton would have used the setup as an opportunity to play out gags and then top them. Vidor might have revealed new aspects of the characters' personalities. Murnau would have formed an objective correlative, using lighting and editing to suggest emotional changes. Fejos, on the other hand, seems stumped by his plot, unsure how to get his characters to the next stage in their drama.

According to Fejos, Laemmle, Sr., was against the project from the start, and even the director had to admit that his story "sounds corny, but let's say it was high corn." But Fejos remembers the elder Laemmle crying so much during a screening that his secretary had to go get a fresh handkerchief. Hopes were so high for the film that after its initial release it was brought back so Fejos could insert color sequences (some stenciled, others hand-colored), and, capitalizing on a new craze, film three sound sequences. "It was sheer horror," he said.

Lonesome was one of the first Universal features to be released with a synchronized score, which included some sound effects and adaptations of popular songs like Irving Berlin's "Always." You can detect chestnuts like "(There'll Be a) Hot Time in the Old Town Tonight" and "Yes Sir That's My Baby" throughout the film, and Universal even supplied a closing theme song, "Lonesome."

The sound sequences pointed out the limitations of adapting a silent style to a new technology. In a silent sequence, two lovers on the beach can ignore the bell that signifies the closing of their dressing rooms. They, and the viewers, literally can't hear it, even if Fejos cuts to an insert of a hand ringing the actual bell. In a sound scene, the bell would be heard by everyone, and make the lovers' actions nonsensical.

The sound segments also pointed out the limitations of technology in the late 1920s. The actors had to huddle around a microphone and speak *slowly* and *distinctly*, the cinematographer could no longer move the camera, and the film stock itself was flat and unappealing.

Lonesome did well enough for the Laemmles to offer Fejos *Broadway*, an adaptation of a George Abbott musical with a $5 million budget, a Technicolor finale, and a 28-ton steel camera crane mounted on a six-wheel truck chassis. Fejos described the shoot as an unhappy experience, and ultimately was blacklisted from Universal after arguing about *The King of Jazz*, a musical starring Paul Whiteman and his orchestra. ("He's a man inordinately fat," Fejos complained to the junior Laemmle. "I don't think you can hang a love interest on him.") At MGM, he directed foreign-language versions of *The Big House* (1930), but soon returned to Europe.

There Fejos embarked on expeditions to Madagascar, Siam, and Latin America, beginning a career as an ethnographic filmmaker. Later he was president and director of research for the Wenner-Gren Foundation for Anthropological Research. He also taught anthropology at Stanford, Yale, and Columbia, and was for a time on the board of directors for Electrolux.

Laemmle, Jr., continued focusing on high-profile films, like *All Quiet on the Western Front* (1930, a Registry title). His strategy paid off at first, but unlike his rival MGM, Universal lacked the theaters to exhibit its products. (It didn't have a first-run theater in New York City to show *Lonesome*, for example.) Ultimately the Laemmles would be forced out of the studio.

The Front Page

This frame enlargement of Matt Moore from *The Front Page* indicates the poor quality of existing prints.

United Artists, 1931. Sound, B&W, 1.37. 35mm. 100 minutes.

Cast: Adolphe Menjou (Walter Burns), Pat O'Brien (Hildy Johnson), Mary Brian (Peggy Grant), Edward Everett Horton (Bensinger), Walter L. Catlett (Murphy), George E. Stone (Earl Williams), Mae Clarke (Molly), Slim Summerville (Pincus), Matt Moore (Kruger), Frank McHugh (McCue), Clarence H. Wilson (Sheriff Hartman), Freddie Howard (Schwartz), Phil Tead (Wilson), Gene Strong (Endicott), Spencer Charters (Woodenshoes), Maurice Black (Diamond Louie), Effie Ellsler (Mrs. Grant), Dorothea Wolbert (Jenny), James Gordon (The Mayor).

Credits: Directed by Lewis Milestone. Play by Ben Hecht and Charles MacArthur. From the Play as Produced by Jed Harris. Adaptation by Bartlett Cormack. Additional dialogue by Charles Lederer. Assistant director: Nate Watt. Photography: Glen MacWilliams. Settings: Richard Day. Film Editor: W. Duncan Mansfield. Sound Engineer: Frank Grenzbach. Production Manager: Charles Stallings. A Howard Hughes presentation of a Lewis Milestone production.

Additional cast: Gustav von Seyffertitz (Professor Max J. Engelhoffer), Richard Alexander (Jacobi), Lewis Milestone, Herman J. Mankiewicz.

Additional credits: Cinematography: Hal Mohr, Tony Gaudio. Premiered New York City March 19, 1931.

Other versions: Remade as *His Girl Friday* in 1940 by Howard Hawks, starring Cary Grant and Rosalind Russell. Billy Wilder directed *The Front Page*, starring Walter Matthau and Jack Lemmon, in 1974. Ted Kotcheff directed *Switching Channels*, an adaptation of *His Girl Friday* set in a cable news studio and starring Burt Reynolds, in 1988.

Available: The Library of Congress.

Filmmakers started moving cameras instead of shooting from fixed positions almost as soon as the medium was invented. Directors and cinematographers relished changing the frame—by tilting or panning the camera, or mounting it on vehicles—because they felt it involved viewers in the action while building an illusion of realism. Pulling in closer to actors or panning to reveal another character allowed directors to shape or punctuate scenes. Moving the camera added to the grammar of film, giving directors a wider array of strategies for presenting their material.

The transition from silent to sound movies marked the single greatest interruption to filmmaking since it began. Learning how to adapt cinematic technique to the demands of a new technology proved just as difficult as figuring out how to successfully record dialogue, music, and effects. Sound stymied directors formerly adept at presenting stories in a visual manner. Many of them fell back to older methods, reducing plays and musicals to inert tableaus.

Several directors experimented with using silent techniques (usually with silent cameras) while making sound films. At first this was the only successful means of moving a camera restricted by the demands of sound technology. The Registry titles *Applause* and *Hallelujah!* (both 1929) included lengthy montages and extended tracking shots, some with sound.

But for every successful stab at liberating the sound camera, we find stiff, stodgy talkies peopled by anxious actors who over-pronounce their lines with the meticulous diction and dull monotone preferred by speech coaches. Even as lively a movie as *The Public Enemy* (1931) is marred by poorly paced and acted stretches of dialogue.

What sets *The Front Page* apart from many of its contemporaries is the freedom with which director Lewis Milestone used sound. At the end of his career, Milestone spoke about his approach to adapting a hit Broadway play for film. "We shoot the way we've always shot," he told his crew. "The big sound revolution" was that simple: "all the tracking shots, for example, were done with a silent camera."

What Milestone left unstated was his insistence on using sound to support the film, not dominate it. The director respected the source material, but didn't allow dialogue to determine the visual structure of his movie. Where Rouben Mamoulian fetishized visuals in *Applause*, using cranes to move the camera above, below, and around his actors, Milestone and his crew figured out how to supplement tracking shots with sound—not the other way around.

Furthermore, Milestone was willing to sacrifice clarity to heighten the reality of a scene. Just like some directors would blur action with short shots and quick cuts in order to increase suspense, Milestone didn't mind losing a line or two of dialogue if it helped keep his scene moving. Unlike the typical film of the time, with dialogue delivered in a careful staccato, Milestone let his actors step over each others' lines, the way real people do when they're angry and upset.

Of course it helped that Milestone was working with one of the fastest-paced plays of its time. Written by Ben Hecht and Charles MacArthur, *The*

Front Page was an immediate hit after it opened on Broadway on August 14, 1928. Hecht, born in New York City but raised in Racine, Wisconsin, had already established himself as a journalist, foreign correspondent, novelist, and playwright in Chicago when he moved back to New York in 1924. The son of an itinerant clergyman, MacArthur ran away from school in Nyack, New York, becoming a salesman, journalist, and member of the Army, serving in Europe during World War I. After the war he worked as a journalist again in Chicago before moving to New York to work on plays.

In his memoir *Charlie*, Hecht remembered meeting MacArthur, whose play *Lulu Belle* had just opened, on the street and agreeing to write a play about their Chicago newspaper days. Over the following weeks of work in Hecht's apartment, they condensed their plot into a single night in a press room of a city jail where a mentally unstable prisoner is to be hung the following dawn (despite pleas to hurry the proceedings by reporters on deadline). "We were both writing of people we had loved, and of an employment that had been like none other was ever to be," as Hecht put it.

Hecht marveled over MacArthur's drive—"I have never known since in anyone the inventiveness and certainty, the burst of creation, Charlie brought to *The Front Page*."—but also his judgment. They hashed out speeches together, MacArthur playing parts while Hecht scribbled notes. The end result was cruel, cynical, even morbid, but the authors' affection for their characters was always evident. (Hecht also took pains to credit producer Jed Harris for the success of the play.)

As writers, the two may have been reworking their experiences in Chicago, but they were also tailoring their material for Broadway. *What Price Glory* had run for 435 performances before being adapted to film, and Hecht and MacArthur were smart enough to see that they could incorporate a similar narrative "engine" into *The Front Page*. In fact, it was an engine that Hecht would use throughout his career: the love affair between two aggressive males who can't stand each other but can't stand to be apart. In Hecht's hands, every-thing from *Underworld* (1927) to *Scarface* (1932) and *Gunga Din* (1939) in some ways revolved around similar male relationships.

Milestone had made good use of the *What Price Glory* formula as well, in a rowdy service comedy called *Two Arabian Knights* (1927) which he filmed for millionaire movie mogul Howard Hughes and his Caddo Pictures. The success of *Two Arabian Knights* led to a contract for Milestone to direct *All Quiet on the Western Front* (1930, a Registry title) for Universal.

And the international success of *All Quiet...* convinced Hughes that Milestone was the man to direct a screen version of *The Front Page*. Hecht and MacArthur were happy to sell the rights to their play to Caddo Pictures, but had no interest in working on it. Hughes hired Bartlett Cormack, yet another Chicago journalist, and Charles Lederer to adapt a screenplay. Cormack had written *The Racket*, a Broadway hit that helped make a star of Edward G.

Robinson. (Coincidentally, Milestone directed the screen version for Hughes.) Lederer, the nephew of movie star Marion Davies, would later collaborate with Hecht and several other notable screenwriters.

While it teems with Chicago types, from a venal mayor to cynical reporters, with an unbalanced killer, disillusioned prostitute, and a variety of civil servants thrown in, *The Front Page* revolves around the love-hate relationship between editor Walter Burns and reporter Hildy Johnson. Milestone later said he wanted James Cagney or Clark Gable for Johnson, unlikely choices at the time as Cagney was under contract to Warner Bros. and Gable had yet to make a name for himself on screen.

Hughes instead cast Pat O'Brien, who had appeared in a Chicago production of the play, but had little film experience. His performance in *The Front Page* reveals his strengths and weaknesses as an actor. O'Brien had a blunt presence and forceful delivery, and his wide face and stocky figure helped him portray a string of fast-talking but sincere cops, priests, coaches, and sidekicks later in his career. But on film O'Brien had trouble conveying nuance. He gets his lines right, but not the irony and self-loathing in Johnson's role. (Hecht wrote, "There was never a better actor for a part than Lee Tracy for Hildy.")

Osgood Perkins played Walter Burns on stage, winning over the initially dubious Hecht and MacArthur. The urbane Adolphe Menjou took the role on screen, and his aloof, supercilious persona suited Burns perfectly. The script provides several outstanding parts for character actors, notably Edward Everett Horton, Frank McHugh, and Mae Clarke, soon to be seen encountering a grapefruit at the hands of James Cagney in *The Public Enemy*.

Milestone and his writers opened the play up a little, adding a scene in a speakeasy where Burns tries to blackmail Johnson, about to leave town to get married, into returning to work. Some material was cut, notably a speech about Communism and a bit in which a cop tries to analyze the sources of crime.

But mostly Milestone remained true to the play. He adds some directorial flourishes—quick cuts among reporters to highlight how they bring their own biases when describing a stand-off, long tracking shots following characters through locations—but for the most part moves the camera because the play calls for it. Milestone's interpretation of the material was so incisive that Howard Hawks copied much of it for his own version.

Lacking his own distribution company, Hughes released *The Front Page* through United Artists. The film was a bona fide hit, with many reviewers singling out Milestone's use of sound. Other studios rushed their own newspaper movies into production: *Five Star Final* (1931) and *Blessed Event* (1932) from Warner Bros., *Platinum Blonde* (1931) from Columbia, *Washington Merry-Go-Round* (1932) from Universal. Snappy patter became a fixture in Hollywood films, as did cynical, grubbing reporters, like the

Oscar-winning turns by Clark Gable in *It Happened One Night* (1934) and James Stewart in *The Philadelphia Story* (1940, both Registry titles). Universal eventually purchased most of Howard Hughes' releases, but not *The Front Page*. Before it was purchased by MGM, United Artists was notoriously lax about renewing the copyrights of the titles in its film library. As a result, the 1931 version of *The Front Page* is in the public domain, although its source material and its many remakes are not. Because most of Hughes' films were withdrawn from circulation, but also because of the success of *His Girl Friday*, Milestone's film was overlooked for years. It wasn't until a joint restoration project by the American Film Institute and Staatlichen Filmarchiv DDR that the film became available again.

And yet when he assembled a series on "The Newspaper Picture," Bruce Goldstein, director of Repertory Programming at New York's Film Forum, learned that no 35mm print of *The Front Page* could be found in the United States. Goldstein considers this a perfect example of an "orphan" film, because no commercial distributor will consider investing the funds necessary to restore and preserve it.

A Study in Reds

The start of what promises to be a long and grim lecture on Soviet Russia.

Miriam Bennett, 1932. Silent, B&W, 1.33. 16mm. 17 minutes.

Cast includes: Miriam Bennett, Verna Dixon, Ruth Dyer, Jean Dyer Reese, Mrs. Barney.

Credits: Screen story (if any) by Miriam Bennett, assisted by Verna Dixon, Ruth Dyer.

Available: Wisconsin Historical Society, www.wisconsinhistory.org.

The 1930s and 1940s marked the heyday of amateur filmmaking. In contrast to home movies, which documented people and events for personal use, amateur filmmakers had higher ambitions. They made movies with themes and narratives, and intended them for a wider audience than family and friends. Founded in 1926, the Amateur Cinema League (ACL) provided a crucial community for amateur film. The 1949 edition of the ACL's *Guide to Making Better Movies* could cite advice and aid to "more than 100,000 home movie makers."

The Tuesday Club stretches back even further, to 1881 in Fort Atkinson, Wisconsin, for example. A women's study group with chapters in several Wisconsin locations, the Tuesday Club offered programs in which members would deliver lectures on various topics, followed by afternoon tea. A

Wisconsin Dells chapter dates from at least 1902, when it helped finance the Kilbourn Public Library.

Kilbourn City, later named Wisconsin Dells, was the site of H.H. Bennett's photographic studio. Born in Canada in 1843, he moved to Wisconsin in 1857. A Civil War veteran, he purchased a tintype studio in 1865, and was selling stereoscopic views of the remarkable area landscapes a few years later. He contributed photographs to guidebooks, tourist brochures, and other promotional materials, helping develop the Wisconsin Dells as a resort destination. Bennett was also an innovator, inventing a stop-action shutter and a portable darkroom. A widower, he married Evaline H. Marshall in 1890. They had two children, Miriam (1891–1971) and Ruth Bennett Dyer (1895–1982). When Bennett died in 1908, his wife and daughters took over his studio.

Miriam and Ruth certainly had the technical expertise to make *A Study in Reds*, an amateur film sponsored by the Tuesday Club in 1932. Shot on 16mm black-and-white negative, the seventeen-minute film features eighteen members of the Tuesday Club in a comic fantasy prompted by worries that Communists were infiltrating society.

A Study in Reds is further proof that ours is not the smartest or most sophisticated generation. Engaging on a technical level, the film is even more successful for its sly, deadpan humor. An opening intertitle announces that the club is about to experience "a feast of reason," but it's followed by the same dull, repetitive establishing shots that make up most home movies. A woman stands by a dining room table. She fusses over table settings, pours water into a goblet, rearranges a napkin, then drops her apron as she responds to something off-screen.

As all eighteen members of the Tuesday Club enter a living room, we seem to be trapped in a potentially endless talk about "what I did on my vacation"—a prospect made more frightening by the speaker's pile of weighty sociological tomes. But Miriam Bennett, most likely the principle filmmaker here, has an astute eye for drawing out characters, like the member who pauses over her makeup at the doorway. Bennett punctuates her shots with quick, unselfconscious gags, chooses unusual camera angles, and (for the most part) keeps her cast under control and in character.

The lecture for the night concerns "reddest Russia" and its "famous Soviets." The jokes start coming quicker, like an insert shot of Negley Farson's *Black Bread and Red Coffins* among the speaker's reference books, or the hands spinning around on a table clock. Members stifle yawns, feet tap impatiently, and poor Mrs. Barney's head starts to nod. As the lecture continues, Bennett even adds a brief bit of animation.

Bennett's entry into the film's fantasy sequence is especially adroit. After a pan across the room, a member takes off her glasses. The next shot, out of focus at first, gradually resolves to the members now dressed in "Russian" clothes. It's a strange new world—as an intertitle announces, "The comrades will eat cabbage soup and like it!"

The film moves to exteriors shot in the neighborhood. In this Russia, mothers are separated from their children, or "freed from domestic shackles." Bennett frames a mother imprisoned for being too affectionate like a shot from a D.W. Griffith melodrama. (One of the "G.P.U." police is dressed in a Keystone Kops costume.)

As the women go off to work, Bennett's camera gets freer, panning, tilting, and at one point traveling on the back of a sleigh. Further scenes take place in snowy woods, in a printing office, a tool shop, and an "egg and milk factory," or farm. This last location allows Bennett—who, like every good filmmaker, knew how popular animals are with viewers—to work in shots of cows, pigs, horses, and chickens.

Once *A Study in Reds* reaches its satisfying conclusion, Bennett cuts to the Amateur Cinema League logo. The ACL held contests for films, and this would have been an excellent entry. With a camera that moves, animation, dissolves, smart intertitles, a game cast, intriguing locations, and a topical storyline, *A Study in Reds* shows just how advanced amateur moviemaking could get.

Miriam Bennett made several other movies, working into the 1960s. Her subjects included her family and friends, but also local events of interest: harvest scenes, fashion parades, "Horse and Buggy Days" in 1949, a park dedication, etc. *A Study in Reds* remained popular with members through the years, and was featured periodically in newspaper stories. Ruth Bennett Dyer's daughter Jean, who played one of the children exiled to a Soviet nursery school, recalled in a 2001 article how one scene was shot in an empty swimming pool.

The film also became a favorite in academia. It was referenced in *Mining the Home Movie: Excavations in Histories and Memories* (University of California Press, 2007), edited by Karen L. Ishizuka and Patricia R. Zimmerman. Zimmerman, a professor in the Department of Cinema, Photography, and Media Arts at Ithaca College, and Pamela Wintle, senior film archivist for the Human Studies Film Archives, Smithsonian Institute, screened *A Study in Reds* at the Second Annual TFMS Film Series at St. Mary's College of Maryland in 2009. With support from Mark Rhoda, a co-organizer of the series, and his Film History class, Ms. Wintle nominated *A Study in Reds* for the National Film Registry in the spring of 2009.

Jean Dyer and her husband Oliver Reese eventually took over the Bennett studio, preserving her grandfather's collection of negatives and continuing to offer prints struck from his glass plates until the 1990s. The Reeses donated the studio and the Bennett collection to the Wisconsin Historical Society. Some 650 Bennett photographs can be viewed online at the WHS site. The H.H. Bennett Studio is now a Wisconsin Historical Society Historical site.

The WHS plans to make *A Study in Reds*, including some previously unavailable outtakes, available on DVD.

It's a Gift

A dark moment for a downcast W.C. Fields.

Paramount, 1934. Sound, B&W, 1.37. 35mm. 68 minutes.

Cast: W.C. Fields (Harold Bissonette), Kathleen Howard (Amelia Bissonette), Jean Rouveral (Mildred Bissonette), Julian Madison (John Durston), Tom Bupp (Norman Bissonette), Baby LeRoy (Baby Dunk), Tammany Young (Everett Ricks), Morgan Wallace (James Fitchmueller), Charles Sellon (Mr. Muckle), Josephine Whittell (Mrs. Dunk), T. Roy Barnes (Insurance Salesman), Diana Lewis (Miss Dunk), Spencer Charters (Gate Guard), Guy Usher (Harry Payne Bosterly), Del Henderson (Mr. Abernathy).

Credits: Directed by Norman McLeod. Screen Play by Jack Cunningham. From "The Comic Supplement" by J. P. McEvoy. Based upon a Story by Charles Bogle [W.C. Fields]. Produced by William LeBaron. Photographed by Henry Sharp. Western Electric Noiseless recording. An Adolph Zukor presentation.

Additional cast: Jerry Mandy (Vegetable man), James Burke (Ice man), Billy Engle (Scissors grinder), William Tooker (Old man), Edith Kingdon (Old woman), Patsy O'Byrne (Mrs. Frobisher), Jane Withers (Hopscotch girl), Jack Mulhall (Butler), Chill Wills and the Avalon Boys (Campfire singers).

Additional credits: Screenwriting: Garnett Weston, Claude Binyon, Paul Gerard Smith, Howard J. Green, John Sinclair, Lou Breslow, Eddie Welch, Harry Ruskin. Executive producer: Emanuel Cohen. Art direction: Hans Dreier, John B. Goodman. Sound: Earl S. Hayman. Released November 30, 1934.

Other versions: Remake of *It's the Old Army Game* (1926).

Available: Universal Home Video DVD *W.C. Fields Comedy Collection* (2004). ISBN: 1–4170–1574–8. UPC: 0–25192–57812–0.

W.C. Fields was fifty-four when he made *It's a Gift*, a bleak, slice-of-life comedy about an unhappy New Jersey grocer. Among his contemporaries, only Charlie

Chaplin and Buster Keaton could claim as much training as Fields, who had been touring as a juggler and comic since the turn of the twentieth century. Over thirty years' worth of experience went into the writing and filming of *It's a Gift*, making it perhaps the most succinct and deeply felt of Fields' movies. (For more about Fields' background and career, see the Registry entries *So's Your Old Man*, 1926, and *The Bank Dick*, 1940.)

It's a Gift was the last of five features Fields released in 1934, during his resurgence after a period of box-office decline at the beginning of the 1930s. Many of these movies reworked his silent films, which in turn were based on skits he had performed daily during the seasonal runs of showman Florenz Ziegfeld's *Follies*. It may seem odd today that Fields would ransack his catalogue so thoroughly, performing essentially a handful of skits throughout his career. But each new version enabled him to add and refine jokes, to adjust timings, to block out new stagings. More important, Fields grew into his roles, developing more nuanced characterizations as he learned more about human psychology. The most remarkable aspect of *It's a Gift* may be how few actual "jokes" are in the movie. With slightly different staging, most of the film could play as a drama, and a singularly dark drama at that.

According to biographer James Curtis, *It's a Gift* is the one Fields film that he wrote primarily by himself, although several other writers worked on it. Fields' treatment was based on *The Comic Supplement*, a play J.P. McEvoy had written with the comedian in mind back in 1924. (The play was also the basis for *It's the Old Army Game*, 1926.) Called *Back Porch*, the eleven-page treatment included all of the scenes in the final movie, as well as several that weren't filmed.

Fields drew on his old routines in the treatment, such as "The Family Ford," a skit he wrote in 1919. It featured the Fliverton family, especially its harried husband, encountering trouble on a trip in a new car. In it, a blind man accidentally smashes a headlight with his cane. Fields opened the *Back Porch* treatment in a grocery run by Mr. Fliverton. A blind customer, Mr. Muckle, enters by breaking the store's glass door with his cane. After a scene that gave the treatment its name, Fields returned to "The Family Ford" and its sequel, "The Sport Model," reworking gags for a cross-country trip the family takes, including an extended picnic scene that he also used in *It's the Old Army Game*.

Fields submitted the treatment to Paramount producer William Le Baron, who in turn handed it over to contract writers. Jack Cunningham received credit for the screenplay (with the story credit going to Fields' pseudonym as "Charles Bogle"), but several other writers contributed, including *Follies* veteran Paul Gerard Smith. The second treatment, thirty-nine pages, added a shaving scene from another McEvoy play, *The Potters*; a car chase that was later discarded; the introduction of Carl LaFong; and much of the final dialogue. Fliverton was now Bissonette, a name taken from a golfing companion.

Cunningham worked the treatments into a shooting script, adding transitional scenes and material for a romantic subplot involving Bissonette's daughter Mildred and her boyfriend.

Rehearsals began on September 5, 1934. Norman McLeod, the nominal director, had worked on two Marx Brothers vehicles, where he proved a good judge of improvisation. But to the cast and crew, Fields was in charge. He knew this material intimately, and had learned what would work and what wouldn't, when a scene needed more business, which character to focus on. Which isn't to say *It's a Gift* is a stale or lifeless recreation of a stage piece: Fields had three gag writers on the set, including his longtime friend Johnny Sinclair, and would tip crew members, like prop man Harry Caplan, $100 for ideas.

The business of comedy is tough, and *It's a Gift* went behind schedule as Fields and the cast and crew worked out scenes. They spent an entire morning perfecting one shot of Mr. Muckle, for example, and it took two hours to shoot his exit from the grocery. After production started, Fields and McLeod agreed that the Bissonette family needed a son instead of a young daughter, replacing Shirley McClellan with Tom Bupp.

Fields felt so much pressure from the studio that he had the Back Porch skit, which he felt was "awful" in *It's the Old Army Game*, shot at Lasky Mesa, a ranch used for Westerns, so that executives couldn't hound him. To save time, he filmed with three cameras, a technique that would later be used for television sitcoms. The picnic scene, the highlight of "The Family Ford," was filmed at Busch Gardens in Pasadena. Fields had elaborated on this skit in *It's the Old Army Game*, deliberately trashing the Palm Beach grounds of banker Edward T. Stotesbury. The version here seethes with repressed hostility instead, an approach that shows how Fields' technique had matured.

Cast and crew, and Fields himself, spoke frequently about his drinking while filming. (Slapstick pioneer Mack Sennett felt that Fields was an "indecisive" performer without alcohol.) Fields drank on the set, with his friend Tammany Young and at times with McLeod, but as production records show, he could not have worked this hard had he been seriously impaired.

Fields did not pay much attention to casting minor roles in his films. For the part of Mildred, he wanted a "Joan Marsh" type (Marsh had played his daughter in *You're Telling Me!* earlier that year). He got Jean Rouveral instead. Angry at being pulled from Max Reinhardt's production of *A Midsummer Night's Dream* at Warners, Rouveral gave a very convincing performance as a spoiled, petulant young woman. Child star Baby LeRoy, Fields' nemesis in *The Old Fashioned Way* (1934), returned for two scenes. Fields hated working with LeRoy, worried that the child was stealing scenes. According to McLeod, "He used to swear at the baby so much in front of the camera that I sometimes had to cut off the ends of the scenes in which they both appeared."

Kathleen Howard had played a haughty society matron in *You're Telling Me!*; here she has a key role as Fields' wife Amelia. A contralto who sang with the Metropolitan Opera, Howard was also fashion editor for *Harper's Bazaar* until she left print for acting. Her regal bearing and piercing voice complemented the henpecked, downtrodden Harold Bissonette perfectly. Fields and his writers concocted wonderful lines for her: "I don't know why every time I try to talk to you, you're in another part of the house." When Bissonette is accosted by an insurance salesman, she declares, "Harold, if you and your friend wish to exchange ribald stories, please take it downstairs."

But it is Fields who ultimately makes *It's a Gift* such a memorable film. His Bissonette is the world's worst grocer, an equally bad investor in real estate, a browbeaten husband, and an incompetent father. Touchingly, he is still a dreamer with faith in a better future. His soft moans, muttered curses, and expressions of despair are a case study in frustration. And yet, at his lowest ebb the worst he can say is, "Everything goes at once."

In his later films Fields leaned more on sentimentality and slapstick, concocting bizarre characters in outlandish situations. With *It's a Gift* he delivered a paean to losers, a timeless, pitiless examination of human nature.

The Revenge of Pancho Villa

A scene from the Universal serial *Liberty* appropriated for *The Revenge of Pancho Villa*.

Félix and Edmundo Padilla, 1936. Silent, B&W, 1.33. 35mm. 60 minutes.

Cast includes: Raoul Walsh (Pancho Villa), Marie Walcamp ("Amelia"/Liberty), G. Raymond Nye (Pancho Lopez).

Credits: Assembled and edited by Félix and Edmundo Padilla. Compiled from *The Life of Pancho Villa* (1914), *Liberty* (1916), *The Birth of a Nation* (1916), various newsreels. Original footage by Félix and Edmundo Padilla.

Additional credits: Spanish title: *La Venganza de Pancho Villa*. Preservation by Kim Tomadjoglou, at the time Curator for the American Film Institute Collection at the Library of Congress.

Available: *Los Rollos Perdidos de Pancho Villa* (2003 DVD, distributed by SubCine, 611 Broadway, Suite 616, New York, NY 10012).

When we watch movies today, we are participating in a business model already largely in place when the film industry consolidated production and distribution in the 1920s. Whether we attend a theater or stream a digital file to computers, we are "end users" of a system that tailors mass market entertainment for the widest audience possible.

But when movies were still being invented, another model put consumers in a different position. In this example movies were made for specific audiences, small groups interested in topical material. Rather than distribute one film nationwide through a chain of theaters, this model saw many

48

filmmakers making regional movies for individual screenings, editing them to fit different markets.

Filmmakers as diverse as J. Stuart Blackton, Billy Bitzer, and King Vidor made movies of local attractions and inhabitants that they would exhibit in local theaters. Today historians refer to a class of "itinerant filmmakers." What was a widespread practice at the turn of the twentieth century became less practical as theaters were bought up by chains and audiences came to expect more polished studio product. But some filmmakers continued to focus on local markets, especially those areas underserved by Hollywood distributors.

The Registry has already highlighted the work of H. Lee Waters, an itinerant filmmaker who worked mostly in North Carolina, Tennessee, and Kentucky (cf., *Kannapolis*, 1940–41). The Padilla family, Félix and his son Edmundo, operated in northern Mexico and southwest United States. Félix, who came from Ciudad Juárez, Chihuahua, bought or rented silent films from distributors in Mexico City or Los Angeles. He would travel by truck to outlying areas to screen the films in theaters or in outdoor plazas, offering musical accompaniment from his collection of 78 rpm records.

According to Gregorio C. Rocha, a film historian who is largely responsible for bringing *La Venganza...* to light after decades of neglect, the Padillas showed slapstick shorts and feature dramas like *En la hacienda* (1922) to audiences in Ciudad Juárez, Gomez Palacio, Durango, and Coyote, Coahuila, among many other places. In the 1930s, when they moved to El Paso, they decided to assemble a film about Pancho Villa, transitioning from exhibitors to actual moviemakers. What distinguishes their Villa film is how casually they mixed original and "found" footage, anticipating by decades the repurposing of materials into something that might contradict the meaning of the appropriated content.

In the region the Padillas were serving, few figures could stir up as much passion and controversy as Pancho Villa. In early 1914, when Villa was considered an ally of the United States government, he signed a contract with Mutual Film Corporation for a biographical movie to be called *The Life of Pancho Villa*. Biographical films were a mainstay of the industry at the time, but no one yet had tried to capitalize on a figure who was in the process of attempting to overthrow a government. Villa received new uniforms, a promise of 20% of the profits from the film, and cash. In return, he granted exclusive rights to Mutual for photographing a battle in Ojinaga (later known as "the battle fought to be filmed"), and even promised to conduct the fighting at day rather than night to facilitate filming.

The Life of Pancho Villa was produced by D.W. Griffith and directed by William Cabanne. Starring was Raoul Walsh, who would play John Wilkes Booth in *The Birth of a Nation* (1915) and later become a significant director (his Registry titles include *Regeneration*, 1915, *The Thief of Bagdad*, 1924, *The Big Trail*, 1930, and *White Heat*, 1949.)

Much of *The Life of Pancho Villa* was shot in California, some scenes at the same locations Griffith would use for *The Birth of a Nation*'s Civil War battles. Mutual also sent four cameramen on location to Mexico. L.M. Burrud and Tracy Mathewson covered the Constitutionalists; Charles Rosher and Herbert Dean, the Federales. (Charles Pryor, an independent filmmaker, also shot footage at Ojinaga.) *The Life of Pancho Villa* opened at the Lyric Theatre in New York City, and later played throughout the country.

But in 1916, the U.S. government threw its support behind Venustiano Carranza for President. In retaliation, Villa attacked Columbus, New Mexico, killing civilians. The incident prompted President Woodrow Wilson to authorize U.S. troops under General John Pershing to invade Mexico. Formerly a hero, Villa was now seen as a villain, at least by gringos. Universal responded with *Liberty*, a serial in which a thinly disguised "Pancho Lopez" attacks the town of "Discovery," in the process threatening the virginity of Liberty, the heroine played by Marie Walcamp.

The Life of Pancho Villa is now considered a lost film, although snippets of it turn up in *La Venganza...* So do sequences from *Liberty*, Mexican and World War I newsreels, *The Birth of a Nation*, and footage the Padillas shot themselves with friends and neighbors outside El Paso. The Padillas also prepared their own intertitles, as well as borrowing intertitles from at least three sources.

Amazingly, the story they constructed makes sense. Perhaps even more remarkably, they show Villa as both hero and villain. He is a youth drawn into rebellion after his sister is forced to commit suicide rather than submit to the advances of Federales; but he is also a corrupt leader who conducts a sneak attack in which infants are snatched from the arms of their mothers. (Mariano de la Torre, Félix Padilla's grandson, remembers that the Columbus, New Mexico, sequence would have Mexican audiences yelling, "Viva Villa! Mueran los gringos!")

According to Rocha, the Padillas prepared at least three versions of their Pancho Villa film. The first, *El reinado del terror (*The Reign of Terror*)*, they exhibited in the early 1930s. The second, *Pancho Villa en Columbus*, was tied specifically to Villa's attack in New Mexico. These were "open-ended" films in that the Padillas would add or subtract to them based on how audiences responded to screenings (and on whether or not new footage turned up).

After Félix died in 1936, Edmundo prepared *La Venganza...*, the definitive Padilla account of Pancho Villa's life. New to this version were sequences lifted from *Historia de la Revolución Mexicana* (1928), a documentary by Julio Lamadrid. In his commentary, Rocha points out how Edmundo would use documentary or newsreel footage to establish a setting, then cut to a battle scene from *Liberty*, equating truth with fiction while playing to his viewers' biases about events.

It is a virtuoso job of editing, not the least because Edmundo always kept his viewers in mind when constructing sequences. *La Venganza...* starts on an action-packed note and rarely lets up, with the abduction of an innocent girl leading to bizarre acrobatics from a prisoner in a jail cell—material that wouldn't feel out of place in a Hong Kong martial-arts film. Robberies, attacks, betrayals, gunfights, and chases follow—the sort of crowd-pleasing entertainment that might be hard to find in a dusty border town without its own movie theater.

But are we supposed to like Villa or hate him? He robs a rich hacienda, killing the very workers whose exploitation he vowed to end. He gives to the poor in one shot and steals from them in the next. He "exterminates" Federales who are sabotaging a railroad line, then kills two peasants in cold blood and sets their shack afire. Padilla then cuts to admiring footage of Villa's soldiers marching in formation.

According to Rocha, leaflets from the Padilla files indicate that the last screening of *La Venganza...* was in October, 1937. Logbooks show that the film earned $1280 over a nine-month period, around 12,000 customers at ten cents a ticket. The Padilla family donated the film and accompanying materials to the University of Texas at El Paso, but *La Venganza...* might have disappeared forever if it hadn't been for Rocha, who stumbled across the collection while searching for *The Life of Pancho Villa*. Ironically, the Padillas may have destroyed one of the last remaining prints of *The Life of Pancho Villa* to make *La Venganza...*

Make Way for Tomorrow

Beulah Bondi and Victor Moore as parents hemmed in by fate.

Paramount, 1937. Sound, B&W, 1.37. 35mm. 92 minutes.

Cast: Victor Moore (Barkley Cooper), Beulah Bondi (Lucy Cooper), Fay Bainter (Anita Cooper), Thomas Mitchell (George Cooper), Porter Hall (Harvey Chase), Barbara Read (Rhoda Cooper), Maurice Moscovitch (Max Rubens), Elisabeth Risdon (Cora Payne), Minna Gombell (Nellie Chase), Ray Mayer (Robert Cooper), Ralph Remley (Bill Payne), Louise Beavers (Mamie), Louis Jean Heydt (Doctor), Gene Morgan (Carlton Gorman).

Credits: Directed by Leo McCarey. Screen Play by Viña Delmar. Based on a novel by Josephine Lawrence and a play by Helen and Nolan Leary. Musical direction: Boris Morros. Original music by Victor Young and George Antheil. Photographed by William C. Mellor. Special photographic effects by Gordon Jennings. Art direction by Hans Dreier and Bernard Herzbrun. Edited by LeRoy Stone. Sound recording: Walter Oberst and Don Johnson. Interior decorations by A.E. Freudeman. Western Electric noiseless recording. An Adolph Zukor presentation of a Leo McCarey production.

Additional cast includes: George Offerman Jr. (Richard Payne), Tommy Bupp (Jack Payne), Ferike Boros (Mrs. Sarah Rubens), Nick Lukats (Boyfriend), Terry Ray (Usherette),Gene Lockhart (Mr. Henning), Ruth Warren (Secretary), Dell Henderson (Auto salesman, Ed Weldon), Paul Stanton (Hotel manager, Mr. Horton), Granville Bates (Mr. Hunter), Byron Foulger (Mr. Dale), Avril Cameron (Mrs. McKenzie).

Additional credits: Screenwriting: Howard J. Green. Song "Make Way for Tomorrow" composed by Sam Coslow, Leo Robin, Jean Schwartz. Production began January 11, 1937. Hollywood premiere: May 7, 1937.

Available: Criterion Collection DVD (2009). UPC: 7–15515–05241–2.

Critics love to write about *Make Way for Tomorrow*, usually with a hectoring tone. They can't understand why the film isn't better known, implying that something is wrong with moviegoers for not embracing it. The public, on the other hand, had little use for a film so painful and despairing. After it completed its theatrical run, *Make Way for Tomorrow* was a difficult film to see. Art-house programmers would occasionally pair it with other works by Leo McCarey, but it did not fit comfortably with titles like *Duck Soup* (1933) or *The Awful Truth* (1937, both on the Registry). Although it is made with the same easygoing virtuosity as those movies, *Make Way for Tomorrow* is a film that may ask too much of its viewers.

The screenplay was adapted from *Years Are So Long*, a 1934 novel by Josephine Lawrence. Born in 1889 in Newark, Lawrence wrote poems and stories as a child, then entered journalism in 1915 as editor of the children's page for a Newark newspaper. She later edited the household page and ran a question-and-answer column devoted to family issues. Between 1919 and 1934 she wrote at least fifty children's novels, many under pseudonyms. She also wrote a radio show for children. Her first novel for adults, *Head of the Family*, came out in 1932. Her second, *Years Are So Long*, was a Book of the Month Club selection.

Lawrence viewed domestic problems in terms of social issues, and her books could be seen as "message dramas," instructional if not downright didactic. *Years Are So Long* concerned the problems adult children faced caring for their elderly parents, a topic she had covered in her question-and-answer column.

A domestic drama was not a typical subject for director Leo McCarey, who was considered one of the best comedy directors in Hollywood. (For more about McCarey's career, see *The Awful Truth*, 1937). But while making *The Milky Way* (1936) with Harold Lloyd, McCarey became deathly ill after drinking contaminated milk. He was so sick that he couldn't attend his father's funeral. As he related to Peter Bogdanovich in an interview, *Make Way for Tomorrow* came about because "I had just lost my father and we were really good friends; I admired him so much."

McCarey went to Palm Springs to recuperate, and in a casino there met Viña Delmar, who had just published a story "about old folks" in *Cosmopolitan* magazine. Delmar had written several semi-scandalous magazine serials and the best-selling novel *Bad Girl* (1928), which was filmed in 1931 by Frank Borzage. She got along so well with McCarey that he hired her for *Make Way for Tomorrow*.

Adapting Lawrence's novel proved difficult, even though McCarey told the *New York Times* that he went off salary and offered to direct at a flat rate "because he was excited about the picture and wanted to take plenty of time." In fact the film took almost a year to produce; in December, 1936, McCarey and writer Howard J. Green were still struggling to make the script less depressing.

No one in the cast of *Make Way for Tomorrow* would have been considered a star at the time, although filmgoers of the time would have been familiar with character actors like Thomas Mitchell and Fay Bainter, both of whom would soon win Oscars. Victor Moore had been a popular vaudeville performer and the star of several amusing silent shorts. In a *Saturday Evening Post* column some ten years later, he would identify this as "The Role I Liked Best." Beulah Bondi would continue portraying the silently sacrificing mother she played here throughout her career, in films like *Of Human Hearts* (1938) where she pleads with President Abraham Lincoln to spare her son from execution, and *It's a Wonderful Life* (1946, a Registry title), where she tries to reassure her son that he hasn't wasted his life.

The premise of *Make Way for Tomorrow* is simple: due to financial reversals, an elderly couple are forced to live with their offspring, the husband (played by Moore) in the Midwest, the mother (Bondi) with her harried daughter in an urban apartment. In his comic shorts, McCarey started from realistic situations—a Sunday dinner, moving a piano—and then spun out jokes based primarily on frustration and repression. The father has accidentally cooked a neighbor's prized chicken, for example, or two movers have to carry a piano up endless flights of stairs.

McCarey uses the same tactic in *Make Way for Tomorrow*, but instead of jokes he finds anger and sorrow. The mother, quaint and fidgety, upsets her daughter's social plans; the father, a blustering blowhard, embarrasses his son. Part of the pleasure in watching McCarey's comedies is that the solutions to narrative problems seem so easy. Mom might win over her daughter's friends, or Dad might find a way to become useful. The catch in *Make Way for Tomorrow* is that there was no solution, no honest answer for the problems McCarey posed. Instead, the story forces the children to betray and abandon their parents because nothing else is possible.

"I made a career out of that picture," McCarey said later. It's obvious that *Make Way for Tomorrow* was a labor of love for him, and that the cast and crew knew it at the time. Moore wrote later that many crew members were moved to send "long-delayed letters" to their parents. "One old lady, after hanging up the extras' clothes on a line, said to me, 'You and Beulah are acting this story. I'm living it.'"

Moore also noted that Paramount production head Adolph Zukor "was on the set most of the time" and wanted a happier ending. Ten years later, the director's daughter Mary McCarey reduced *Make Way*'s plot to: "Why are children so mean to their parents?" The way Leo McCarey poses it, it's a lopsided argument in favor of Moore and Bondi. The story omits the demands, the illnesses, the bad sleep, the medicines and special diets the elderly require, the needs that can be so hard to fill. Instead, McCarey seems to be saying if children were only nicer, or richer, their parents wouldn't have to suffer.

(The film also doesn't explain how the parents got into their mess, an omission that lets critics from both sides of the political spectrum to praise it. Some leftists have found it a Marxist film that criticizes capitalism, a conclusion that would have infuriated the notoriously right-wing director.)

McCarey kept insisting that customers would want to see *Make Way for Tomorrow*. "This picture certainly was a heart tugger," he wrote in a special issue of *The Hollywood Reporter* that summed up the year in movies. "But the thing that made it great, I think, was the subtle comedy that Victor Moore, Beulah Bondi and others in the cast were able to inject into their performance."

Perhaps what makes *Make Way for Tomorrow* so great, or at least so memorable, is the hope that McCarey holds out for viewers. He's using the same smooth, improvisational style of his silent comedies. It was a style that adapted easily to sound comedies like *Six of a Kind* (1934), which features an older married couple not unlike Moore and Bondi here, and *Ruggles of Red Gap* (1935), which twisted its characters into seemingly intractable dilemmas only to free them at the last moment. McCarey's comedies had happy endings, and right up to the final scene of *Make Way for Tomorrow* it seems as if a happy ending is possible here as well.

At the time, no one wanted to see the film. *Variety* complained how its "lighter mood [was] saved until last," how McCarey "might well have sacrificed the bitterly sad ending," how there were no stars. The *Chicago Tribune* critic Mae Tinée wrote, "I cried quietly all the way through it." While giving the film his highest rating, *New York Post* critic Archer Winsten noted, "I don't think you will enjoy it, I don't think any one could." When he helped distribute the film in France, future director Bernard Tavernier wrote, "We had implored critics not to summarize its plot, to find a literary way of describing the film's emotional tone…but our pleas often fell on deaf ears. And once the film's plotline was disclosed, the positive effect of the critics' praise was wiped out."

Tavernier said his wife at the time cried when she was typing up the subtitles. My wife cried when she first saw it, and then burst into tears again when she tried to describe it to coworkers. It's difficult not to tear up even explaining how the film was made. Bogdanovich quoted Orson Welles as saying, "It would make a stone cry."

But do moviegoers really want to know how sad life is, even if sugar-coated by someone actor Charles Laughton called "the greatest comic mind now living"? *Make Way for Tomorrow* was not the first "serious" film McCarey directed (Bogdanovich cites *Wild Company* from 1930). It was the last film of any sort he made at Paramount, however. Zukor fired him soon after its release.

McCarey moved to Columbia for his next film, *The Awful Truth*.

Jezebel

Bette Davis won an Oscar for her interpretation of Southern belle Julie Marsden.

Warner Bros., 1938. Sound, B&W, 1.37. 35mm. 104 minutes.

Cast: Bette Davis (Julie [Marsden]), Henry Fonda (Preston Dillard), George Brent (Buck Cantrell), Margaret Lindsay (Amy), Donald Crisp (Dr. Livingstone), Fay Bainter (Aunt Belle), Richard Cromwell (Ted), Henry O'Neill (General [Theophilus] Bogradus), Spring Byington (Mrs. Kendrick), John Litel (Jean La Cour), Gordon Oliver (Dick Allen), Janet Shaw (Molly Allen), Theresa Harris (Zette), Margaret Early (Stephanie Kendrick), Irving Pichel (Huger), Eddie Anderson (Gros Bat), Stymie Beard (Ti Bat), Lou Payton (Uncle Cato), George Renevant (De Lautruc).

Credits: Directed by William Wyler. Screen Play by Clements Ripley, Abem Finkel and John Huston. From the play by Owen Davis, Sr. Music by Max Steiner. Photography by Ernest Haller. Technical advisor: Dalton S. Reymond. Art director: Robert Haas. Film editor: Warren Low. Sound by Robert B. Lee. Musical director: Leo F. Forbstein. Costumes by Orry-Kelly. A William Wyler Production.

Additional cast: Georgia Caine (Mrs. Petion), Fred Lawrence (Bob), Ann Codee (Madame Poulard), Jacques Vanaire (Durette), Daisy Bufford (Black flower girl), Jesse A. Graves (Black servant), Frederick Burton (First director), Edward McWade (Second director), Frank Darien (Bookkeeper), Suzanne Dulier (Midinette), John Harron (Jenkins), Lucky Hurlic (Erronens), Dolores Hurlic (Errata), Davison Clarke (Deputy sheriff), Trevor Bardette (Sheriff), George Guhl (Fugitive planter), Maurice Brierre (Drunk), Tony Paton (Drunk), Jack Norton (Drunk), Alan Bridge (Man with gun); Franco Corsaro, Roger Volmy, Louis Mercier, George Sorel, Vic Demoruelle, Louis La Bey.

Additional credits: Producers: Hal B. Wallis, Henry Blanke. Screenwriting: Lou Edelman. Principal filming: October 21, 1937–January 17, 1938. Reshoots: February 4, 1938. Opened Radio City Music Hall, March 10, 1938.

Awards: Oscars for Best Actress (Davis), Best Supporting Actress (Bainter)

Available: Warner Home Video DVD (2006). UPC: 012569678781.

Although it starred Miriam Hopkins, the Broadway staging of Owen Davis's play *Jezebel*, a melodrama about the pre-Civil War South, closed after only a month. One of the people who saw it was director William Wyler, on a working vacation after finishing *Counsellor-at-Law* for Samuel Goldwyn. Wyler believed the story would work better as a movie because an adaptation could include material only alluded to in the play. He wanted Goldwyn to cast Margaret Sullavan in the lead.

Script readers at Warner Bros. thought the play might work for Ruth Chatterton, but Hopkins owned the rights and did not want to give them up to another actress. When Hopkins sold the rights in January 1937, she did not realize that producer Hal Wallis had already promised the lead to Bette Davis. The project was a peace offering of sorts to the actress, who had lost a highly publicized lawsuit with Jack Warner over her studio contract. Warner not only paid Davis's legal fees, he gave *Jezebel* an $800,000 budget (later upped to $1.25 million) and a 12–week shooting schedule.

The script had not been finished when Wallis hired Wyler for $75,000 to direct. Early in her career, after he had filmed her in a screen test, Wyler had criticized Davis as vulgar. According to the actress, on the first day of shooting for *Jezebel*, he made her do forty-eight takes for a scene in which she hooked up her riding habit with a crop. Davis was furious until she saw the rushes and realized what Wyler was trying to achieve. He wanted to strip away her actorly devices to reach a point where he, and the audience, could believe what her character was doing instead of how the actress was performing.

Davis embraced Wyler's methods enthusiastically, to the point where Wyler had to warn her that not every scene was equally important. Behind the scenes the two began an intense romance. Studio executives, meanwhile, were apprehensive about how Wyler would treat star Henry Fonda, who was playing Davis's unrequited love interest. Both men had married and divorced Sullavan. But Fonda, who had already worked with Davis in the film *That Certain Woman* (1937), never publicly complained about the director.

Unsatisfied about the script, Wyler had Wallis hire John Huston to polish it, and to act as a sort of liaison with the producer. (Huston also directed some second-unit material, including scenes of Davis and Eddie Anderson in a swamp.) The director shot the most expensive scenes first. The Olympus Ball sequence, a turning point in the story, showed off how much money Warners was spending on the project. At a time when Warners would typically build only half or a quarter of a set to cut back on costs, art director Robert Haas designed a set that filled an entire soundstage, extending up over two stories. Wyler spent five days filming what had been scheduled to take a half-day, perhaps in an attempt to outdo a similar scene in the recently released *Prisoner of Zenda* (1937, a Registry title).

Unlike his usually restrained approach to filmmaking, Wyler went all out in several sequences, using Warners' deep pockets to construct lengthy tracking shots and montages. For example, he keys the film's opening shot, which travels down a studio version of street life in New Orleans, circa 1852, to horses and carriages who move in the middle distance at the same speed and in the same direction as the camera. By building several planes of action into the shot, the director suggests a world whose depth extends beyond sound-stages. Wyler would use scenes and moments from *Jezebel* later in his career, notably in *Wuthering Heights* (1939) and *The Heiress* (1949, both Registry titles), but also in his two subsequent collaborations with Davis: *The Letter* (1940) and *The Little Foxes* (1941). In all these examples Wyler chose a more pared back, or perhaps toned-down, style of shooting.

Exteriors for *Jezebel* were filmed at Chatsworth, a ranch outside Burbank owned by Warner Bros. But almost all of the movie, including its swamp and bayou scenes, were shot on soundstages. This was not unusual for a Hollywood feature in 1937, but it inevitably adds a layer of artificiality to the story.

What's surprising about the film is how artificial its story line is. "The Passing of the Old South" had been the subject of countless melodramas, and had also been mocked mercilessly by comedians like Buster Keaton, who took special delight in parodying Southern gentility. *Jezebel* not only takes the Old South seriously, it swathes the era with an almost Gothic sensibility. No matter how many writers contributed to the script, the film still seems stagebound, a theatrical artifact that foreshadows its twists with monotonous regularity. In the end, *Jezebel* is more convincing at portraying Davis as a force of nature than it is as a discussion of the factors that led to the Civil War.

Wyler was still a subtle, incisive director, but you have to search for his touches among all the Warner Bros. glitz. Fay Bainter, Julie Marsden's "Aunt Belle," gives an extremely appealing performance, for example. After hearing a Southern gentleman intone a pompous platitude, she turns to a companion and complains, "I don't know what to say to people." By delivering her thinly disguised insult in the most plaintive of tones, Bainter shows just how an aristocratic woman had to operate within Southern protocol. Bainter's choices not only provide a contrast to Davis's character, but comment on Davis's performance as well.

Jezebel's 800–pound gorilla is of course *Gone With the Wind*, which *Zenda* producer David O. Selznick was trying to mount at the same time. Selznick threatened the Warners with a lawsuit, complaining about a film "permeated with characterizations, attitudes, and scenes which unfortunately resemble *Gone with the Wind*," even while considering Davis for the role of Scarlett O'Hara. Selznick wound up using *Jezebel*'s cinematographer, Ernest Haller, and composer, Max Steiner, for *Wind*.

Steiner, one of the first of the European émigré composers to reach Hollywood, had already worked on such landmark films as *King Kong* (1933, a Registry title). His score for *Jezebel* showed both his economical technique and his wide range of influences. He used several variations on Stephen Foster's

"Beautiful Dreamer" for Davis's character, quotes elegantly from Chopin's "Etude in E Op. 10, No. 3" for a scene in which a character contracts yellow fever, and adds his own waltz to one by Johann Strauss in the Olympus Ball sequence.

Wyler finished filming on January 17, 1938, some twenty days over schedule. (Reshoots took place on February 4th.) The film was an immediate hit when it opened that March. Davis, who was featured on the cover of *Time* magazine, would go on to win Best Actress at the Academy Awards. "Willy is really responsible for the fact that I became a box-office star," she said later. In her memoir *Lonely Life*, Davis went further: "I earned the Oscar I received for *Jezebel*. The thrill of winning my second Oscar was only lessened by the Academy's failure to give the directorial award to Willy. He made my performance. He made the script. *Jezebel* is a fine picture. It was all Wyler."

Although its reputation remains high, *Jezebel* has not aged well. Some critics want you to ignore its patently false locations, the actors' terrible accents, the over-determined plotting, the high-priced frivolity, the glorification of plantation culture and its concomitant excuses for slavery—perhaps to concentrate on Davis before her acting devolved into mannerisms, or catch Wyler on the verge of his best work. But *Jezebel* is so nakedly cynical about its goals, and how they are achieved, that it ultimately becomes an oppressive experience. Author Jeanine Basinger referred to *Jezebel* as Warners' attempt to produce a "prestige" picture. All the film really proved is that the studio could make movies just as pretentious as its rivals.

Under Western Stars

Roy Rogers, the King of the Cowboys.

Republic, 1938. Sound, B&W, 1.37. 35mm. 65 minutes.

Cast: Roy Rogers, Smiley Burnette (Frog), Carol Hughes (Eleanor Fairbanks), Maple City Four, Guy Usher (John D. Fairbanks), Tom Chatterton (Congressman Edward H. Marlowe), Kenneth Harlan (Richards), Alden Chase (Tom Andrews), Brandon Beach (Senator Wilson), Earl Dwire (Mayor Briggs), Jean Fowler (Mrs. Wilson), Dora Clemant (Mrs. Marlowe), Dick Elliott (Congressman William P. Scully), Burr Carruth (Larkin), Charles Whitaker (Tremaine), Jack Rockwell (Sheriff), Frankie Marvin (Deputy Pete).

Credits: Directed by Joe Kane. Screen Play by Dorrell and Stuart McGowan, Betty Burbridge. Original story: Dorrell and Stuart McGowan. Associate producer: Sol C. Siegel. Production manager: Al Wilson. Unit manager: Arthur Siteman. Photography: Jack Marta. Film editor: Lester Orlebeck. Musical director: Alberto Colombo. Songs "Send My Mail to the County Jail," "When a Cowboy Sings a Song," "Back to the Backwoods" by Jack Lawrence, Peter Tinturin. "Rogers for Congressman" by Eddie Cherkose, Charles Rosoff. RCA Victor "High Fidelity" Sound System. A Republic Pictures production.

Additional cast: Earl Hodgins (Master of ceremonies), Trigger.

Additional credits: Production began mid-March, 1938. Released April 20, 1938.

Available: Sinister Cinema, www.sinistercinema.com

To many children growing up in the 1950s, Roy Rogers was the embodiment of American values. Wholesome, respectful, and brave, Rogers promoted patriotism and self-reliance in comic books, television shows, lunch boxes, and over a hundred movies. Their parents had grown up with Roy themselves through the tail end of the Depression. Few realized how hardscrabble a life he led. Rogers was born Leonard Slye in Cincinnati, Ohio, in 1911. He grew up on a farm in Duck Run while his father worked in factories in Portsmouth. Slye dropped out of school at seventeen to work in a shoe factory, then convinced his family to move to California in 1930. He drove a truck and picked fruit until an appearance on an amateur show, "The Midnight Frolic," got him a job as a singer with the Rocky Mountaineers.

Other bands followed, none of them very successful. They performed for free on radio in exchange for publicity, touring the Southwest for low- or no-paying gigs in dance halls, schools, or outdoors. In his memoirs, Rogers spoke about hunting rabbits and blackbirds for food, the fear of returning to migrant labor driving him on. It wasn't until he formed the Pioneer Trio with Bob Nolan and Tim Spencer that he found a formula that clicked: smooth, simple versions of traditional cowboy songs performed in precise, three-part harmony. Nolan and other writers provided new songs like "Tumbling Tumbleweeds" and "Away Out There" that fit so comfortably into the genre that they seemed traditional as well.

After the addition of Native American brothers Rob and Hugh Farr on guitar and violin, the Pioneer Trio evolved into the Sons of the Pioneers, the third act to be signed to the fledgling Decca Records. The Sons were at the forefront of a new boom in country-and-western music, and were instrumental in the growth of the Western Swing genre as well. With the success of Gene Autry (whose *Melody Ranch*, 1940, is on the Registry), studios began to shoot their own "singing cowboy" movies. The Sons of the Pioneers appeared in *The Old Homestead* (1935) for the tiny Liberty Films, as well as in three Charles Starrett Westerns, four Gene Autry vehicles, and *Rhythm on the Range* (1936) with Bing Crosby at Paramount.

Rogers, under his Slye name or as Dick Weston, pursued acting as well, appearing as the villain in Autry's *The Old Corral* (1936). Obtaining an audition with Republic Pictures through producer Sol Siegel, Rogers signed a contract with the studio on October 13, 1937. He left the Sons of the Pioneers, who signed with Columbia Pictures, but kept a close professional relationship with the group for years after. Along with Republic head Herbert Yates, Sol Siegel and his brother Moe persuaded Slye to become Roy Rogers on screen. (Slye changed his name legally to Rogers in 1942.)

Republic already had Gene Autry, so Rogers didn't see much work at first. But Autry had signed a punitive contract with Yates, who was receiving a percentage of the singer's earnings from records and tours. When Autry quit the studio on the first day of shooting *Washington Cowboy*, Yates had Rogers ready to step in. "The fact that I replaced him when he walked out made it easy to imagine we saw each other as enemies," Rogers wrote about Autry. "We've gotten along just fine over the years. We're different sorts of people, that's for sure—I like the outdoors, hunting, and such; he was always more of a businessman—but we're two human beings, and we respect each other."

Rogers' writing style matched his screen persona in *Washington Cowboy*: warm friendliness wrapped around guile and ambition. He plays the "buckaroo" son of a deceased Congressman in a rural farm district that is being exploited by a water company. During the film Rogers fakes newsreel footage, masterminds a hold-up and kidnapping, and decks a half-dozen or so security guards, all in the name of protecting farmers and their ranches. ("Your methods are not only unethical, they're phenomenal," says one excited politician.)

He also sings the tunes that had been intended for Autry, including one, "Dust," that Autry wrote with his friend Johnny Marvin, and another, about "That Pioneer Mother of Mine," meant to evoke Autry's breakthrough hit "That Silver-Haired Daddy of Mine." Autry's subsequent lawsuit was settled out of court when he returned to Republic in 1938.

The film was directed by B-movie stalwart Joe Kane, one of his nine features released in 1938. Kane, who had worked frequently with Autry, was a quick, efficient craftsman with a sly sense of humor. The opening credits of *The Old Barn Dance* (1938) make fun of Autry's radio fans, and here, Kane inserts quick but amusing bits during songs, like the peg leg keeping time during "Rogers for Congressman." The director's style might be described as low-budget professional. Except for chases, he rarely moved the camera, and generally avoided expressive lighting. But each Rogers film included at least some stunning outdoors vistas.

Republic changed the name of *Washington Cowboy* to *Under Western Stars*, but the film was more of an Autry vehicle than one for Rogers, even down to the use of Autry's regular sidekick Smiley Burnette. One big difference was Rogers' riding ability, exploited in several thrilling traveling shots of him riding at a gallop. His horse, Golden Cloud, had been used by Olivia de Havilland in *The Adventures of Robin Hood* (1938, a Registry film). Rogers bought the palomino for $2500 (equal to ten months of the actor's salary at the time) and renamed him Trigger.

Rogers, Burnette, and the Sons of the Pioneers attended the premiere of *Under Western Stars* in Dallas, then supported the film on tour for the next three months. The film did well enough for Republic to develop more films for the actor. He began a grueling performance schedule, starring in 36 movies between 1938 and 1942 while also singing on radio and touring rodeos and fairs with Trigger. Thanks to a handshake deal with Art Rush from the William Morris Agency, Rogers was soon making ten times his movie salary from his other appearances.

Rogers tried to separate his films from Autry's. "Gene always played himself, and his movies were all set in modern times with cars and radios and bad guys in business suits. Most of my early pictures after *Under Western Stars* were set in the past, and I played someone else, not Roy Rogers." When

Burnette returned to Autry's films, Rogers found a new sidekick, Gabby Hayes, who had previously teamed with William Boyd's Hopalong Cassidy movie character. With lines like "them dab-nagged persnickety women," Hayes became a fixture in Rogers films.

As his credits mounted up, Rogers developed an agreeable screen presence, although he always downplayed his skills. "I eventually learned acting pretty much the way I learned music—by ear," he wrote. "I would read a script and I'd hear it a certain way in my head, and that's the way I did it. If I was a bad guy, I didn't smile; if I was a good guy I had plenty of pleasant personality and a lot of smiles. That was about it: I never tried any fancy trick acting on screen. I was just me."

Rogers also downplayed romance in his films, although he did star in six films with Mary Hart. (Yates changed her name from Lynn Roberts so he could bill the pair as "Republic's own Rogers and Hart.") In 1944, he made *The Cowboy and the Señorita*, the first of 35 films with Dale Evans (born Frances Smith). Although they were clearly a couple, on screen Evans acted more like a sitcom housewife than a lover, alternately amused by and nagging Rogers. She helped Rogers remain at or near the top of Western box-office polls until 1954. The pair married in 1947, a year after Rogers lost his first wife due to complications from childbirth.

Like Autry, Rogers switched to television in the early 1950s. Along with his films, which were syndicated by Republic, his television series made Rogers a ubiquitous presence on TV. (The 16mm dupes sold "for the life of the print" to individual stations became the source of many of the bootlegged videotape and DVD copies of his films.) Rogers also made a few mainstream film appearances, including *Dark Command* (1940) with John Wayne and *Son of Paleface* (1952) with Bob Hope.

Although he never retired from the screen, in the 1960s Rogers began to concentrate on his museum in Apple Valley, California, and on his personal appearances. Rogers died in his sleep of congestive heart failure in 1998, six months after his fiftieth wedding anniversary.

The Mark of Zorro

The foppish Don Diego hides a dark side: Tyrone Power in *The Mark of Zorro*.

Twentieth Century-Fox, 1940. Sound, B&W, 1.37. 35mm. 94 minutes.

Cast: Tyrone Power (Diego), Linda Darnell (Lolita Quintero), Basil Rathbone (Captain Esteban Pasquale), Gale Sondergaard (Inez Quintero), Eugene Pallette (Fray Felipe), J. Edward Bromberg (Don Luis Quintero), Montagu Love (Don Alejandro Vega), Janet Beecher (Senora Isabella Vega), George Regas (Sergeant Gonzales), Chris-Pin Martin (Turnkey), Robert Lowery (Rodrigo), Belle Mitchell (Maria), John Bleifer (Pedro), Frank Puglia (Proprietor), Eugene Borden (Officer of the Day), Pedro de Cordoba (Don Miguel), Guy D'Ennnery (Don Jose).

Credits: Directed by Rouben Mamoulian. Screen play by John Taintor Foote. Adaptation by Garrett Fort and Bess Meredyth. Based on the Story "The Curse of Capistrano" by Johnston McCulley. Music by Alfred Newman. Director of photography: Arthur Miller. Art direction: Richard Day, Joseph C. Wright. Set decorations: Thomas Little. Film editor: Robert Bischoff. Costumes: Travis Banton. Sound: W.D. Flick, Roger Heman. Western Electric Mirrophonic recording.

Additional cast includes: Fred Malatesta, Fortunio Bonanova, Jean Del Val, Joseph Villard (Sentries); Harry Worth, Gino Corrado, George Sorel, Lucio Villegas (Caballeros); Paul Sutton, Art Dupuis (Soldiers).

Additional credits: Executive producer: Darryl Zanuck. Associate producer: Raymond Griffith. Screenwriting: William A. Drake, Dorothy Hechtlinger. Premiered in Cincinnati November 1, 1940. Opened November 8, 1940.

Other versions: *The Mark of Zorro* with Douglas Fairbanks (1920). (Fairbanks starred in a sequel: *Don Q Son of Zorro*, 1925.) Sequels to this film include *The Son of Zorro* (1947) and *The Ghost of Zorro* (1949). Between 1957 and 1959, Guy Williams starred in 78 half-hour episodes of *Zorro* for Walt Disney. In 1960, Disney released four one-hour *Zorro* specials. Over the next fifteen years, some 26 features were made starring Zorro, including *Zorro* (1974) starring Alain Delon. Frank Langella and Ricardo Montalban starred in the TV movie *The Mark* *of Zorro* (1974). George Hamilton starred in the spoof *Zorro, the Gay Blade* (1980). In 1998 TriStar released *The Mask of Zorro*, starring Antonio Banderas. He repeated his role in *The Legend of Zorro* (2005).

Available: Twentieth Century Fox Home Entertainment DVD (2005): UPC: 0–24543–20511–1.

The success of movies like *Captain Blood* and *Mutiny on the Bounty* (1935) helped convince Hollywood executives that they could film swashbucklers just as well as they could during the silent era. Studios rushed to develop more adventures, including Twentieth Century-Fox, where production chief Darryl Zanuck was overseeing script conferences on *The Mark of Zorro* as early as 1936.

Zorro was the creation of Johnston McCulley, author of hundreds of stories and some fifty novels, many of them featuring masked avengers like the Green Ghost, the Scarlet Scourge, and the Crimson Clown. A former reporter and contributor to the *Police Gazette*, Johnston had moved from New York to California by the time he first introduced Zorro, in a five-part serial called *The Curse of Capistrano*. When movie star Douglas Fairbanks read the serial en route to Europe, he bought the screen rights and also suggested a new title. McCulley published *The Mark of Zorro* in 1924, dedicating it to "Douglas Fairbanks, the original Zorro of the screen."

The Fairbanks adaptation of *The Mark of Zorro* (released 1920) was enough of a success to merit a sequel, *Don Q Son of Zorro*. McCulley meanwhile wrote four additional Zorro novels and a total of 57 Zorro short stories and novellas, the last, "The Mask of Zorro," appearing five months after his death in 1958. (McCulley also wrote screenplays for Western stars like Gene Autry and Hopalong Cassidy.)

The serial, which first appeared in *All-Story Weekly*, was an unapologetic potboiler about Don Diego de Vega, an aristocratic fop whose alter ego, a sort of masked Robin Hood, defended peons against cruel Spanish overseers. The plot, which took place in a fantasy world of senoritas and caballeros lolling about haciendas, relied on mistaken identities, secret passages, hairsbreadth escapes, horseback chases, and several scenes of swordplay, broken up by comic relief as Don Diego toys with his rivals, and with his betrothed, Lolita.

The Scarlet Pimpernel by Baroness Orczy (published in 1905) was a likely inspiration. McCulley may have taken his setting from Helen Hunt Jackson's novel *Ramona*, or from John Steven McGroarty's *The Mission Play*, first performed in 1911 at Mission San Gabriel. Tyrone Power, Sr., grandson of a famous actor also named Tyrone Power, appeared in *The Mission Play* in 1917; for many years his wife Patia was the heroine in Act III. Tyrone Power, Jr., was ten years old when he played "Juanito, an Indian boy" in the 1924 season.

Born in Cincinnati in 1914, Tyrone, Jr., spent years developing his acting skills, appearing with his father in *The Merchant of Venice* before moving to New York City to work with Katherine Cornell. (Tyrone, Sr., moved to Hollywood, where *The Miracle Man* helped make him a star. He appeared in films like *Where Are My Children?*, 1916, a Registry title, but died unexpectedly of a heart attack in 1931.) Tyrone, Jr., signed with Fox after a screen test in 1936, debuting that year in *Girls' Dormitory* with Simone Simon. Director Henry King, a friend of his father, cast Power in *Lloyds of London*, the studio's top grossing film of the year.

Zanuck needed a follow-up hit for Power, but producing another version of Zorro was not an obvious choice. Zorro the character had remained popular after the Fairbanks films. In 1936, Republic released the first talking Zorro film, *The Bold Caballero* (it was also the first in color). He starred in three film serials (and was closely copied in four others). A contemporary version featuring Diego's grandson James Vega, *Zorro Rides Again*, was released in 1937. Critics Robert Morsberger and Katharine Morsberger consider *Zorro's Fighting Legion*, set in 1824 Baja Mexico and starring the dean of Hollywood stuntmen Yakima Canutt, to be "the best of all the Republic serials." It was still playing in theaters when the new feature went into production.

Bess Meredyth had prepared an outline in 1936; Garret Fort, who had worked with director Rouben Mamoulian on *Applause* (1929), wrote an adaptation that did not please Zanuck, who thought Zorro's mask was "phony" and "hokey." The producer also didn't trust Mamoulian's ear for dialogue, calling for revisions to make the lines less ornate and more realistic. Several characters were dropped, notably Zorro's nemesis Captain Ramón. Don Diego's love interest Lolita became a niece instead of a daughter to foe and comic relief Luis Quintero. To replace McCulley's evil governor, the writers introduced Esteban, a corrupt commandant who uses torture and intimidation to control the local populace.

And to establish Power's manliness to viewers who might not be familiar with the story, the writers added a prologue set in Madrid, where Don Diego is attending a military academy. Here we see military exercises reminiscent of those in *Gunga Din* (1939, a Registry title), before meeting the star, who juggles duels and romantic assignations while his classmates look on enviously. Reminded that he is to meet a rival at three, Power slaps his head and says, "Santa Maria, it had slipped my mind!" — a line so whimsical that author Michael Wood appropriated it as the subtitle for his *America at the Movies*.

This lighthearted approach was not typical for Mamoulian, better know for the more earnest side he displayed in films like *Applause* and *The Song of Songs* (1933). Biographers take pains to note that Mamoulian's stylistic contributions to *The Mark of Zorro* were minimal, but you can see his work in the rhythm and pacing of the opening sequences, and in the often formal staging of scenes involving five or more actors. (Mamoulian had considerably more artistic leeway in his next project with Power, *Blood and Sand*, 1941).

Perhaps more than a Mamoulian film, *The Mark of Zorro* could be considered a Fox film, with a rousing Newman score, good cinematography, efficient work from the studio's contract actors, and the sort of sly writing that might have been found earlier in an Ernst Lubitsch film. "Esteban is always thrusting at this and that," Quintero complains at one point, and throughout the film the innuendo behind swordplay (like "a firm wrist behind a true point") is never neglected for very long. When Zorro, disguised as a monk, tells Lolita that she might be more "useful" outside a convent, she replies disarmingly, "You mean in serving God?" Later, Mamoulian has the camera climb up the walls of a hacienda and in through her window, mimicking what Zorro does when he breaks into her bedroom.

Weirdly, censors like Reverend John J. McClafferty, Executive Secretary of the National Legion of Decency, complained more about Eugene Pallette's portrayal of a Franciscan friar as a "piratical character" and the frequent exhortations of "Madre de Dios" than the script's risqué situations. Zanuck, on the other hand, was concerned about thinly veiled criticism of the film industry's animosity towards unions.

What concerned viewers were the actors and the action. As lit by Arthur Miller, Power and Darnell exhibit an unearthly beauty that places them on an entirely different plane than the other performers. Viewers knew from their opening scenes that they were destined for each other. As for the action, much of *The Mark of Zorro* leans more towards suspense than adventure, with some of the early California scenes staged almost like a horror film.

The film includes one memorable chase and some that are merely filling time. It's the swordfights that set *The Mark of Zorro* apart from other swashbucklers. In a film like *The Prisoner of Zenda* (1937) and *The Adventures of Robin Hood* (1938), the swordfights flow through massive, multi-level sets teeming with extras. Protecting the stars required careful choreography with stunt doubles. The big fight in *The Mark of Zorro* takes place on a single set, with a minimum of stunts or trickery. It's just Power and Basil Rathbone (the swashbuckling villain of choice for his insolent sneer, perfect diction, and skill at fencing) slashing at each other. Choreographed by fencing master Fred Cravens, it's an intense scene shot much tighter than expected, and it succeeds because Power and Rathbone are so physically adept. As Rathbone said later, "Power was the most agile man with a sword I've ever faced before a camera. Tyrone could have fenced Errol Flynn into a cocked hat."

Power teamed with Mamoulian again for *Blood and Sand*, a remake of a Rudolph Valentino bullfighting melodrama, but World War II disrupted his career. (He was a lieutenant in the US Marine Air Corps.) Mamoulian returned to the stage, directing the Broadway hit *Oklahoma!*

Zorro, meanwhile, flourished, starring in movies, serials, and a hit television series produced by Walt Disney and broadcast on ABC. He appeared in 26 movies between 1960 and 1975, and returned to the big screen in 1998 in the TriStar box-office hit *The Mask of Zorro*. Each generation finds a new Zorro to embrace.

Tarantella

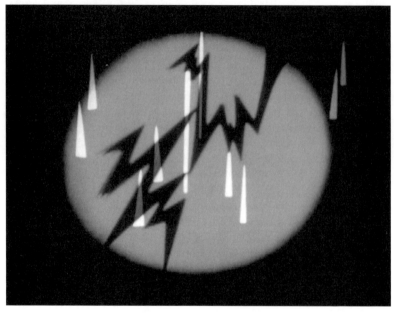

One of the more percussive passages from Mary Ellen Bute's *Tarantella*.

Ted Nemeth Studios, 1940. Color, sound, 1.37. 35mm. 4 minutes.
Credits: Visual: Mary E. Bute. Music: Edwin Gerschefski.
Additional credits: Produced by Theodore Nemeth. Animation by Norman McLaren.
Available: Image Entertainment DVD (2005): *Unseen Cinema: Early American Avant-Garde Film 1894–1941*.

The creative possibilities available to computer animators may seem infinite, but to filmmakers of an earlier age, animating strategies were more limited. For abstract artists, the choices were even fewer: essentially geometric forms and fields of color instead of the characters or narratives used by their commercial counterparts. Abstract animators could place lines and shapes in a frame and then give the illusion that they were moving up or down, in and out, at a fast or slow place. They could change colors and make shapes brighter or darker; they could merge them, stack them, distort them.

These were all time-consuming processes that used stop-motion or that required drawing or painting one frame at a time. Working independently, several animators developed strikingly similar ideas, in Europe starting with

68

Walter Ruttmann and progressing through Len Lye (whose *Free Radicals*, 1979, is on the Registry), Francis Bruguière and Oskar Fischinger (his *Motion Painting No. 1*, 1947, is also on the Registry).

The Houston-born Mary Ellen Bute followed a similar path in the United States. What set her apart is that she actually got people to see her films, which were screened alongside Hollywood features in mainstream movie houses. Growing up on a ranch in Texas, Bute pursued painting, attended art school in Philadelphia, then studied stage lighting at Yale. In 1929 she apprenticed with inventor Leon Theremin in New York. In 1932, they collaborated on a demonstration of synchronizing light and sound.

Theremin introduced Bute to Joseph Schillinger, a Russian émigré musician who believed that music could be composed according to mathematical formulas. (Schillinger's students eventually included George Gershwin, Benny Goodman, and Glenn Miller.) Bute said of this time: "Visual composition is a counterpart of sound composition, and…I began to seek a medium for combining these two and found it in films."

Bute started a movie project with Schillinger and Lewis Jacobs, but it had to be abandoned because the animation proved too complex. Instead, she collaborated with Melville Webber (one of the directors of the Registry title *The Fall of the House of Usher*, 1928) on *Rhythm in Light* (1934). Shot in black and white, "[i]t was mostly three-dimensional animation, pyramids, and ping pong balls, and all inter-related by light patterns," she explained later. Bute synchronized their work to music from Grieg's *Peer Gynt Suite*. The film was shot by Ted Nemeth, a cinematographer whose trick photography was seen primarily in trailers and advertising. (Bute and Nemeth eventually married and raised two sons.)

Bute synchronized a number of her subsequent films to classical music, making use of Schillinger's theories while doing so. To some critics, this became a sort of crutch. Classical music not only gave Bute the equivalent of a metronome, it also provided a narrative for her animation. And it added a veneer of respectability to her efforts. The opening titles of Bute's films often announced, with touching insistence, that the viewer was getting was "a new art form." *Rhythm in Light* was "A PICTORIAL ACCOMPANIMENT in abstract forms"; *Synchromy No. 2* was "designed by a modern artist to create MOODS THROUGH THE EYE." You can almost hear the barker crying, "Step right up…"

For most amateur or independent filmmakers, simply getting a project finished was battle enough. Few thought of exhibiting their work beyond friends and cinema clubs. Perhaps because of her privileged upbringing (her father, Col. E.M. House, was a member of President Woodrow Wilson's "kitchen cabinet") or because of her experiences in academia (she wrangled a world tour while at Yale), Bute took a different approach. She understood the value of connections, and was aggressive in pursuing them. She pushed to have her shorts screened at Radio City Music Hall, where they were covered by the press.

Because Bute also grasped the importance of publicity. She was the subject of a profile in the *New York World-Telegram* that referred to her as "highly personable," with "a flashing smile like the toothpaste ads." She's quoted as saying, "We can take a mathematical formula and develop a whole composition exactly synchronized—the sound and the color following a chromatic scale," but the reporter also points out that she's "a girl with a winsome face and a well-turned ankle."

Bute first used color in *Escape* (1937), set to Bach's "Toccata and Fugue in D Minor." *Spook Sport* (1939) was, according to film historian Jan-Christopher Horak, Bute's most successful film, running for months at Radio City Music Hall. That may have been because it was the easiest of her films for a mainstream moviegoer to comprehend, with ghostly figures dancing to Saint-Saëns' "Danse Macabre." (Dudley Murphy and Francis Bruguière used the same music in 1922's *Danse Macabre*, as did Walt Disney in his 1929 Silly Symphony *The Skeleton Dance*.) Bute hired Norman McLaren to help animate the film.

Tarantella, her follow-up, also in color, was conceived as a choreographed piece that would mimic the Neapolitan dance. (Opening credits carefully define both Tarantella and tarantula, shown here as an orange, nine-legged bug.) For the music, Bute turned to another Schillinger associate, composer and pianist Edwin Gerschefski. Born in Meriden, Connecticut, he trained at Yale and in Europe before completing his studies with Schillinger from 1936–38.

Since Bute and Gerschefski were both working from Schillinger's principles, *Tarantella* has an unusually close synchronization between music and animation. Bute generally avoids a note-for-note correspondence, although the pacing and editing match and even amplify the tempo of the playing. The visuals develop along the same paths as Gerschefski's piano, with circles, parallel lines, waves and spirals echoing the musician's chords and triplets. Bute keeps her color palette relatively simple: three or four blues offset by an orange, or white backgrounds splashed with reds and blues.

The middle section of *Tarantella* uses some of McLaren's animation left over from *Spook Sport*. It's followed by a radical shift to indeterminate lines that mold themselves into circular shapes, reminiscent of effects used by McLaren in his *NBC Valentine Greeting* (1939–40). Recognizable objects appear: smiling lips, an arrow pointing southwest. Bute then reprises earlier effects for the closing section.

Bute's next film, *Polka Graph*, wasn't completed until 1947. For *Abstronic* (1952), Bute achieved visual effects through an oscilloscope. She continued making abstract films like the amusing *Imagination* (1958), a reworking of the pop song that was broadcast on a Steve Allen television show, and the futuristic

New Sensations in Sound (1959), commissioned by RCA and reminiscent of modern-day attempts to capture a retro look.

But Bute also began working in live-action movies, producing *The Boy Who Saw Through* (1956), directed by George Stoney and featuring Christopher Walken in his film debut. She struggled for years to complete *Passages from James Joyce's Finnegan's Wake* (1965, released in the United States in 1966), and never found financing for a film adaptation of Thornton Wilder's play *The Skin of Our Teeth*. Bute died in New York City in 1983.

Mrs. Miniver

One of the shots that helped win an Oscar for Greer Garson as the redoubtable Mrs. Miniver.

Metro-Goldwyn-Mayer, 1942. Sound, B&W, 1.37. 35mm. 133 minutes.

Cast: Greer Garson (Mrs. [Kay] Miniver), Walter Pidgeon (Clem Miniver), Teresa Wright (Carol Beldon), Dame May Whitty (Lady Beldon), Reginald Owen (Foley), Henry Travers (Mr. [James] Ballard), Richard Ney (Vin Miniver), Henry Wilcoxon (Vicar), Christopher Severn (Toby Miniver), Brenda Forbes (Gladys, housemaid), Clare Sandars (Judy Miniver), Marie De Becker (Ada), Helmut Dantine (German Flyer), John Abbott (Fred), Connie Leon (Simpson), Rhys Williams (Horace).

Credits: Directed by William Wyler. Screen Play by Arthur Wimperis, George Froeschel, James Hilton, Claudine West. Based on the book by Jan Struther. Produced by Sidney Franklin. Director of photography: Joseph Ruttenberg. Musical Score: Herbert Stothart. Song "Midsummer's Day," Gene Lockhart. St. Luke's Choristers, Ripley Dorr, Director. Recording director: Douglas Shearer. Art director: Cedric Gibbons. Associate art director: Urie McCleary. Set decorations: Edwin B. Willis. Special effects: Arnold Gillespie, Warren Newcombe. Gowns by Kalloch. Men's wardrobe by Gile Steele. Hair styles for Miss Garson by Sydney Guilaroff. Film editor: Harold F. Kress. Western Electric sound system. A Metro-Goldwyn-Mayer presentation of a William Wyler production.

Additional cast includes: Billy Bevan (conductor), Aubrey Mather (George, innkeeper), Arthur Wimperis (Sir Henry), Sidney Franklin (Man at flower show), Peter Lawford (Pilot), Stanley Mann (workman).

Additional credits: Screenwriting by R.C. Sherriff, Paul Osborn. Publicity: Howard Dietz. Production dates: November 1941–February 12, 1942. Reshoots March–April 1, 1942. Released in New York City, June 4, 1942.

Awards: Oscars for Best Picture, Director, Cinematography–B&W, Writing–Screenplay, Actress (Garson), Actress in a Supporting Role (Wright).

Other versions: Sequel, *The Miniver Story* (1950).

Available Warner DVD (2004). ISBN: 0–7907–4664–6. **UPC:** 0–12569–51962–6.

In the months leading up to President Franklin Roosevelt's declaration of war, Hollywood studios had to determine how to handle the hostilities. Executives worried about alienating viewers by making overt political gestures, and also faced the loss of a large portion of their European audience. Warner Bros. returned to a strategy that proved successful in the early 1930s: films ripped from the headlines, and told in a brash, breathless style, like *Confessions of a Nazi Spy* (1939) or *A Dispatch from Reuters* (1940).

MGM proved more wary. Firmly under the control of Louis B. Mayer, MGM specialized in glossy, mainstream entertainment—plush, non-threatening, and stuffed with expensive talent. A film like *The Mortal Storm* (1940) might criticize Nazis, but only in terms of a romantic triangle. When it came to adapting *Mrs. Miniver*, the studio initially took a similarly cautious approach.

Married and with three children, Joyce Anstruther had a home in London, a family estate in Scotland, and a cottage near Rye in Sussex. As Jan Struther (a name she chose because both her parents were writers), she published poems in numerous magazines. Asked to write a continuing piece for the *London Times*, she invented Caroline Miniver, an upper-class housewife who, despite the war, became involved in the sort of lighthearted situations that would fuel scores of television sitcoms.

Collected and published in the United States as *Mrs. Miniver*, the stories were promptly snapped up by MGM executive Eddie Mannix for producer Sidney Franklin, who saw them as a vehicle for Norma Shearer. As Franklin put it, "I had the notion that someone should make a tribute, a salute to England, which was battling for its life."

But Shearer objected to playing the mother of grown children. Franklin approached Greer Garson for the lead role. Garson was "discovered" by Mayer in a London stage production of *Old Music* and, after much international haggling, signed to a contract. (At the time, one London magazine referred to her as "The Most Sought After Young Actress in London.") But Garson had trouble adjusting to working in Los Angeles. It wasn't until she returned to London to film *Goodbye, Mr. Chips* (1939) that her value as a screen performer became apparent.

Garson was exceptionally beautiful, but she was also blessed with a smooth, caressing voice and an aristocratic mien, all of which made her perfect for the sort of refined, upper-class leading lady Mayer loved to see on screen. Film historian Thomas Schatz described a sort of mini-studio unit that developed around Garson, consisting of Franklin as producer, often Mervyn LeRoy as director, and, in a number of films, Walter Pidgeon as co-star.

Several writers struggled with *Mrs. Miniver*, including Arthur Wimperis, a real-life air-raid warden in London; novelist James Hilton, whose *Random Harvest* would become another vehicle for Garson; and an uncredited R.C. Sherriff, who wrote the film's pivotal scene set in an air-raid shelter. The script begins where the book ends, in September, 1939, and consists of almost entirely new material.

Franklin persuaded William Wyler to direct *Mrs. Miniver*. According to his daughter Catherine, Wyler saw the project as propaganda. "I was a warmonger," he said. "I was concerned about Americans being isolationist." Wyler cast Teresa Wright, who was under contract to Samuel Goldwyn, as an aristocratic neighbor, and Richard Ney as a Miniver scion who joins the RAF. Ney and Garson fell in love on the set and eventually married after the film's release.

Wyler was notorious in the industry for his treatment of actors, and while the filming of *Mrs. Miniver* never devolved into the clash of egos found on the set of *Jezebel* (1938, a Registry title), Garson still faced tough moments. (*Jezebel* star Bette Davis encouraged Garson to trust her director.) But after the December 7 attack on Pearl Harbor, the cast and crew of *Mrs. Miniver* found a new level of support from the studio. (Wyler also enlisted in the Army Signal Corps.)

The film's approach to the Minivers was seen as subtle—even guarded—at the time, presenting the family as enviably happy (and extremely wealthy). Bit by bit their lives are compromised by distant forces, until minor aggravations escalate into personal threats. Critics praised a war movie that had no battles, some pointing to a subplot about a contest for champion roses at a village festival as a "key" to understanding England. Told that the war will prevent such festivals, stationmaster Ballard (played by Henry Travers) responds indignantly, "Don't talk silly. You might as well say goodbye England. There will always be roses."

But what viewers of the time really responded to was Garson's performance as a full-blooded woman whose desires were thwarted by fascist interlopers. Wyler and cinematographer Joseph Ruttenberg framed Garson as carefully as at any time in her career, turning her into an icon of femininity who took out Germans single-handedly, towered over the other women in the story, yet could still be seen as subservient to her husband.

To intensify the focus on Mrs. Miniver as an object of desire, Wyler cut a scene in which she complained about male politics, and another which showed her wedding during World War I. For the director the heart of the story was a scene inside an air-raid shelter, almost nine minutes long and shot over several days. In some thirty edits, Wyler showed the war in personal terms, closing in relentlessly on the characters as bombs rained over them.

One of Wyler's last tasks on the film was reshooting a sermon delivered by the vicar. Henry Wilcoxon had already enlisted in the Navy, and had to obtain permission to return to the *Mrs. Miniver* set. He and Wyler stayed up all night rewriting the sermon. They "hardened the speech," as Wyler remembered later.

Mrs. Miniver was the top-grossing film of 1942, and second only to *Gone With the Wind* in terms of profits for MGM. Garson was in the midst of an extraordinary box-office run, but within a decade, when she appeared in *The Miniver Story*, her appeal had dimmed. Wyler's next film was *The Memphis Belle* (1944, a Registry title), a wartime documentary. In later years he downplayed *Mrs. Miniver*, saying that it "only scratched the surface of the war. I don't mean it was wrong. It was incomplete."

A Tree Grows in Brooklyn

Francie Nolan (Peggy Ann Garner) and her father Johnny (James Dunn) in a pivotal scene from *A Tree Grows in Brooklyn.*

Twentieth Century-Fox, 1945. Sound, B&W, 1.37. 35mm. 128 minutes.

Cast: Dorothy McGuire (Katie Nolan), Joan Blondell (Aunt Sissy), James Dunn (Johnny Nolan), Lloyd Nolan (Officer McShane), James Gleason (McGarrity), Ted Donaldson (Neeley Nolan), Peggy Ann Garner (Francie [Nolan]), Ruth Nelson (Miss McDonough), John Alexander (Steve Edwards), B. S. Pully (Christmas tree vendor).

Credits: Directed by Elia Kazan. Screen Play by Tess Slesinger and Frank Davis. Adapted from the Novel by Betty Smith. Produced by Louis D. Lighton. Music: Alfred Newman. Orchestral Arrangements: Edward Powell. Director of Photography: Leon Shamroy. Art direction: Lyle Wheeler. Set Decorations: Thomas Little. Associate: Frank E. Hughes. Film editor: Dorothy Spencer. Costumes; Bonnie Cashin. Makeup artist: Guy Pearce. Special photographic effects: Fred Sersen. Sound: Bernard Freericks, Roger Heman. Western Electric recording.

Additional cast includes: Ferike Boros (Grandma Rommely), Charles Halton (Mr. Barker), J. Farrell MacDonald (Carney, the junkman), Adeline deWalt Reynolds (Mrs. Waters), George Melford (Mr. Spencer); Mae Marsh, Edna Jackson (Tynmore sisters); Vincent Graeff (Henny Gaddis), Susan Lester (Flossie Gaddis), Johnnie Berkes (Mr. Crackenbox), Lillian Bronson (Librarian), Alec Craig (Werner), Al Bridge (Cheap Charlie).

Additional credits: Dialogue coach: Nicholas Ray. Production dates: May 1 to August 2, 1944. Opened New York City February 25, 1945.

Awards: Oscar for Best Supporting Actor (Dunn), honorary Oscar to Garner for "outstanding child performer of 1945."

Available: 20th Century Fox Home Video DVD set *The Elia Kazan Collection* (2010). UPC: 024543706465.

When the film industry elite embraced the war effort in the early 1940s, Hollywood changed in two drastic ways, first in the types of movies that were made, second in the people who made them. With directors like John Ford, William Wyler, and Frank Capra, and stars like Clark Gable, James Stewart, and Gene Autry in various branches of the armed services, opportunities arose for younger, less experienced directors and actors.

Many of those directors wound up at Twentieth Century-Fox. Darryl Zanuck, its head of production, gave starts to such future award-winners as Joseph Mankiewicz, Otto Preminger, and Henry Hathaway. Elia Kazan, a veteran of New York's Group Theater, was at the tail end of an unpromising acting career in movies when he drew attention in Hollywood for directing the New York stage version of *The Skin of Our Teeth*. He remembers fielding offers from producer Jerry Wald at Warners and from Louis D. Lighton at Fox. Lighton, a screenwriter-turned-producer, was working on a screen version of *A Tree Grows in Brooklyn*.

Zanuck had also established a winning formula at Fox by adapting best-selling novels into prestige movies. Like Warner Brothers did in the 1930s, when he worked there on films like *I Was a Fugitive from a Chain Gang* (1932), Zanuck leaned toward the controversial: *The Grapes of Wrath* (1940) and *The Ox-Bow Incident* (1943). But he also favored coming-of-age tales like *How Green Was My Valley* (1941; all four are Registry titles). Wary of alienating viewers, he took pains to soften the edges of *How Green Was My Valley* and ultimately threw up his hands over *Ox-Bow*'s commercial prospects.

Betty Smith's *A Tree Grows in Brooklyn*, a coming-of-age novel set among the urban poor at the turn of the twentieth century, was ideal material for the studio, which purchased the screen rights before the book was published. (Twentieth Century-Fox was developing the best sellers *A Bell for Adano* and *The Razor's Edge* at the same time.) It was the fourth most popular novel in the country in 1943, and the third in 1944; during the war it ranked behind only *The Robe* in overall sales. Its story of endurance through poverty and death was both inspirational and comforting to mainstream readers.

Tree, Smith's first novel, contained autobiographical elements from her childhood in Brooklyn. But the book was more than a memoir. The author honed her technique through some seventy one-act plays she wrote after ending a marriage and relocating to Chapel Hill, North Carolina. Writing plays taught her how to develop character through dialogue and action, and how to focus on dramatic elements within scenes. As a result, adapting her book was an easier process than a novel like *How Green Was My Valley*, which had to be radically restructured for film.

Kazan liked the script, seeing in it "material I knew something about, the streets of New York and the lives of the working class," but said he did not meet screenwriters Tess Slesinger and her husband Frank Davis. They wrote an adaptation of Pearl S. Buck's *The Good Earth* (1937) at MGM, and for RKO,

Dance, Girl, Dance (1940), a Maureen O'Hara vehicle and Registry title. Lighton, himself a screenwriter of note, added to the adaptation, improving it in Kazan's thinking.

The end result simplified Smith's novel, which used a flashback structure to explain how singing waiter Johnny Nolan charms an Irish lass into marrying him. The script still captures the flavor of Smith's writing, and many of her best scenes. Despite a life of unremitting poverty, Katie Nolan raises her two children, Francie and Neeley, strictly. All of the characters face setbacks in the course of the film, but the script hinges on Francie's relationship with her father, in particular her faith in him.

Although Kazan had directed *People of the Cumberland*, a documentary, he did not know much about Hollywood filmmaking. He praised Lighton as "very kind and patient. He surrounded me with help in the various areas where I was uncertain, like the camera, where I did not know one lens from another." In fact, Kazan claimed that cinematographer Leon Shamroy asked Lighton for a co-directing credit. "There was some justice in what he said," Kazan admitted, "because I just staged the scene as I would a theatre scene and then he determined where to put the camera and so on. I owe a lot to him."

Whatever his technical limitations at that stage of his career, Kazan saw that the key to *A Tree Grows in Brooklyn* was Francie. For a story so awash in pathos, the director had to find a realistic core, a character viewers could believe and understand, and not just feel sorry for. As he put it, "The outside has to be there, but what is important is that I get the light in that little girl's eyes, the expression on her face, the feeling in her soul." Kazan felt that Peggy Ann Garner played Francie so well because of her own personal problems, including a father overseas in the war.

"She was not pretty at all, or cute or picturesque, only true," Kazan said, downplaying his own contributions. Through rehearsals, the director built an atmosphere of trust and cooperation. "I read first, and worked slowly and built each scene very carefully," and in fact *A Tree* moves with a focus and purpose that is unusual for its time. Each scene operates on several levels, advancing the plot but also putting characters in emotional peril, often while others watch obliviously. Shamroy's camera, remarkably unobtrusive, manages to draw in and out at precisely the right moment, without calling attention to itself, allowing the emotional truth Kazan helped forge to emerge for viewers.

Perhaps nowhere is this skill more apparent than the scenes at Christmas time, first between Katie and Johnny in the kitchen, and then between Johnny and Francie by her bed. Although Kazan felt that Dorothy McGuire was miscast as Kathy, she pushes across a difficult moment without trying to hold onto viewers' sympathy. James Dunn, "uncertain and so dependent on me," acts as if caught in the lights, almost frozen by the demands of his role. It is a brilliant interpretation of a man torn by self-doubt, one that helped win him an Oscar.

Kazan staged the kitchen scene in only two shots (one of those a brief reaction shot) in order to sustain the emotional tension between Katie and Johnny. The next scene is structured more carefully, in part to protect a young actress, but also to enhance the script's most poignant moment. This is the heart of the film, a scene that brings both Francie and Johnny to the brink of despair. The lighting and camera angles help support the actors, but it was Kazan who got them to deliver such heartfelt accounts of themselves, their doubts as well as dreams.

"I wouldn't direct this movie at all in the same way now," Kazan said years later. "I haven't got the same vocabulary now—it is a sentimental story and I don't believe in that now." What's striking about *A Tree Grows in Brooklyn* is how little its own characters believe in themselves or their futures. Francie holds onto her youth because the alternative is so dismal, Kathy her discipline because to waver is to fail. Johnny can't live up to what his wife or children want, but can he be a failure if so many people love him?

A Tree Grows in Brooklyn has its shortcomings, notably an insistent score of turn-of-the-century chestnuts like "Annie Laurie" and some plot twists that seem too pointed. But its influence extends from obvious examples like *I Remember Mama* (1948) to more subtle works like *A Raisin in the Sun* (1961, a Registry title). It also established Kazan as a Hollywood director. He would win an Oscar for *On the Waterfront* (1954), and embark on a series of films in the 1950s that have been selected to the National Film Registry, such as *A Streetcar Named Desire* (1951) and *A Face in the Crowd* (1957).

Story of G.I. Joe

Lt. Bill Walker (Robert Mitchum) and Ernie Pyle (Burgess Meredith) get news from the front in *Story of G.I. Joe*.

United Artists, 1945. Sound, B&W, 1.37. 35mm. 108 minutes.

Cast: Burgess Meredith (Ernie Pyle), Robert Mitchum (Lieutenant [Bill] Walker), Freddie Steele (Sergeant Warnicki), Wally Cassell (Private Dondaro), Jimmy Lloyd (Private Spencer), Jack Reilly (Private Murphy), Bill Murphy (Private Mew), and as themselves, combat veterans of the campaigns in Africa, Sicily, and Italy.

Credits: Directed by William A. Wellman. Screen play by Leopold Atlas, Guy Endore, Philip Stevenson. Produced by Lester Cowan. Director of photography: Russell Metty. Sound recording: Frank McWhorter. Associate art director: James Sullivan. Associate musical director: Louis Forbes. Set decorator: Edward G. Boyle. Make-up: Bud Westmore. Film editor: Albrecht Joseph. Assistant director: Robert Aldrich. Research: Paige Cavanaugh. Production manager: Ray Heinz. Supervising film editor: Otho Lovering. Associate producer: David Hall. Musical score by Ann Ronell, Louis Applebaum. Technical guidance for the Army Ground Forces: Lt. Col. Roy A. Murray, Jr., 4th. Ranger Bn.; Lt. Col. Edward H. Coffey, A.G.F.; Lt. Col. Robert Miller, 34th. Inf. Div.; Maj. Walter Nuye, 4th Ranger Bn.; Capt. Milton M. Thornton, 1st. Inf. Div.; Capt. Charles Shunstrom, 1st. Ranger Bn. Grateful acknowledgement: Lt. Gen. Lesley J. McNair. For the combat correspondents: Don Whitehead, Associated Press; George Lait, International News Service; Chris Cunningham, United Press; Hal Boyle, Associated Press; Sgt. Jack Foisie, Stars and Stripes; Bob Landry, Life magazine; Lucian Hubbard, Reader's Digest; Clete Roberts, Blue Network; Robert Reuben, Reuters. Western Electric Mirrophonic recording. A Lester Cowan presentation of a William A. Wellman production.

Additional cast: Billy Benedict (Soldier), Dorothy Coonan (Elizabeth "Red" Murphy), Shelley Mitchell (Voice of "Axis Sally"), Pat Friday (Singer on radio), Yolanda Lacca (Amelia, Italian café girl), Tito Renaldo (Lopez), William Self ("Gawky" Henderson), Bob Landry (Himself), Clete Roberts (Himself), Dick Rich (Sergeant at showers).

Additional credits: Title on screen: *G.I. Joe*. Also known as *Ernie Pyle's Story of G.I. Joe*. Based on the books *Here Is Your War* (1943) and *Brave Men* (1944) by Ernie Pyle. Directing by Leslie Fenton. Screenwriting: Clifford Odets, Arthur Miller, Alan LeMay, Albert Maltz, John Huston, Burgess Meredith, Ernie Pyle. Cinematography by Archie Stout. Technical advisors: Paige Cavanaugh, Capt. Frederick D. Greist, Sgts. Kenny Thorpe and George Yahlem, Cpl. Enrico Dorazzio, Pfc. Clarence Cohen, Pvt. Edward Lawson. Production dates: March 14 to May, 1944; November 15, 1944 to January, 1945. Reshoots: April 15, 1945. Released July 13, 1945.

Available: Image Entertainment DVD (2000). UPC: 014381905823.

War was a creative spur for William Wellman.

A veteran of World War I, "Wild Bill" spent the early 1930s directing competent but largely unmemorable programmers at Warner Bros., as well as one bona fide gangster classic, *The Public Enemy* (1931, a Registry title). (For more about Wellman's background, see *Wings*, 1927.) Leaving Warners, Wellman worked briefly for David O. Selznick and then at Paramount, Twentieth Century-Fox, MGM, and United Artists. He had already directed two war pictures, the aviation-themed *Thunder Birds* (1942) and *This Man's Navy* (1945), when he was asked by producer Lester Cowan to direct a troubled project about infantry soldiers.

In September 1943, Cowan approached the Army for permission to make a film about "ground forces" which would be based on a play by Clifford Odets. The picture he eventually produced as *Story of G.I. Joe* shows just how important collaboration is to the filmmaking process. The project changed shape repeatedly as different people became involved, and it wasn't until a core group coalesced around Cowan that the motion picture he wanted could emerge.

Cowan apparently originally envisioned a movie that would follow rookie troops through training. Over time, the project evolved into a story of war correspondent Ernie Pyle's experiences in Europe. Born in Indiana in 1900, Pyle dropped out of college to write for a newspaper, eventually working in New York City and in Washington, DC. He became a roving reporter for the Scripps-Howard chain of newspapers, turning in six columns a week on subjects of his choosing for the last ten years of his life. He traveled to London in 1940 to cover the Battle of Britain, and continued on through war zones in Africa, Europe, and the Pacific. Pyle's writing was simple, direct, and compassionate. He saw how young soldiers became killers, how war shattered their lives, how choices made thousands of miles away led to violent disasters. He was by consensus the country's best correspondent during the war, and the best-loved among the troops.

In his autobiography, playwright Arthur Miller wrote that Cowan asked him to turn Pyle's *Here Is Your War* into a screenplay. Miller quit the project when Cowan teamed him with Alan LeMay, a writer who would later make his mark with Westerns. (Miller turned his script into his first published book, *Situation Normal*.) Several other writers contributed to the project, including John Huston, who was considered at one point as director.

Cowan signed Gary Cooper to play Pyle, but the actor dropped out due to script delays. Cowan also considered James Gleason, Walter Brennan, and, intriguingly, Fred Astaire. Burgess Meredith, who had contributed to the script in June, 1944, was Pyle's choice. Meredith signed in November; at that point a Captain in the Army, the actor was placed on inactive duty during shooting. Meredith unfortunately is the weak link in the film, portraying Pyle with saintly forbearance that seems too forced today.

Actor Robert Mitchum was under contract at RKO when he was signed to play "Bill Walker," a thinly disguised version of Captain Henry T. Waskow, the subject of one of Pyle's most famous columns. Mitchum had small parts in several films before *G.I. Joe*, but Walker earned him an Academy Award nomination and made him a star. Mitchum never seems to be acting, but he exudes toughness and authority. Former boxer Freddie Steele, whose massive jaw and surly, slitted eyes made him a menacing screen presence, was hired for the important part of Sgt. Warnicki.

Under director Leslie Fenton, shooting began near Yuma, Arizona, in March, 1944. After six weeks, Cowan shut down the production for a month so the script could be rewritten to cover unfolding developments in the war (such as the Allies' march through Italy). As the weeks stretched on, however, Cowan had to make arrangements to cover the Allies' imminent victory in Europe. Fenton left the project, and although records are spotty, some of his battle and location footage most likely ended up in the final film.

In Wellman's autobiography, he wrote that he resisted Cowan's entreaties to take over the film until he spent time with Pyle at his home in New Mexico. "He told of men, and kids that were men, that had been killed fighting our war, and a lot about a lot that were alive, and *still* fighting," Wellman remembered. Pyle flew out to Hollywood to help Wellman with a new version of the script. "We worked together day after day, and it gradually became a great shooting script. Cruel, factual, unaffected, genuine, and with a heart at big as Ernie's. This was *the* story of G.I. Joe."

"Dialogue and adventure, battles and heroics, letters and heartbreaks, boredom and, above all, exhaustion"—this is what Wellman tried to capture in his version. Perhaps inevitably, the director filtered Pyle's experiences through his own as an aviator during World War I. As biographer Frank T. Thompson wrote, Wellman "understood the camaraderie and love that exist between people under duress, the loyalty laced with fatalism that accepts the death of a friend with a stoic shrug and a lifetime of memories."

In practice, this meant Wellman's infantrymen adopt a carefree, joshing tone, complaining about rain, mud, and bad food, but never questioning the politics that brought them to the fields of death. A rescued puppy, an impromptu marriage (Wellman cast his own wife as "Red," the bride), comic business with Italian villagers—bits like these flesh out the film, and while they may have been based on incidents Pyle observed, they are also familiar from years of Hollywood movies about war.

The film's battle sequences are jarring, ugly, full of nervous energy. They build on similar scenes from documentaries like *The Battle of San Pietro* (1945) and *Why We Fight* (1944–46, both Registry titles), and include some newsreel footage. Wellman chose not to show the worst fighting. Instead, he concentrated on Pyle's reactions as troops leave and return from their deadly patrols.

Although professional characters were cast for the lead roles, when Wellman began shooting in November, 1944, he also used some 150 real-life soldiers, most of them veterans of the Italian campaign. The soldiers stayed at the temporary Camp Baldwin in Los Angeles for the six weeks of shooting, then were sent to the South Pacific. As Wellman tersely noted, "None of them came home."

Pyle won a Pulitzer for his writing while *G.I. Joe* was still being shot. Wellman staged a version of how he heard about the award for the movie. Here's how the director referred to Pyle's columns: "The writing, poetry of the doughfoot, cruel poetry but so honest, so tragic, so miserable, so lonely, and so many wonderful kids gone." Pyle was killed by a sniper on Ie Shima, an island near Okinawa, on April 18, 1945.

Since it wasn't released until July, 1945, *G.I. Joe* followed several other war films and documentaries into theaters. Some of these, like *Back to Bataan* (released that May) or *Wake Island* (1942), were forceful, hard-hitting movies that resisted upbeat, jingoistic attitudes. But *G.I. Joe* drew special attention from the press. Reviewers of the time noted the film's lack of sentimentality (or "hokum," in *Variety*'s terms); James Agee, a movie critic for *The Nation*, called it "an act of heroism." General Dwight D. Eisenhower said it was "the greatest war picture I've ever seen."

Wellman said that *Story of G.I. Joe* "is the best picture I ever made in my whole life," but added, "It's the one picture of mine that I refuse to look at." The fact that so many of the extras died later made him "feel lousy," he wrote. "We had a lot of laughs together, a lot of work, a lot of drinks, and I got them a little extra dough. It all seems so futile now."

Let There Be Light

John Huston used special lighting and a camera on tracks to film an orientation class at the Army's Mason General Hospital in Brentwood, Long Island.

US Army, 1946. Sound, B&W, 1.37. 35mm. 60 minutes.

Featuring: Col. Benjamin Simon.

Credits (not on screen): Directed by John Huston. Screenplay by John Huston and Charles Kaufman. Narration voiced by Walter Huston.

Additional credits: Music by Dimitri Tiomkin.

Available: National Archives, the Internet Archive (www.internet.org).

Most Hollywood directors who joined the armed services during World War II were content to report on the war, often concentrating on regions, like John Ford did in the South Pacific, or on specific areas of fighting, as William Wyler did with aviation. But in his three principal war-time documentaries, John Huston moved beyond reporting to investigate the effects of war on soldiers and civilians. *Report from the Aleutians* (1943), *The Battle of San Pietro* (1945, a Registry title), and *Let There Be Light* form a remarkable trilogy in which Huston struggles to find a meaning for the devastation of war.

Huston volunteered for the Signal Corps shortly after Pearl Harbor, completing most of the feature *Across the Pacific* (1942) before receiving his first assignments. He had little interest in a documentary about the making of a B-25 airplane, dismissing his contributions to the film in his autobiography *An Open Book*. In September, 1942, he flew to Alaska with a five-man crew, including cameramen Rey Scott and Jules Buck. His father Walter Huston narrated the resulting film, *Report from the Aleutians*, which showed the building of an air base at Adak.

Along with Frank Capra, Huston helped shoot faked footage of troops landing in Africa, later combined with genuine British footage, for *Tunisian Victory*. The director was next stationed in England where he received orders to "make a film of the Allies' triumphant march into Rome." Instead, he made *The Battle of San Pietro*.

Cameraman Rey Scott suffered from shell shock after the bombardment of Caserta in Italy. He received treatment at the Army's Mason General Hospital in Brentwood, Long Island. While working at studios in nearby Astoria, Huston visited him there, and became intrigued about the treatment of soldiers with psychological injuries.

The director was asked in the spring of 1945 to make a film about psychologically disturbed soldiers. Huston at first referred to the film as *The Returning Psychoneurotics*. The Army had very specific goals for what it called "film on the Nervously Wounded." Huston was to tell viewers that there were very few psychoneurotics in the armed services; that their symptoms weren't as exaggerated as had been previously reported in the press; and that someone might be considered psychoneurotic in the Army, but a "success" as a civilian.

Like many of his contemporaries, Huston had a smattering of knowledge about Freud, Adler, and Jung, enough, as he put it, to attempt the project without really knowing what he was doing. Given access to all of the facility, he decided to follow a typical group of patients through its treatment.

Two classes of seventy-five patients each entered the hospital each week for an eight-week course. Huston placed sound cameras in receiving rooms and in classrooms where group therapy sessions were held. Patients were told that they were being filmed for a documentary. According to Huston, the cameras had a positive effect: the soldiers were more responsive and recovered more quickly when they were being filmed.

For scenes in which patients received one-on-one consultations, he used a two-camera set-up. One camera was directed at the patient; the other showed a reverse angle of the doctor counseling him. This allowed Huston and his crew to film entire sessions uninterrupted, "thousands of feet" as he put it. From this footage, he selected testimony from a dozen or so soldiers.

Finally, Huston famed some scenes of soldiers receiving treatment, consisting of sodium amytol injections or hypnosis. (He found the electro-shock treatments too troubling to work into the movie.) In his autobiography, Huston praised Col. Benjamin Simon as the best hypnotizer on the staff; the director admitted that he learned how to hypnotize patients as well, and often jumped in when Simon wasn't present.

Huston filmed these scenes with special lighting, synchronized sound, and equipment like dollies that enabled his cameramen to travel up and down aisles during therapy sessions. (A few other scenes had synch sound as well, such as an impromptu guitar jam in a recreation room.) Huston's crew also filmed several locations without sound: wood shop, a baseball field, dormitories, etc. The director used this material to help familiarize viewers with the layout of the hospital, and to break up the extended therapy scenes.

Dolly shots, usually taken from a low angle looking up at patients listening intently to doctors, not only turned the soldiers from abstractions into individuals, but showed the immensity of the challenge facing Mason General. One shot travels down a corridor past a half-dozen interrogation rooms, each with a doctor tape-recording a session with a patient.

Huston's approach gave *Let There Be Light* the polish of a Hollywood feature. The director worked on individual scenes carefully, editing the patients' descriptions to their most pertinent details. He cuts back and forth between doctor and patient, switching to close-up lenses to increase tension as patients divulged details both sad and grisly: the loss of friends, thoughts of suicide. Huston cuts among different sessions, using conventional Hollywood devices like close-ups of typewriters and dictaphones for editing. Piling up the sessions this way gives them a hopeless feel, as if the soldiers could never be cured.

But the point of *Let There Be Light* wasn't to overwhelm viewers, it was to reassure them about the eventual fates of the patients. Huston spent so much time at first detailing the problems because later he would show that the Army had found out how to solve them, largely through drugs. The film covers some individual treatments in considerable detail, again with a two-camera setup and special lighting. In one, a soldier suffering from "conversion therapy" has lost the use of his legs; in another, a patient has trouble speaking because, as Huston puts it, the "ess" sound has become "the sound of death."

These and the other soldiers in the film are cured, perhaps too conveniently by modern standards. No matter how much viewers may want to believe in them, the miraculous recoveries are the weakest element of *Let There Be Light*. Our understanding of psychology today precludes the possibility that one injection of sodium pentathol, or three minutes of hypnotherapy, will erase trauma from a shell-shocked soldier. It's doubtful that Huston believed this himself, yet he had to present to the public a story in which such cures were indeed possible.

While editing the footage at the Signal Corps studios in Astoria, Huston and screenwriter Charles Kaufman worked out a genuinely moving narration which would eventually be delivered by Walter Huston. The documentary was considered an important enough story to be covered in magazines like *Life*, which ran photographs from the film, and *Harper's Bazaar*, but as the release date approached Huston began to encounter opposition from Army brass. Signed release forms from the patients suddenly disappeared, an excuse used to stop a scheduled screening of the film at the Museum of Modern Art in June, 1946.

While some critics at the time saw *Let There Be Light*, the public didn't. The War Department shelved the film. Huston complained, "The authorities wanted to maintain the 'warrior myth,' which said that our American soldiers went to war and came back all the stronger for the experience. Only a few weaklings fell by the wayside."

But as writer Richard Ledes points out, the film Huston delivered to the War Department presented a highly selective account of psychoneurotic soldiers. In his choice of patients, Huston seemed to be blaming their problems on three issues: the war itself, race, and unemployment. What's more, "Every man has his breaking point," as his narration announced.

The Army, on the other hand, wanted a film that blamed shell-shock on actual shells, and not intractable social problems. In fact, Army psychologists were in the process of identifying "transient situational personality disorder," which tied soldiers' mental troubles specifically to their war traumas. (The Army, and Huston, may also have had second thoughts about the complete absence of psychoanalysis, as opposed to drugs and hypnosis, in the film.)

Huston was discharged on February 13, 1946. "It gave me a sense of human behavior," he wrote about the experience later. "It also inculcated in me a vast desire to work away from the studios." *Let There Be Light* may also have inspired Huston to film *Freud* (1962), a biography of the analyst starring Montgomery Clift.

It took concerted lobbying from Jack Valenti, at the time the head of the Motion Picture Association of America, and producer Ray Stark (who was involved with Huston in the making of *Annie*, 1982) to persuade Vice President Walter Mondale to order the release of *Let There Be Light* in 1981. A new generation of critics wasn't impressed, perhaps expecting more thrills than Huston was willing to offer. In retrospect, *Let There Be Light*, for all its flaws and analytical shortcuts, provides as sympathetic and insightful a picture of veterans as can be found in movies of its time.

The Lead Shoes

An anamorphic lens distorts the images in *The Lead Shoes*.

Workshop 20, 1949. Sound, B&W, 1.33. 16mm. 16 minutes.

Cast: Jeremy Anderson (Father), Elsa Barrett (Mother), Jack Klough (Edward).

Credits: Directed by Sidney Peterson. Produced through Workshop 20, California School of Fine Arts. Sound: "The Three Edwards and a Raven." Crew: Benjamin Chan, Becky Johnston, Wirth McCoy, Nadine Richards, Frank Wright, James Johnston.

Additional credits: Premiered at the Art in Cinema program, San Francisco Museum of Art, October 14, 1949.

Available: *Avant Garde 3: Experiment Cinema 1922–1954*, Kino International DVD (2009). UPC: 7–38329–05832–6.

One of the key figures in American avant-garde film, Sidney Peterson followed a style of filmmaking that encapsulated the strengths and weaknesses of experimental cinema. Born in Oakland, California, in 1905, Peterson worked as a newspaper reporter after graduating from college. He moved to Paris to study sculpture and painting, lived in France for several years, and returned to California a widower. Remarrying, he moved to San Francisco, where he met poet James Broughton.

Peterson and Broughton collaborated on a play about John Sutter, whose discovery of gold helped set off the California Gold Rush, but abandoned it to concentrate on making a movie. Shot over the summer of 1946, *The Potted Psalm* reworked the surrealism of European filmmakers like Luis Buñuel and René Clair in American terms. A screening at the San Francisco Museum of Art caused enough consternation among viewers that Douglas MacAgy asked Peterson to lead a class in avant-garde filmmaking at what was then called the California School of Fine Arts. (It would later be named the San Francisco Art Institute.)

Broughton, who also ended up teaching at the institute, continued making movies on his own, including *Mother's Day* (1948) and *Four in the Afternoon* (1951), works based on his poems and inspired in part by the films of Jean Cocteau.

Peterson found his classes filled with veterans who had returned to school on the G.I. Bill, students who did not have a thorough grounding in modern art, let alone the fundamentals of filmmaking. To give them production experience, Peterson formed Workshop 20, through which he planned to make one film per semester. A total of five films came out under the Workshop 20 name, starting with *The Cage* in 1947. Students not only helped with lighting, set design, and sound, they also performed in the cast.

The Cage elaborated on ideas in *The Potted Psalm*, with Buñuel and Salvador Dali again obvious inspirations. Peterson used "every trick in the book and a few that weren't," including adjusted camera speeds, animated collages, lenses that distorted images, iris effects, etc. From *Entr'acte* (1924), a French film directed by René Clair, he got the idea of swinging the camera in an arc. He also filmed in reverse, at times having his cast move backwards to further disorient viewers.

For *The Petrified Dog* (1948), Peterson used sound for the first time, assembling a *musique concrète* soundtrack of found and manufactured noises. Although some critics have described it as a variation on *Alice in Wonderland*, its narrative resists explication. Film historian K.A. Westphal quotes Peterson as asking, "Do you suppose movie audiences will ever learn to take works as experiences instead of merely as expression, what does it mean? etc.?"

Peterson's unwillingness to construct a narrative that would make sense to mainstream viewers was based in part on the restrictions he faced as a filmmaker. Working with inexperienced students; using silent, 16mm cameras with minimal lighting and minuscule budgets for casts and sets; and unable to synchronize sound to picture, Peterson would have been forced into narrative compromises even if he hadn't been attracted to surrealism.

Viewers can still make narrative connections, of course. Much of *The Cage* seems to deal with an artist who loses control over his eye after he removes it. The eye wanders through town, peering fuzzily at people, objects, movement. In *The Petrified Dog*, an artist stands before a lush garden and "paints" the scene on a nonexistent canvas. If the symbolism seems trite, or the imagery secondhand, Peterson was working largely on his own, with a meager tradition of avant-garde cinema to draw from.

According to P. Adams Sitney, Peterson based *Mr. Frenhofer and the Minotaur* on a Balzac short story, "Le Chef d'Oeuvre Inconnu," as well as a Picasso painting and a monologue by James Joyce. In shooting the film, Peterson made extensive use of an anamorphic lens, which enabled him to distort images in specific and reproducible ways.

For the last of the Workshop 20 films, Peterson allowed his students to participate in creating the script. Starting in the summer of 1949, he and his class assembled materials and story ideas. Peterson remembers a couple from Virginia, Becky and James Johnston, suggesting that the class film a ballad. One student brought in a diving suit; another, hamsters. Peterson decided to pull these diverse elements together in a film that would deconstruct two traditional ballads, "Edward" and "The Three Ravens."

"Edward" was derived from an older ballad, "Lord Randall," in which a son tells his mother that he killed his father. "The Three Ravens" is told from the point of view of the birds as they watch a dying knight carried from a battlefield. In Peterson's hands, the diving suit became a suit of armor, the ravens turned perhaps into hamsters, and the "narrative" featured a mother who digs her son up out of the sand on a beach and then drags him back to her apartment. Punctuating the story are shots of a girl playing hopscotch.

At least that is an interpretation offered by film critic Parker Tyler, who in his notes to a 1950 Cinema 16 screening goes on to point out the presence of Cain and Abel, the emotional implications of hopscotch, and the use of castration anxiety, drawing the conclusion that the film "suggests the historical fact that Greek tragedy derived from Dionysian revel." Adams calls *The Lead Shoes* a spherical form with a narrative drift, citing the Greek terms *sparagmos* and *omophagia*. In filmmaker Stan Brakhage's words, "Every attempt at symbolic or historic understanding of *The Lead Shoes* is bound to destruct against the multiplicity of meanings."

Writers may struggle to explain how *The Lead Shoes* works, but even for viewers who aren't conversant in Freudian psychology or Greek mythology, the film can be an inexplicably powerful and unsettling experience. The borrowed symbolism of Peterson's earlier films is still there, as well as his defiant resistance to basic storytelling strategies. But *The Lead Shoes* has an atmosphere of dread, a deeper understanding of suspense and terror, that is missing from shock-at-all-costs films like *The Cage* and *The Petrified Dog*.

Part of this dread comes from Peterson's use of anamorphic lenses. Like Broughton, Peterson often drew from early cinema: his characters' makeup and costumes, their often histrionic acting, even how they are posed within frames wouldn't feel out of place in an Edison film from 1905. But twisting and distorting the image serves to cloud our understanding of what is happening.

Peterson's choice of shots seems more inspired as well. Close-ups in *The Lead Shoes* are almost *too* close, making it difficult to place them in context. As shot by Peterson, wriggling toes and fingers, grimacing mouths, and averted heads build a sense of hysteria in part because we can't associate them with normal narrative methods. Similar shots would emerge in science fiction and horror films of the 1950s.

Technically, *The Lead Shoes* is more advanced than other Workshop 20 entries. A shot of a child drawing a chalk line on a sidewalk, recorded by a camera inches from the ground, weaves for several seconds, the equivalent of suspending time, or holding one's breath. Peterson runs it in reverse, compounding the shot's mysterious pull, and intercuts a shot of a couple dancing on a beach.

Peterson even alludes to earlier filmmakers, such as the slapstick comedians beloved by surrealists. A sequence in which a woman tries to pull a diving suit onto a bed uses the same gags Buster Keaton employed in *Spite Marriage* (1929).

Perhaps the most unnerving element in *The Lead Shoes* is its music, a perfect aural correlative to Peterson's imagery. According to Adams, Peterson assembled a band of students and faculty that improvised on themes from the ballads "Edward" and "The Three Ravens." A trumpet, drums, and incantatory singers emerge from a muddy sound mix. Lyrics are sometimes discernible, often buried. The music shapes itself into a driving beat before collapsing into pieces. The soundtrack has the feel of a country blues song from the 1920s: primitive, unearthly, forbidding. It's the sort of morbid howling that Darby & Tarlton used on "Frankie Dean" back in 1930, or that Harry Smith would extol in his *Anthology of Folk Music*. You can hear guitarist John Fahey attempt something similar in his adaptations of "Will the Circle Be Unbroken" and "Sail Away Ladies." For that matter, it's hard to watch David Lynch's *Eraserhead* (1977, a Registry title), without thinking of *The Lead Shoes*.

With *The Lead Shoes*, Peterson may have felt he developed this style of filmmaking as far as he could. Leaving school, he tried to work within the system, making documentary films and working as a cartoonist for Walt Disney. He also wrote a novel, *A Fly in the Pigment* (1961), and worked as a consultant for the Museum of Modern Art. He moved from New York to Santa Fe to Los Angeles before returning to San Francisco. His film output dropped considerably, although he continued to release titles like *The Invisible Moustache of Raoul Dufy* (1955) and *The Day of the Fox* (1956). His book *The Dark of the Screen* (1980, published by Anthology Film Archives) discusses his theories of film.

Peterson died in 2000 at the age of 94.

The Incredible Shrinking Man

Actor Grant Williams amid oversized props.

Universal–International, 1957. Sound, B&W, 1.85. 35mm. 81 minutes.

Cast: Grant Williams (Scott Carey), Randy Stuart (Louise Carey), April Kent (Clarice), Paul Langton (Charlie Carey), Raymond Bailey (Doctor Thomas Silver), William Schallert (Doctor Arthur Bramson), Frank Scannell (Barker), Helene Marshall (Nurse), Diana Darrin (Nurse), Billy Curtis (Midget).

Credits: Directed by Jack Arnold. Screenplay by Richard Matheson from his novel. Produced by Albert Zugsmith. Director of photography: Ellis W. Carter. Art Direction: Alexander Golitzen, Robert Clatworthy. Set decorations: Russell A. Gausman, Ruby R. Levitt. Sound: Leslie I. Carey, Robert Pritchard. Film editor: Al Joseph. Gowns: Jay A. Morley, Jr. Hair Stylist: Joan St. Oegger. Make-up: Bud Westmore. Assistant director: William Holland. Special photography: Clifford Stine. Optical effects: Roswell A. Hoffman, Everett H. Broussard. Music supervision by Joseph Gershenson. Trumpet soloist: Ray Anthony. Westrex Recording System.

Additional cast: Lockhart Martin (Giant), Luz Potter (Midget).

Other versions: A sequel, *The Fantastic Little Girl*, was planned but never filmed. *The Incredible Shrinking Woman* (1981) used the premise for comedy. Universal announced a remake starring Eddie Murphy in 2009; as of this writing it is scheduled for a 2012 release.

Available: Universal Studios DVD set *The Classic Sci-Fi Ultimate Collection* (2008). UPC: 025195033015.

One of the least flamboyant of the 1950s science fiction movies, *The Incredible Shrinking Man* is also one of the most moving and thought-provoking. Adapted by Richard Matheson from his novel, it one-upped competing science fiction films by reversing their strategies. Instead of highlighting monstrous, oversized opponents—giant ants in *Them!* (1954), a giant tarantula in *Tarantula* (1955), a giant woman in *Attack of the 50 Ft. Woman* (1958)—this film was about getting smaller. And instead of an outside force that threatened our existence, Robert Scott Perry was fighting himself, struggling to retain his identity even as it slipped out of his grasp. "For its time, it was quite unique," Matheson said years later.

Matheson was born in Allendale, New Jersey, in 1926, and raised in Brooklyn. After serving in the Army during World War II, he studied journalism at the University of Missouri. Working as a linotype operator during the day, he wrote short stories at night. It was the tail end of the golden age of pulps and fiction magazines, and Matheson could soon commit to being a freelance writer in California.

Matheson worked in a wide range of genres: horror, science fiction, war, Westerns, suspense. Many of his stories satirized politics and society; others examined moral issues facing everyday protagonists. Paranoia, both imagined and real, became a dominant theme.

The author found commercial success almost immediately. One of his first novels, *I Am Legend* (1954), became the basis of three movies—starring Vincent Price in *The Last Man on Earth* (1964), Charlton Heston in *The Omega Man* (1971), and Will Smith in *I Am Legend* (2007)—and influenced George Romero's *Night of the Living Dead* (1968, a Registry title). Several of his subsequent novels and short stories were adapted to film and television, and he is responsible for some of the most famous episodes from *The Twilight Zone* series.

Inspiration for the novel *The Shrinking Man* came from *Let's Do It Again*, a 1953 comedy starring Jane Wyman, Ray Milland and Aldo Ray. (It was actually the fourth film version of an Arthur Richman play called *The Awful Truth*; the 1937 film, starring Cary Grant and Irene Dunne, is on the Registry.) Matheson remembered one scene in particular, where Ray Milland, leaving Jane Wyman's apartment in a huff, accidentally put on Aldo Ray's hat, which sank down around his ears. "Something in me asked, 'What would happen if a man put on a hat which he knew was his and the same thing happened?' Thus the notion came."

In *The Shrinking Man*, businessman Scott Carey begins to lose stature after he passes through a mysterious cloud on a boating holiday. The novel gains its power through Matheson's attention to realistic details. The writer describes at length the medical tests that Carey undergoes, the immediate consequences to his wife and daughter, and his difficulties in coping with day-to-day routines.

When the novel was optioned by Universal-International, Matheson was signed to write his first screenplay. Now called *The Incredible Shrinking Man*, the script followed the same story line as the novel, with the elimination of some potentially troublesome subplots (like an encounter with a pedophile). Like the novel, the film was particular, even insistent, about detail. *The Incredible Shrinking Man* wanted to persuade viewers that its premise wasn't just possible, but plausible.

The project was filmed under great secrecy to hide plot twists but also to protect Universal's proprietary special effects camerawork. Some of the photographic effects proved so difficult that production had to be halted twice. In all, the effects took almost five months to shoot.

Yet some of the scenes in the film used techniques dating back to *Princess Nicotine, or the Smoke Fairy* (1909, a Registry title), in particular the use of oversized props. In the novel, Carey battled a black widow spider; here, he fights a tarantula, perhaps because Universal had access to what its press department referred to as one of the world's only trained tarantulas. ("Tamara" had already starred in Universal's *Tarantula*.)

Director Jack Arnold, who worked with Tamara in *Tarantula*, had built a solid background in science fiction films, although he started in show business as a performer. Born in 1916 in New Haven, he was a dancer in vaudeville as well as a Broadway actor. Enlisting in the Air Corps after Pearl Harbor, he was assigned to a film unit under documentary director Robert Flaherty, who trained him on the camera.

After the war Arnold formed Promotional Films Company with a squadron friend. They made educational and fundraising films for the State Department, the Jewish Consumptive Relief Society, and *The Road* for the Jewish Anti-Defamation League. Other titles included *Chicken of Tomorrow* and *Beachwood Package Home*. *These Hands*, which covered fifty years in the history of the International Ladies Garment Union, was released theatrically, and received an Academy Award nomination.

These Hands won Arnold a contract at Universal, where he made message dramas and Westerns until he was asked to direct a 3D version of a Ray Bradbury story. *It Came from Outer Space* was so successful that Arnold was pigeon-holed as a sci-fi director. "The more I did of these films the more I liked it because the studio left me alone," Arnold told writer John Brosnan. Like Matheson, Arnold obsessed over details, striving for realism. "In most of my sf films I tried to create an atmosphere," he said. "[To] ask an audience to believe things that are bizarre—you have to make them believe it. You can't do this with the story or actors alone, you have to create a kind of atmosphere while shooting it in which the audience's credibility will be suspended."

With *The Creature from the Black Lagoon* (1954) and its follow-up *Revenge of the Creature* (1955), Arnold introduced one of the few horror creatures to catch on with the public since Universal's heyday back in the 1930s. He attributed at least part of the success of his science fiction films to the financial support Universal gave them. For example, *The Incredible Shrinking Man* was technically a "B" movie. But according to Arnold, "We spent about seven to eight hundred thousand dollars, which was a lot of money for a film in the 1950s. That's what made the difference between our science fiction films and many that followed—such as the ones that American International Pictures made."

The production values in *The Incredible Shrinking Man*—the back projection footage of a house cat, for example, or the sets which made up Carey's cellar—are above average. But it's the script that sets the film apart from others of its period. Despite its giant cats and spiders, *The Incredible Shrinking Man* has no real villain, no one to blame for Carey's predicament. Nor is there a solution or answer to the film's premise. Even though it's disguised as mainstream entertainment, the film is as existential as they come.

Nowhere is this more apparent than in the film's closing scenes. As he moves into the night, Carey tries to understand what he is becoming. "Was I still a human being?" he asks. "I felt my body dwindling, melting, becoming nothing." These are fears that stretch beyond threats from technology or enemy governments. Carey is questioning his role in the universe, and by extension, ours. "All this vast majesty of creation," he says, "it had to mean something." But what if it doesn't, the film seems to ask. Where are we then?

A cultural bias against science fiction films muted the critical reception for *The Incredible Shrinking Man* when it was released. Matheson professed to dislike the film until the 1970s. Arnold also distanced himself from the science-fiction genre, turning to films like *High School Confidential!* (1958), a drugs-and-juvenile-delinquency expose that featured John Barrymore's son and Jerry Lee Lewis. But over the years *The Incredible Shrinking Man*'s reputation has grown. Arnold's simple, even prosaic style, the modest but persuasive special effects, and the mainstream settings all give the film an atmosphere of sincerity that is missing from its sci-fi competition. And in its closing scene, *The Incredible Shrinking Man* climbs out of the genre ghetto onto an entirely new level of artistry.

The Cry of Jazz

Frame enlargement from a concert montage in *The Cry of Jazz.*

KHTB Productions, 1959. Sound, B&W, 1.33. 16mm. 34 minutes.

Cast: George Waller (Alex), Dorothea Horton (Natalie), Linda Dillon (Faye), Andrew Duncan (John), Laroy Inman (Louis), James Miller (Bob), Gavin McLadyen (Bruce).

Credits: Directed by Edward O. Bland. Writers: Edward O. Bland, Nelam L. Hill, Mark Kennedy. Script consultants: Eugene Titus, Madeline Tourtelot, Frank McGovern. Based in part on the book *the fruits of the death of jazz* by Edward O. Bland. Produced by Edward O. Bland and Nelam L. Hill. Director of photography: Hank Starr. Film editor: Howard Alk. Assistant director: Nelam L. Hill. Music written by Le Sun Ra, Paul Severson, Julian Priester, Eddie Higgins, Norman Leist. Additional photography: Jonathan Chernoble. Lighting: Valentin Scheglowski. Stills: Valentin Scheglowski, Betty McCarthy. Art director: Bernard Goss. Script consultants: Eugene Titus, Madeline Tourtelot, Frank McGovern. Sound crew: Garry Harris, Timmy Harris, Nelam L. Hill. Copyright 1959 by KHTB Productions, Inc., Chicago, Illinois.

Available: Atavistic DVD (2004).

Combining fictional scenes with documentary footage, *The Cry of Jazz* is the cinematic equivalent of an essay. A subject of heated controversy when it was released, this *sui generis* film is valuable today as a time capsule of cultural assumptions and conflicts, and as the only known contemporary film record of musicians like Sun Ra. "It was a film we *had* to make," said director Edward Bland. "One way or another we were going to do it."

Born in Chicago, Bland served in the Navy during World War II. He studied at the University of Chicago and the American Conservatory of Music, and worked on projects ranging from arranging pop music to composing classical pieces. Hired to score documentary films, Bland learned first-hand about small budgets. "It was quite easy to make a film without spending much money," he remembered. "Film is such a powerful medium, I thought, 'Why not throw my money that way?'"

Bland and three friends—novelist Mark Kennedy, mathematician Eugene Titus, urban planner Nelam Hill—hammered out a treatment that would use a fictional music appreciation society to examine jazz as a cultural force. "We all lived in the Hyde Park/University of Chicago area," he said. "A big nightlife, students and ex-students talking and arguing over beers. Among those ongoing arguments were arguments about jazz. And it seemed to some of us black kids that the whites were claiming all kinds of creative ownership of the music. To correct this cultural misconception, that was one of our motivations. We knew there would be some ruffled feathers."

Bland approached Sun Ra, who agreed to perform in the film for free. In fact, Bland came up with a total of sixty-five people who worked without pay on *The Cry of Jazz*, including Melinda Dillon, a future star of the Registry entry *Close Encounters of the Third Kind* (1977).

Scenes set in the "Parkwood Jazz Club," an integrated jazz appreciation society, were filmed over the course of four weekends. These were rehearsed and blocked before shooting, and featured professional lighting and sound work. Bland also shot Sun Ra and other musicians in nightclub settings, with cinematographer Hank Starr drawing from films like *Jammin' the Blues* (1944, a Registry title) for compositions and lighting effects.

Finally, Bland and Starr embarked on what Bland referred to as "excursions": seven or eight sorties into Chicago neighborhoods. In some ways the most remarkable material in *The Cry of Jazz*, this footage was often shot at night, without lighting, from a moving car, capturing street scenes with the immediacy of a newsreel and the artistry of a Edward Weston or Robert Frank. "We figured if we slowed the car down, quite a bit, we might be able to get usable footage," Bland said. He explained a certain "timidity" in some of the shots because they were worried at the time about obtaining releases: "They'd want us to release some money to them, too," he said.

This material gives an indelible, if brief, look at life in Chicago at the end of the 1950s. A couple sways in front of a jukebox, silhouetted by the machine's lights; a child twirls on a sidewalk, an adult sprawled on the ground behind him; patrons hurry in and out of bars and groceries; a hustler plays pool in a smoky hall. It's as if Richard Wright suddenly had the use of Helen Levitt's camera; perhaps not coincidentally, Bland knew both artists.

According to Bland, filming *The Cry of Jazz* went smoothly, but the editing took months. No one on the project had worked with synchronized dialogue before. It wasn't until Howard Alk arrived that the film began to take shape. (Alk was a key figure in Chicago improvisational comedy, working with Mike Nichols and Elaine May in the Compass Players and helping found Second City.) Bland remembered that Alk "seemed mystified by the whole project," but credited the editor with bringing "all kinds of help" to the project.

In a promotional note, Bland wrote that the film was broken into seven parts, four with actors discussing the film's topics, and parts 2, 4, and 6 made up of documentary footage accompanied by a voice-over. Alk's editing smoothed these parts into a whole, often by cutting to the musical soundtrack. He used a shot of a car by a sidewalk—blurred, unlit, only 16 frames long—to maintain the tempo of one street montage, for example. Alk finished editing on New Year's Eve, 1958.

The producers hoped to market *The Cry of Jazz* to film clubs and art houses. Bland remembered the initial response as muted. ("We didn't expect to make any money," he said, "and we didn't.") But a producer showed a print to Amos Vogel at Cinema 16, at the time one of the most influential film societies in the country. Vogel scheduled a screening on February 24, 1962. Among those in attendance were jazz critics Nat Hentoff and Marshall Stearns and novelist Ralph Ellison. The reception was stormy. "I expected everyone to be angry," Bland admitted. As for Ellison, "He hated it."

As a provocateur, Bland delights in strong reactions. Asked at a recent screening what Sun Ra thought of the film, Bland replied, "I didn't care what Sun Ra thought because I knew him as a person. He was unavailable to me intellectually." It's easy to take issue with many of the statements in *The Cry of Jazz*. "A joyous celebration of the present is the Negro's answer to America's ceaseless attempts to obliterate him." "Jazz is merely the Negro's cry of joy and suffering." But Bland was making a polemic, a manifesto, not a how-to film, which is why *The Cry of Jazz* begins right where most music documentaries would end.

Bland and his partners advertised *The Cry of Jazz* in magazines devoted to art films before Cinema 16 took over its distribution. Cinema 16 in turn was sold to Grove Press, which continued to rent the film through the 1990s, when Bland lost track of the negative, an internegative, and other original elements. Still, he noted an "incremental increase in rentals, more and more curiosity" before signing with Atavistic for a DVD release in 2004.

The Anthology Film Archives had kept an archival reversal print of *The Cry of Jazz*. With support from The Film Foundation, Anthology oversaw a restoration of the film and its eventual blow-up by Colorlab to 35mm. The Orphans Symposium offered additional support by arranging for a pro-bono audio restoration by Universal/BluWave Audio. "It looks like a film now," was Bland's comment. He plans to release a remastered DVD version.

Pillow Talk

The calm before the storm: Doris Day and Rock Hudson in *Pillow Talk*.

Universal International, 1959. Sound, color, 2.35. 35mm. 102 minutes.

Cast: Rock Hudson (Brad Allen/Rex Stetson), Doris Day (Jan Morrow), Tony Randall (Jonathan Forbes), Thelma Ritter (Alma), Nick Adams (Tony Walters), Julia Meade (Maria), Allen Jenkins (Harry), Marcel Dalio (Pierrot), Lee Patrick (Mrs. Walters), Mary McCarty (Nurse Resnick), Alex Gerry (Dr. Maxwell), Hayden Rorke (Mr. Conrad), Valerie Allen (Eileen), Jacqueline Beer (Yvette), Arlen Stuart (Tilda), Perry Blackwell (Perry), Robert B. Williams (Mr. Graham), Muriel Landers (Heavy woman), William Schallert (Hotel clerk), Karen Norris (Miss Dickenson), Lois Rayman (Jonathan's secretary), Don Beddoe (Mr. Walters).

Credits: Directed by Michael Gordon. Screenplay by Stanley Shapiro and Maurice Richlin. Based on a story by Russell Rouse and Clarence Greene. Produced by Ross Hunter and Martin Melcher. Director of photography: Arthur E. Arling. Art director: Richard H. Riedel. Set decorations: Russell A. Gausman, Ruby R. Levitt. Sound: Leslie I. Carey, Robert Pritchard. Color consultant: Henri Jaffa. Film editor: Milton Carruth. Make-up: Bud Westmore. Hair stylist: Larry Germain. Assistant director: Phil Bowles. Special photography: Clifford Stine and Roswell Hoffman. Music by Frank de Vol. Music supervision by Joseph Gershenson. "Pillow Talk" words and music by Buddy Pepper and Inez James. "Roly Poly" by Elsa Doran and Sol Lake. "Inspiration," "I Need No Atmosphere," "Possess Me," "You Lied," by Joe Lubin and I.J. Roth. Gowns for Doris Day by Jean Louis. Miss Day's Jewels by Laykin et Cie. Westrex recording system. An Arwin Productions, Inc. presentation.

Awards: Oscar for Best Screenplay.

Available: Universal DVD (2004). UPC: 025192508424.

Although it was his first romantic comedy, Rock Hudson received top billing over Doris Day in *Pillow Talk*. Hudson was coming off an Oscar nomination for *Giant* (1956, a Registry title); Day, 35 at the time, was searching for a new screen identity after years under contract to Warner Bros. *Pillow Talk* helped make Day a "professional virgin," a career woman who resisted men on what she saw as moral principles. (In Hollywood terms, she just hadn't met the right man yet.) It was a move that kept her a bankable star for another decade.

In the 1950s, producer Ross Hunter developed a strategy of updating old Universal titles and formulas with new stars and new moral codes, many made in collaboration with director Douglas Sirk. (*All That Heaven Allows*, 1955, is a Registry title.) Not all of these films were melodramas: Hunter released Westerns and action films like *The Spoilers* (1955) and *Taza, Son of Cochise*

(1953), the latter starring Hudson. Hunter also produced comedies, like a remake of *My Man Godfrey* in 1957, and *Tammy and the Bachelor* that same year. The "Tammy" character, an attractive but innocent, even naive girl who finds herself in provocative situations, provided a sort of template for Day's role in *Pillow Talk*.

Pillow Talk was based on an unproduced script and stage play by Russell Rouse and Clarence Greene. They sold it to Martin Melcher, Day's agent and third husband, in 1958, by which point its premise of antagonistic phone customers sharing a party line was pretty outdated. In Hunter's hands, the script, rewritten by Stanley Shapiro and Maurice Richlin, would be a chance for both Hudson and Day to redefine themselves as comedians. (The two writers had worked the previous year on *Hey, Jeannie!*, a television sitcom whose star, Jeannie Carson, often burst into song.)

Both stars were apprehensive about making *Pillow Talk*, Day because her previous three films had been unsuccessful, Hudson because he had never done comedy. Hudson was born Roy Scherer in Winnetka, Illinois. After serving in the Navy, he changed his name to Roy Fitzgerald and made the rounds at film studios. An agent gave him the name Rock Hudson; a contract at Universal got him small roles in several films. His turning point came with *Magnificent Obsession* (1954), a remake directed by Douglas Sirk and produced by Hunter. Hudson considered Hunter a friend, which gave him some confidence about *Pillow Talk*. He credited director Michael Gordon with giving him the key to his role: "Play it straight, and let the audience find the comedy."

Hudson was also a closeted homosexual, a fact most moviegoers of the time were unaware of, but which inevitably colors our viewing of the film today. When Hudson's character, a songwriter pretending to be a Texas businessman, muses, "I don't know how long I can get away with this," it's difficult not to consider the line and situation in coded terms.

But *Pillow Talk* has many codes to crack. Day's role as a successful but sexually repressed career woman spoke to Hollywood's longtime disdain of working women, but few viewers of the time would have known of her desperate background. Born Doris von Kappelhoff in 1925, she had studied to be a dancer until her leg was shattered in a car accident. Twice divorced, she became a big band singer, touring with Les Brown and His Band of Renown in part to escape an abusive ex-husband. (In 1945, she recorded her biggest hit, "Sentimental Journey," with Brown.) Day's marriage to Melcher ended in 1968, when the star discovered that he had cheated her out of millions and signed her to calamitous contracts.

This was the first film directed by Michael Gordon since *The Secret of Convict Lake* in 1951, when he was blacklisted after the House Un-American Activities Committee hearings. Gordon had been a member of the Group Theatre, acting in productions like *Waiting for Lefty*, before becoming a stage and screen director. His Broadway production of *The Home of the Brave* led to a series of mid-budget Hollywood films, including *The Lady Gambles* (1949) with Barbara Stanwyck and *Cyrano de Bergerac* (1950), which won an Oscar for José Ferrer. Gordon brought out his actors' talent, letting them play up to their abilities. He drew an easy, unaffected performance from Hudson, for example, as well as from the veteran character actors in the cast. Nick Adams, on the other hand, flounders in a part that calls for more sophistication. (In his defense, Adams was a last-minute replacement for an ill Dwayne Hickman.) Gordon also had a good grasp of technical details, useful in this case because *Pillow Talk* required extensive split-screen work. Gordon and editor Milton Carruth used two and three screens faultlessly, at times suggestively, throughout the movie.

Pillow Talk basic narrative strategy can be traced to the screwball comedies of the 1930s and romantic melodramas of the 1940s, in which virtuous heroines are besieged on all sides by predatory males. She may have been a salesclerk in *Bachelor Mother* (1939), a secretary in *The More the Merrier* (1944), or an executive in *Honeymoon in Bali* (1939), but the working woman was always an open target. It wasn't a question of when, but to whom she would fall.

The more generous screwball comedies are those in which the women have a fighting chance, or in some instances are actually in complete control of the plot. In *The Awful Truth* (1937) or *Ninotchka* (1939, both Registry titles), for example, Irene Dunne and Greta Garbo toy with their male counterparts, participating as eagerly in romantic hijinks as their costars Cary Grant and Melvyn Douglas.

Doris Day, on the other hand, is tormented throughout *Pillow Talk*, by college students, telephone workers, policemen, and millionaire playboys, all of whom seem to be in league together. If she won't agree to be seduced, it's because she has "bedroom problems"—a stigma that never be attached to screwball stars like Barbara Stanwyck in the Registry title *The Lady Eve* (1941). Sex in *Pillow Talk* is a game for men, but for women the consequences in the 1950s were real.

Even the comeuppance, a classic part of the screwball formula, feels weak in *Pillow Talk*. Day made two more comedies with the same team of Hudson and the indispensable Tony Randall—*Lover Come Back* (1961) and *Send Me No Flowers* (1964)—and in both she is given better opportunities to turn the tables on her aggressors.

Day plays an interior designer in *Pillow Talk*, giving viewers a look at what Ross Hunter thought was chic in 1959. Hunter's taste could charitably be described as big: later in his career he would oversee such bloated disasters as *Thoroughly Modern Millie* (1967) and a 1972 remake of *Lost Horizon*. Here Day's orange-themed bedroom, mauve wallpaper, and avocado appliances, and Hudson's knickknack-strewn bachelor pad, point to a time of strident vulgarity. Even an intimate little piano bar is gigantic (in part to give the CinemaScope cameras room to move). Was it intentional irony to surround an interior designer with such excess, or to expose a songwriter to hack novelty tunes like "Roly Poly"?

Filmgoers of the time lapped *Pillow Talk* up, although the audience for this type of comedy began to split along demographic lines. Movies like *Will Success Spoil Rock Hunter?* (1957, a Registry title) and *The Girl Can't Help It* (1956) skewed younger, leading to teen-oriented titles like *Where the Boys Are* (1960), *Bachelor in Paradise* (1961), and the *Beach Blanket Bingo* (1965) movies.

Day targeted older viewers, soldiering on opposite Cary Grant, James Garner, David Niven, Rod Taylor, and Hudson in increasingly artificial and unsatisfying comedies. She attracted the same audience that went to titles like *Under the Yum Yum Tree* (1963), *How to Murder Your Wife* (1965), and *A Guide for the Married Man* (1967)—films that in the long run could no longer lure their target viewers away from their television sets. In 1968, Day left the movies, working on television for a stretch before retiring entirely from performing. Since then she has devoted herself to animal rights.

The Exiles

Yvonne Williams in a movie theater near Bunker Hill. Courtesy of Milestone Film & Video.

Kent Mackenzie, 1961. Sound, B&W, 1.37. 35mm. 72 minutes.

Cast: Yvonne Williams, Homer Nish, Tommy Reynolds. Rico Rodriguez, Clifford Ray Sam, Clydean Parker, Mary Donahue, Eddie Sunrise, Jacinto Valenzuela, Ann Amiador, Delos Yellow Eagle, Louis Irwin, Norman St. Pierre, Marilyn Lewis, Bob Lemoyne, Ernest Marden, Frankie Red Elk, Chris Surefoot, Sedrick Second, Leonard Postock, Eugene Pablo, Matthew Pablo, Sarah Mazy, Gloria Muti, Arthur Madbull, Ted Guardipee, Ned Casey, Jay Robidaux, I.J. Walker, Julia Escalanti, Danny Escalanti, Della Escalanti, Tony Fierro.

Credits: Written, produced and directed by Kent Mackenzie. Photography: Erik Daarstad, Robert Kaufman, John Morrill. Additional photography: Sven Walnum, Nicholas Clapp. Archive photographs: Edward Curtis. Editing: Kent Mackenzie, Warren Brown, Tom Conrad, Erik Daarstad, Thomas Miller, Beth Pattrick. Music: Anthony Hilder, The Revels, Eddie Sunrise, Robert Hafner. Sound: Sam Farnsworth. Production: Ronald Austin, Sam Farnsworth, John Morrill, Erik Daarstad, Robert Kaufman, Beth Pattrick, Sven Walnum, Paula Powers. Crew: Marvin Walowitz, Lawrence Silberman, Stuart Hanisch, Mindaugas Bagdon, Vilis Lapenieks, Charles Smith, Ken Nelson, Ron Honthaner, David McDougall, James Christensen, Stanley Follis, Ramon Ponce, Judy Bradford.

Available: Milestone Film & Video DVD (2009). ISBN: 978–1–933920–08–5. UPC: 7–84148–01094–6.

Before he died in 1980, Kent Mackenzie directed a handful of films that typified the career path of a film school graduate in the late 1950s. Mackenzie made sponsored documentaries, television episodes, educational films, and an independent feature that failed to receive a national distribution. While struggling for success in the film industry, he developed a distinctive style that combined elements of documentary with the free-form camerawork and editing of the New Wave.

Born in England in 1930, Mackenzie attended college at Dartmouth, where he began to study film. Receiving a draft notice, Mackenzie enlisted in the Air Force, where he served until 1953. The GI Bill and a scholarship helped him attend classes at the University of Southern California Cinema Department, where he was inspired by Professor Andries Deinum to view filmmaking as an art to master rather than a skill or craft to acquire. Mackenzie accordingly practiced writing, editing, directing, and acting, working with an industrial film company, Parthenon Pictures, as well as for the United States Information Agency (USIA) and producer David L. Wolper, whose documentary series *The Story of...* was broadcast on ABC.

Bunker Hill (1956), Mackenzie's graduate film project, covered many of the themes and styles that would appear in *The Exiles*. A documentary short about a Los Angeles neighborhood facing redevelopment, *Bunker Hill* included locations, and even shot compositions, found in *The Exiles*. The film focused on three people who lived in the area, and had them express their thoughts in voice-overs. This technique, common in British documentaries of the time, enabled Mackenzie to film intimate scenes without cumbersome synch-sound equipment.

Mackenzie used a similar approach for *A Skill for Molina*, a USIA film that was designed to explain re-education programs that had been established by the US Department of Labor. Mackenzie focused on a single family in Fresno, California, following Arnold Molina, the father of nine children, as he took classes in welding. Mackenzie had Molina provide a voice-over, although as in *Bunker Hill* the director also recorded wild sound on location, and some synch sound.

Robert Kaufman shot *Bunker Hill*; Erik Daarstad and John Morrill were the cinematographers on *A Skill for Molina*. All three would work on *The Exiles*.

Mackenzie became interested in the plight of American Indians after reading a *Harper's Magazine* article, "The Raid on the Reservations." After visiting a reservation in Arizona, he decided to make a film about the tide of Indians relocating to Los Angeles. In writing what he called *Thunderbird*, Mackenzie sought the support and input of Indians living in the Bunker Hill area. Yvonne Williams, an Apache, Homer Nish, a Hualapi, and Tommy Reynolds, a Mexican-American, became the three central figures in the story. Mackenzie recorded script sessions with them and incorporated their thoughts and experiences into his screenplay. The three would also provide voice-overs for the movie.

Filming began in January 1958, and continued off and on for "3 years and 4 months," according to a press kit. One reason for the delays was the fact that both Daarstad and Morrill served stints in the Army. Another was

Mackenzie's continuing search for funding. The Milestone DVD release of *The Exiles* includes a copy of an eleven-page plea for money that Mackenzie sent to "The Fund for the Republic" in New York City. Among the other groups Mackenzie approached: the American Friends Service Committee, the Apache Tribal Council, the American Civil Liberties Union, and the National Council of American Indians.

No one on the cast or crew of *The Exiles* was paid, but Mackenzie worked out a comprehensive profit-sharing agreement that he was still fulfilling years later.

No evidence of the difficulties in financing *The Exiles*, or its prolonged production schedule, can be seen in the completed film. It opens with a series of Edward Curtis photographs, solemn and portentous, before dissolving to present-day Los Angeles. And then the film takes flight, using extraordinary cinematography to open up every corner of Bunker Hill, turning its desolate buildings and streetscapes into works of art. Mackenzie zeroes in on Yvonne Williams, following her as she shops through the Grand Central Food market, then makes her way up the Angel's Flight hill to home. Inside is her former husband Homer and his friend Tommy, soon heading out for a night of drinking, gambling, and carousing with friends.

Mackenzie follows one after another of these characters, into bars, movie theaters, shops, gas stations. Their thoughts serve as both guides and warnings. "Someone will make me feel different," Yvonne muses. "Maybe happier. It's why I came out to Los Angeles." Homer, on the other hand, searches for direction. "I want to have some kind of excitement," he says. "Get in a fight or something. Walk all over town or something." Tommy is equally puzzled by life. "I'm not jealous, I'm not greedy," but he knows he's not getting anywhere.

Where is there to go? Their lives are defined by their surroundings, by a Bunker Hill of cheap bars and liquor shops, and their experiences are as limited as their finances. It's a measure of Mackenzie's skill that *The Exiles* seems so improvisatory, so light-footed, even cheerful. The film could have been as oppressive as the Registry title *On the Bowery* (1957), but Mackenzie fits in happy, skylarking moments along with the grim. Four friends zoom through a tunnel in a convertible, for example, drinking and driving without any cares, the camerawork offering up a dozen memorable shots that predict the work of the French New Wave master Raoul Coutard.

Mackenzie paints a remarkable portrait of the Indian community that connects it directly to the Curtis photographs that opened the film. Late in the story, during a powwow in Chavez Ravine, a girl leaning on a car wraps herself in a blanket and becomes the past, shedding the present for something approaching iconography. The drinking, the dancing, the casual circles that form and disperse, even the tricksters seem part of traditions that go back centuries.

When shooting was completed, Mackenzie had to rely on contributors like cinematographer Haskell Wexler (whose *Medium Cool*, 1969, is on the Registry) to pay for post-production costs. Mackenzie screened a finished print in April, 1961; a month later, he added the opening montage of photographs. *The Exiles* played in film festivals that year in Venice, Edinburgh, London, and San Francisco. (It also played at the first New York Film Festival in 1964.)

But distributors were unwilling to take on the project. Eventually Pathé Contemporary offered to distribute a 16mm version to the educational market. Within a few years only poorly duped videotapes were available.

When Thom Andersen used clips from *The Exiles* in his compilation film *Los Angeles Plays Itself* (2003), it brought renewed attention to the film. A 35mm restoration was completed in 2009, financed in part by University of Southern California Moving Image Archive, the National Film Preservation Foundation and Milestone Film & Video.

The Pink Panther

Music doesn't seem to help Inspector Closeau (Peter Sellers) with his wife Simone (Capucine).

United Artists, 1964. Sound, color, 1.85. 35mm. 115 minutes.

Cast: David Niven (Sir Charles Lytton), Peter Sellers (Inspector Jacques Clouseau), Robert Wagner (George Lytton), Capucine (Simone Clouseau), Brenda de Banzie (Angela Dunning), Colin Gordon (Tucker), John Le Mesurier (Defense attorney), James Lanphier (Saloud), Guy Thomajan (Artoff), Michael Trubshawe (The Novelist), Riccardo Billi (Greek shipowner), Meri Welles (Hollywood starlet), Martin Miller (Photographer), Fran Jeffries (The Greek "Cousin"), Claudia Cardinale (Princess Dala).

Credits: Directed by Blake Edwards. Screen play by Maurice Richlin and Blake Edwards. Produced by Martin Jurow. Associate producer: Dick Crockett. Music: Henry Mancini. Director of photography: Philip Lathrop. Claudia Cardinale and Capucine's wardrobe principally by Yves St. Laurent. Art director: Fernando Carrere. Set decorators: Reginald Allen, Jack Stevens, Arrigo Breschiu. Make-up: Euclide Antoli, Michele Tremarchi. Hairdressing: Amalia Paoletti. Film editor: Ralph E. Winters. Assistant film editors: Marshall M. Bordern, David B. Zinnemann. Sound: Alexander Fisher. Music editor: Richard Carruth. Sound effects editor: Gilbert D. Marchant. Special effects: Lee Zavitz. Production supervisors: Guy Luongo, Jack McEdward. Assistant director: Ottavio Oppo. Script supervisor: Betty Abbott. Dialogue coach: James Lanphier. Wardrobe consultant: William Theiss. Wardrobe supervisor: Annalisa Rocca. Main title by De Patie – Freleng Enterprises, Inc. Song "It Had Better Be Tonight" ("Meglio Stasera"): Music: Henry Mancini. Lyrics – English: Johnny Mercer. Italian: Franco Migliacci. Sung by Fran Jeffries. Tenor sax solos: Plas Johnson. Technicolor. Technirama. Westrex Recording System. A Mirisch–G-E Production. A Mirisch Company presentation of a Blake Edwards production.

Additional credits: Released March 18, 1964.

Other versions: Sequels: *A Shot in the Dark* (1964), *Inspector Clouseau* (1968), *The Return of the Pink Panther* (1975), *The Pink Panther Strikes Again* (1976), *Revenge of the Pink Panther* (1978), *Trail of the Pink Panther* (1982), *Curse of the Pink Panther* (1983), *Son of the Pink Panther* (1993). Remake: *The Pink Panther* (2006), and its sequel *The Pink Panther 2* (2009).

Available: MGM Home Video (2009). UPC: 883904132332.

A popular comedy franchise in the 1980s, The Pink Panther began some fifteen years before as "The Pink Rajah," a thirteen-page treatment cowritten by Blake Edwards and Maurice Richlin. Richlin, a screenwriter who had worked on projects like the Registry title *Pillow Talk* (1959), approached Edwards with the idea of a comedy based on the type of glamorous cat burglar played by

Cary Grant in Alfred Hitchcock's *To Catch a Thief* (1955). To this premise the authors brought the workings of a West End sex farce, and for financial reasons set the story in Rome.

Born in Tulsa in 1922, Edwards was the son of writer Donald Crump, and was later adopted by actor Jack McEdwards. An actor himself, mostly in uncredited roles, Edwards turned to writing and producing with a pair of low-budget Westerns in the late 1940s. He created a radio series for actor Dick Powell, who later hired him to direct episodes of his *Four Star Playhouse* television series. During the 1950s, Edwards wrote screenplays in a variety of genres, often with future director Richard Quine, and worked in television as well, creating series like *Peter Gunn* (his first collaboration with composer Henry Mancini).

Edwards directed his first feature, *Bring Your Smile Along*, in 1955. His commercial breakthrough came in service comedies like *Operation Petticoat* (1959), at the time Cary Grant's most profitable vehicle. Edwards followed these with mainstream hits like *Breakfast at Tiffany's* (1961) and *Days of Wine and Roses* (1962), technically sophisticated films that succeeded in updating old movie formulas for a younger audience.

The Pink Panther, as the "Pink Rajah" project became known when it was purchased by producer Walter Mirisch, was originally supposed to star Peter Ustinov as Inspector Clouseau, a French detective, and Ava Gardner as his wife. Both dropped out of the cast before shooting started. Edwards replaced Gardner with Capucine, a French model, and Ustinov with Peter Sellers, who had made his reputation as a member of *The Goon Show* and in several supporting roles in British comedies. Sellers, not yet a box-office star, collaborated so well with Edwards that the director and Richlin began to expand his scenes during production.

As shooting progressed, David Niven, cast as a suave jewel thief known as "The Phantom" and the ostensible star of the movie, began to realize that he was being overshadowed by Sellers. (He also may not have been aware at the start how Edwards intended to mock his role.) Although the focus of the plot remains centered on Niven's Sir Charles Lytton, his scenes have a rote feel to them, as if Edwards were spinning them out simply to get back to Sellers. Niven often seems uncomfortable, pushing too hard during his comic scenes and trying to wring emotion from the few moments when he isn't simply a cad. (He is also photographed in unflattering ways.)

Sellers, on the other hand, became immersed in his role. He claimed to have developed Clouseau's character while flying to Rome to meet Edwards for the first time—taking the detective's moustache from a book of matches, for example. Sellers realized that to keep viewers' sympathy, Clouseau had to be more than a bumbling fool. The actor insisted on maintaining the character's dignity no matter what befell him, and it is Clouseau's efforts to recover from pratfalls and insults that make him so appealing.

The moustache also indicated how much Sellers and Edwards reached back to earlier comedies for material. With his precise movements and exasperated expressions, Sellers' Clouseau evoked clowns like Charlie Chaplin and W.C. Fields. Similarly, Edwards turned *The Pink Panther* into a sort of case study in how to update venerable comic situations for new viewers and new technologies. Nowhere is this more apparent than in the three prolonged scenes that allude to centuries of bedroom farces, as well as films like *The Rounders* (1914), *Spite Marriage*, and *The Cocoanuts* (both 1929).

The first scene, less than two minutes, establishes the layout of the ski resort hotel room Clouseau shares with his wife Simone, including a connecting door to the suite taken by Lytton, her lover. The second scene amplifies the jokes in the first, giving Sellers more physical business and stretching situations out with more gags.

Tellingly, many of the jokes unfold off-screen, from a shot that frames the foot of their bed, a window, and the door to the bathroom, for example. This allows Edwards to exaggerate the impact of the wife's increasingly silly demands as she tries to avoid a romantic encounter with her husband. Each request causes Clouseau to rise from his bed, cross the room, and turn on the light before he can act.

What's more, by staging pratfalls off-screen, Edwards avoids dealing with the pain the jokes would cause. One of the charming elements of silent comedies is how its performers were protected from the consequence of their slapstick, cushioned as it were by the absence of sound effects. Working in sound, Edwards doesn't have that cushion. Instead, he finds ways to make sound part of the humor. The director also scales back the pratfalls, reducing his jokes to smaller gestures.

At one point in the second bedroom scene, Clouseau spills a bottle of sleeping pills across the bathroom floor. We don't see it, we hear it, just as we hear them crunch with each of his steps as he walks in or out of the room. Buster Keaton used a similar joke in *Steamboat Bill, Jr.* (1928) when Ernest Torrance tried to sneak across a bedroom floor littered with peanut shells in his bare feet. There Torrance's physical reactions supplied the laughs; here it's how Clouseau tries to pretend that nothing is out of the ordinary as he crunches his way out of the room.

Edwards could spin this scene out, with interludes, for almost ten minutes, using sight gags, dialogue gags, and double entendres that result in an especially satisfying series of jokes about a violin. And he tops this scene with a third bedroom sequence that more closely resembles the slamming doors of a Feydeau farce, adding two hidden lovers, a bellhop, and a chambermaid to the mix. Here Edwards is especially adroit in placing the camera in the best possible position: under the bed, across a bathtub, by an endangered nightstand, etc.

In terms of plot demands and screen time, Sellers has a relatively small part in the film. Too much of *The Pink Panther* is devoted to escapades involving attempts to steal a priceless diamond from an Indian princess played by the Italian star Claudia Cardinale. These scenes occasionally lead to wonderful moments, like a costume party where Clouseau in medieval armor berates a detective in a zebra costume for drinking on duty. Other scenes betray Edwards' tendency, more obvious in his later films, to strain too hard for jokes, notably when he reworks a scene from the Marx Brothers' *Duck Soup* for two jewel thieves dressed in ape costumes.

The Pink Panther is a product of its times, with its twisting jet-setters in metallic minis, its après-ski clubs, its pop songs and conga lines. It is also cruel and misogynistic in ways that aren't fully apparent until after the film is over. In subsequent episodes in the series, Edwards and Sellers played down Clouseau's cuckoldry, relying instead on broader accents, louder slapstick, and introducing a cartoonish nemesis in Inspector Dreyfus (played by Herbert Lom) to temper the original film's cynicism.

A cartoon turned out to be one more masterstroke with *The Pink Panther*. The film's opening credits, designed by De Patie–Freleng Enterprises, Inc., featured an animated panther who disrupted the film behind Henry Mancini's bouncy jazz theme. (De Patie–Freleng operated out of the recently closed Warner Bros. animation department, where Friz Freleng had worked for many years.) The cartoon Pink Panther was so popular that it was soon starring on its own series of shorts, including the Oscar-winning *The Pink Phink* (1964). The Pink Panther became a publicity figure for Owens Corning and other companies, and later hosted his own television series.

Sellers and Edwards reunited for *A Shot in the Dark* when Edwards replaced director Anatole Litvak. They agreed to change the original source for the film, a play that had starred Walter Matthau and Julie Harris on Broadway, into a Clouseau vehicle. Producers Walter and Harold Mirisch, who had the rights to the first *Pink Panther*, tried to interest Edwards and Sellers in a third film, *Inspector Clouseau*, but Sellers proved too recalcitrant and was replaced by Alan Arkin. (The Mirisch brothers hired Bud Yorkin to direct.)

In his memoir, Walter Mirisch detailed the endless squabbling that marked the Edwards–Sellers collaborations, with Edwards insisting on expensive locations that ended up impossible to film, and Sellers denouncing productions as soon as shooting completed. It took years for Mirisch and Edwards to mount *The Return of the Pink Panther*, which became one of the top box-office hits of 1974. The Pink Panther franchise has continued successfully into the twenty-first century in films starring Steve Martin as Clouseau.

The Jungle

Publicity photo of members of the 12th & Oxford Film Corporation. Courtesy Temple University Libraries, Urban Archives, Philadelphia, PA.

12th and Oxford Filmmakers Corporation, 1967. Sound, B&W, 1.33. 16mm. 22 minutes.

Cast: Charlie "Brown" Davis, David "Bat" Williams, Reginald "Reggie" Ackridge, Jimmy "Country" Robinson, David "Spike" Leach, Garfield Peacock, Forrest Outting.

Credits: Directed by Charlie "Brown" Davis, David "Bat" Williams, Jimmy "Country" Robinson. Cameramen: Garfield Peacock, Forrest Outting. Film editors: William Loomer, Phil Galligan. Project director: Harold Haskins. Film specialist: Phil Galligan.

Available: *The Jungle* was distributed on 16mm and video by Churchill Films. Copies are occasionally available in libraries.

North Philadelphia in the 1960s was a textbook example of urban decline. The loss of manufacturing jobs coupled with a shift in population to the suburbs left behind a largely poor underclass living in a decaying infrastructure. The area became a breeding ground for crime. Harold Haskins, at the time a social worker with Temple University, estimated that the city had as many as thirty-five gangs. Because he lived in the neighborhood and worked closely with youth, Haskins was approached by a California philanthropic group interested in making a film about what caused youths to enter gangs. "I realized this would be a great opportunity to see if I could direct them," Haskins said recently about the project, "get them to understand that there's more to life than what they were doing."

Rather than make a film about gangs and their problems, Haskins decided to let the gang members make their own film. "Everybody I knew were doing films that were *about* people, without involving them in the actual work," he remembered. "They would interview some people and then leave the community."

Haskins took a two-pronged approach to the project, obtaining support and materials from city leaders like Ed Bacon, the executive director of the Philadelphia City Planning Commission, District Attorney Arlen Specter, and schools superintendent Mark Shedd. Then, after meeting with gang members, Haskin began assembling groups of interested members. "We started with a group of about twenty-five young men we decided to call 'actors,'" he said. "We told them we were going to do a play, and that they were going to act out parts."

Next, Haskins paired volunteer professionals with specific groups. A cameraman taught three or four youths how to operate a camera, in this case both a 16mm Bolex and an Arriflex. The cameraman's friend taught editing to another group. A third group worked on sound. Another dozen or so members worked up songs for the film, one about drinking wine, another about a sort of theme for the gang. In Haskins' words, "I organized several groups of young men and wrapped around them individuals with skills."

Haskins felt that the key to communicating with gang members boiled down to simple issues: "How do you help these people get a new idea? How do you help them get beyond their community? Help them see there's another world, to see there is something beyond a futile lifestyle of drinking and playing cards and fighting—I never focused beyond that."

The actual filmmaking process was a combination of instruction and improvisation. Haskins's professional volunteers would often "pre-shoot" scenes in order to show their students how to use the equipment. It took between eight and nine months to shoot and assemble the footage, a time Haskins remembered as one of pressure and unexpected problems. "A lot of pain went into putting that together," he said. "A lot of mistakes, a lot of scenes that had to be repeated so many times."

Fights and distractions contributed to delays. The members sought out Sidney Poitier, who was filming *The Lost Man* (1968) nearby, and got him to appear before their cameras. Poitier's footage never made it into the film because it disrupted the story line too much. How the narrative developed was a source of considerable debate. Haskins remembered picking strips of film off the floor and inserting them back into the rough cut himself in order to clarify scenes.

Despite all the problems shooting and editing *The Jungle*, the finished film is tense and powerful, a portrait of dead-end lives in extraordinarily grim settings. The work is filled with creative decisions that were daring at the time but which have since become part of the artistic mainstream: backgrounds of scrawled graffiti, gangster poses and attitudes learned from crime movies, chanted songs that approach hip-hop.

The opening sequence, a gang attack at night, shows how sophisticated the filmmakers are, working in difficult locations, pushing exposure limits, editing to the jumpy percussion soundtrack, using deliberately crude credits. No matter how well thought out the scenes, *The Jungle* never loses its raw, edgy, uncompromising tone.

Hollywood films like *Angels with Dirty Faces* (1938) or *The Blackboard Jungle* (1955) or even *West Side Story* (1961, a Registry title) approached gangs as a problem that could be solved, perhaps through discipline or love. Viewers were taught that stopping gang violence was just a question of reforming a few bad apples. *The Jungle* had a different message: you had to defend yourself against a hostile world, with help from no one except the friends you could gather around you.

"I didn't know what we had," Haskins said when the film was finished, "but it was a simple fact that if they made it, they should own it." The twenty-five or so youths who stayed on the film throughout the production formed the 12th & Oxford Filmmakers Corporation, which received all rights and royalties for *The Jungle*.

The first screening of *The Jungle* took place at the R.W. Brown Boys Club, a community center on Columbia Avenue near 10th Street. A public relations director for the Philadelphia Gas Works, which had facilities across the street, arranged additional screenings. The film was shown at a festival in Watts, and won a Documentary Film Award at the 1968 Festival de Popoli in Italy. As attention grew, *The Jungle* was screened in universities and libraries.

"There must have been a thousand presentations all over the country," Haskins said. "It was such a great experience, but the guys didn't really know what they had." Haskins spoke of a "dark side" to the film's success. "Of course a lot of them died. The more they traveled, the more they got exposed to people who exploited them. Frankly, none of them did drugs before the film. But when they got to Chicago and the Blackstone Rangers, suddenly they were doing heroin. It's a hell of a story."

One gang member and cameraman was murdered after the film's release, possibly as a result of the press coverage of *The Jungle*. The 12th & Oxford corporation did not last long as members fought among themselves about its purpose and how it would be funded. A follow-up film was abandoned before shooting was completed, and no footage is known to survive.

But Haskins points out that many of the participants benefited from *The Jungle*, like a high-school dropout who returned to school to master the math he needed to edit film. For some, it was like "learning how to drive a car before you have one. You know it's something you need, so you learn how."

The 12th & Oxford corporation signed a licensing agreement with Churchill Films to distribute *The Jungle*. Robert Churchill entered film by shooting *Valley Town* in 1939. After serving in the Army Signal Corps during World War II, he cofounded Churchill Wexler Film Productions with Sy Wexler, producing and distributing dozens of educational films. On his own, Churchill also formed Churchill Films and Churchill Media. He sold Churchill Films to American Educational Products in 1994, and died in 1998.

No one seems to know where the negative for *The Jungle* is. "I don't think any of the original elements exist," Haskins said. "Most of the guys are in their fifties now, and they are not interested in going back and doing all the research and finding out exactly what happened to the film."

In 2004, Jay Schwartz, a Philadelphia film collector who curates film screenings under the name "The Secret Cinema," purchased a 16mm copy of *The Jungle* at an auction. He arranged a showing of the film on September 11, with Haskins and some of the filmmakers present. "It was moving," Haskins said. "Having children and grandchildren able to see something that their families, their fathers and grandfathers, did."

Schwartz has searched for the original elements for *The Jungle*, contacting Sy Wexler's son David and Robert Churchill's children Joan (an editor and director herself) and Robert, Jr. The trail ended with George McQuilken, who ran Churchill Films after its sale.

Schwartz campaigned to have *The Jungle* added to the National Film Registry, screening it at the 2008 Summer Symposium of Northeast Historic Films, an archive in Bucksport, Maine. National Film Preservation Board members Dwight Swanson and Dan Streible saw the film there, and asked Steve Leggett of the Library of Congress to borrow the print to show to the full Registry board at the Hollywood screening room of the Academy of Motion Pictures Arts & Sciences. Schwartz scheduled one additional screening on September 11, 2010, after it was named to the Registry. With missing elements, a clouded distribution history and an uncertain chain of ownership, *The Jungle* is a textbook example of an "orphan film."

Haskins has had a distinguished career in education, working at Temple University and then for some three decades as an administrator at the University of Pennsylvania before retiring recently. While he is proud of *The Jungle*, he takes pains to point out that, "It was not the type of film that was made because we were professionals, or trying to get into filmmaking. It was a film made to save kids' lives."

Electronic Labyrinth
THX 1138:4EB

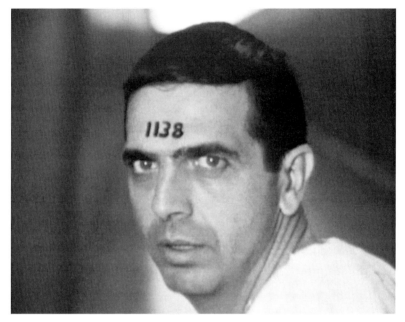

Dan Natchheim tries to escape detection in the future.

University of Southern California, 1967. Sound, color, 1.37. 16mm. 15 minutes.

Cast: Dan Natchsheim (1138), Jay Carmichael (7117), David Munson (2222), Marvin Bennett (0480), Ralph Stell (9021).

Credits: Written & Directed by George Lucas. Photography: F.E. Zip Zipperman. Sound: Daniel Tueth. Production Mgr.: Charles Johnson. Unit Mgr.: Richard Johnson. Asst. Director: Nelson E. Harris. Editing: Dan Natchsheim. Advisor: Gene Petersen. Produced by Navy students in the Navy Production Workshop; U.S.C.

Additional credits: One of three student films featured in *Take One*, screened in New York City in 1970.

Available: Featured extra on the Warner Home Video DVD *THX 1138 The George Lucas Director's Cut* (2004). UPC: 085391116226.

George Lucas made several shorts while attending film school at the University of Southern California. He was studying animation when he made *Look at Life* (1965), a compilation of photographs from *Life* magazine, a new picture appearing every five frames, or 1/8 of a second. In his book *Skywalking*, author Dale Pollock quotes Lucas as saying, "When I did that film, I realized I was able to run circles around everybody else."

Films like *Herbie*, an abstract piece set to a Herbie Hancock soundtrack; *Freiheit*, about a man (Randal Kleiser) fleeing from East to West Germany; and *1:42:08 a man and his car*, a documentary about race car driver and artist Peter Brock, followed. In 1967, he made two films as a graduate student: *Anyone Lived in a Pretty How Town*, based on the e.e. cummings poem; and *The Emperor*, a twenty-minute, black-and-white documentary about a radio disk jockey that, like *American Graffiti* would be later, was crammed with rock hits.

According to Pollock, Lucas's favorite films of the time came from the National Film Board of Canada. Lucas was particularly enamored by *21–87*, a ten-minute piece by Arthur Lipsett. The 1964 film combined New York City street scenes, portraits of consumers, and images of robotics with an almost abstract soundtrack made up of hymns, pleas for freedom, and industrial sound. "I saw that film twenty or thirty times," Lucas remembered later. "I said, '*That's* the kind of movie I want to make—a very off-the-wall, abstract kind of film.' It was really where I was at, and I think that's one reason I started calling most of my movies by numbers."

In the fall of 1966, he talked to fellow filmmakers Matthew Robbins and Walter Murch about how easy it would be to make a futuristic film using existing locations, like Jean-Luc Godard did with *Alphaville* (1965). Lucas wrote a short script about a man escaping from an underground world through a manhole cover.

Gene Peters, Lucas's former camera instructor, arranged for a way to produce the film through a USC program, the Navy Production Workshop, that was designed to train career Navy sailors about film. As an instructor for the class, Lucas would gain access to equipment, color film stock and processing. Navy students would make up the cast and crew. Not incidentally, he would also be allowed to film in the USC computer department. Other locations included an underground parking lot at UCLA, and corridors in the Los Angeles International and Van Nuys airports.

THX 1138:4EB, as the film was originally called, was about how one man escapes from a tightly controlled futuristic society. Lucas chose to tell the story primarily from the point of view of security cameras covering the escape and the personnel monitoring them, a decision that enabled him to disguise how small his budget was. Simply by showing its security apparatus and the people required to keep it running, Lucas can indicate the size and scope of his future empire.

Lucas's narrative strategy also meant that he didn't have to show very many futuristic sets. No living or eating quarters, for example, no transportation, entertainment, or social situations of any kind. He didn't have to "dress" or change sets, and if he used mostly close-ups he wouldn't have to worry much about costumes either.

The director still needed a look and feel that would plausibly suggest the future. He found it on closed circuit security monitors, which at the time delivered low-resolution black-and-white images. Lucas zeroed in on this poor video quality, including image rolls and other technical glitches to add a veneer of realism to his film. As Stanley Kubrick demonstrated in *Dr. Strangelove* (1964, a Registry title), documentary and newsreel footage looks more "real," more "honest," when viewers can see mistakes. Lucas used existing fluorescent lighting to further degrade the image, and often composed off-center shots that looked as if they had been caught by accident.

On many of the shots, Lucas added an optical effect of letters and numbers which he ran at the side and bottom of the frame. Kubrick used a similar effect in *2001: A Space Odyssey* (1968, a Registry title) when filming from the computer HAL's point of view. In *THX 1138:4EB* the effect doesn't make as much sense (who is watching this footage?), but it builds a powerful sense of unease. The effect has become widely used, in everything from the educational film *Powers of Ten* (1978) to *The Terminator* (1984, both Registry titles). Lucas would occasionally use it himself in his various *Star Wars* entries.

One final element was surprisingly advanced for the time, especially for a student film. Like Lipsett did in *21–87*, Lucas constructed a dense soundtrack, using music, industrial noises, snatches of dialogue, distorted broadcasts, and tones to build an aural collage. (The opening theme is from "Still I'm Sad," an obscure track by the British rock band The Yardbirds.) Unlike Lipsett, Lucas layered his sounds together, mixing them in and out of the soundtrack for dramatic effect. This helped him provide a narrative of sorts without having to come up with logistical details, like how security systems of the future actually operated.

Lucas was working on the edge of abstraction, hiding or withdrawing details from viewers so that they would have to construct their own narratives. In a sense he was duplicating experiments in montage conducted by Russian director Lev Kuleshov in the early twentieth century. (Kuleshov showed that by placing shots of food or a coffin next to the same close-up of an actor, he could manipulate what viewers thought the actor was feeling.) Lucas includes several shots in *THX 1138:4EB* that in and of themselves do not mean anything. Spinning computer reels, for example, or a shot of an empty corridor. Seen in conjunction with an escape alert broadcast on the soundtrack, however, the shots gradually build an atmosphere of menace.

While working his day job for Verna Fields at the USIA, Lucas edited on her Moviola at night, finishing *THX 1138:4EB* after twelve weeks. "I didn't expect it to turn out so well," he said later, and in fact the film won first prize for drama at the Third National Student Film Festival.

Director Steven Spielberg later spoke about being influenced by the film's power: "*THX 1138:4EB* created a world that did not exist before George designed it." Based on the short, producer Carl Foreman hired Lucas to shoot a "making of" short for his feature Western *Mackenna's Gold*. Foreman was also instrumental in Lucas receiving a deal from Warner Bros. to expand *THX 1138:4EB* into a feature.

When Lucas included *THX 1138:4EB* in a program of student films screened in New York City in 1970, he added *Electronic Labyrinth* to the title. (Some have speculated that the "THX" in the title was Lucas's phone exchange, 849. The initials later became part of his Dolby brand. Some writers believe that the "EB" means "Earth bred.") *THX 1138:4EB* also screened in a 1974 program at the Whitney Museum of American Art in New York City; a *New York Times* review concluded that "much of the film is just too clumsy to be chilling."

It's tempting to find the seeds of Lucas's later films in *THX 1138:4EB*, in particular the menacing, all powerful Empire of the *Star Wars* movies. Lucas's first feature, *THX 1138*, fleshed out the characters and background for the story and gave the director the opportunity to film the short again with 35mm equipment. But *THX 1138* was a notorious box-office failure that helped lead to the dissolution of a contract between Zoetrope, Francis Ford Coppola's studio, and Warner Bros.

At the time, Lucas's wife Marcia complained about *THX 1138*, saying that it left her emotionally cold. Lucas wasn't concerned. According to author Peter Biskind, he told her, "Emotionally involving the audience is easy. Anybody can do it blindfolded, get a little kitten and have some guy wring its neck." But in all of his subsequent films, starting with the Registry title *American Graffiti* (1973), Lucas has gone out of his way to forge an emotional connection with his viewers, no matter how broad or basic his directing must become to achieve that.

Once Upon a Time in the West

Three killers meet a fourth in *Once Upon a Time in the West.*

Paramount, 1968. Sound, color, 2.35. 35mm. 165 minutes.

Cast: Claudia Cardinale (Jill McBain), Henry Fonda (Frank), Jason Robards (Cheyenne), Charles Bronson (The Man [Harmonica]), Gabriele Ferzetti (Morton), Paolo Stoppa (Sam), Woody Strode (Stony), Jack Elam (Snakey), Keenan Wynn (Sheriff), Frank Wolff (Brett McBain), Lionel Stander (Barman).

Credits: Directed by Sergio Leone. Screenplay by Sergio Donati, Sergio Leone. From a story by Dario Argento, Bernardo Bertolucci, Sergio Leone. Produced by Fulio Morsella. Executive producer: Rino Cicogna. Director of photography: Tonino Delli Colli. Music composed and conducted by Ennio Morricone. Edited by Nino Baragli. Production supervisor: Ugo Tucci. Production manager: Claudio Mancini. Dialogue by Mickey Knox. Make-up supervisor: Alverto De Rossi. Sound engineers: Claudio Maielli, Elio Pacella, Fausto Ancillai. Special effects: Bacciucchi. Sound effects: Luciano Anzilotti, Italo Cameracanna, Roberto Arcangeli. A Rafran/San Marco production. A Sergio Leone film.

Additional cast: Marco Zuanelli (Wobbles), John Frederick (Member of Frank's gang), Enzio Santianello (Timmy), Dino Mele (Harmonica as a boy), Robert Hossein, Benito Stefanelli, Livio Andronico, Salvo Basile, Aldo Berti, Marilù Carteny, Luigi Ciavarro, Spartaco Conversi.

Additional credits: Italian title: *C'era una volta il West.* New York premiere: May 28, 1969. Later rated PG-13.

Available: Paramount DVD (2003). ISBN: 0–7921–7272–8. UPC: 0–9736–06830–4–2.

It may not have been apparent at the time, but the Western genre entered a period of steep decline during the 1960s. Movies with singing cowboys and TV Westerns aimed at kids ran out of steam in the 1950s, severing a connection to a new generation of filmgoers. Demographics for Westerns kept edging upwards as stars and audiences alike aged. Films like *Hombre* and *Ulzana's Raid* tried to introduce harsher story elements and characters, moves that did not sit well with purists.

What younger viewers did like were Spaghetti Westerns, initially a dismissive term for Westerns made by Italian crews. The "Man With No Name" trilogy directed by Sergio Leone became an international sensation and helped turn Clint Eastwood into a major movie star. After the third film, *The Good, the Bad, and the Ugly* (1967), was released by United Artists in the United States, Leone tried unsuccessfully to mount his pet project, a movie eventually released as *Once Upon a Time in America* (1984). When funding failed to appear (or, as Leone put it, "because people are not willing to forgive success"), the director accepted an offer from Paramount to make another Western, one that would be "a reaction to my previous work," as he explained in an interview. *Once Upon a Time in the West* would not just comment on the Western genre, but "see it live its last moments."

Leone had a background in film that could few could duplicate. His father Vincenzo was a director in the silent period; his mother Edvige starred in the first Italian Western in 1914. Leone dropped out of college to work in the industry, starting as a clapper boy and working his way up to assistant director. Leone's training included medium-budget Italian films, but also second-unit work on Hollywood blockbusters like *Ben-Hur* (1959) and *Cleopatra* (1963). He combined these backgrounds in the first of his "Man With No Name" trilogy, *A Fistful of Dollars* (1964). Its success helped revive a moribund Italian film industry.

The script for *Once Upon a Time in the West* started with story sessions with two of Leone's admirers, director Bernardo Bertolucci and movie critic Dario Argento (later a director of cult horror films). Bertolucci had completed two features, but in three years had been unable to start a new project. Years later he spoke about Leone's "double nature," saying he was an artist on the level of director Luchino Visconti, but "his basic ideology is a completely childlike version of life."

The trio spent months constructing a plot and filling it with references to as many of their favorite Hollywood Westerns as they could. Bertolucci encouraged Leone to include a strong female character for the first time in his Westerns. Today most critics see story parallels with *Johnny Guitar* (1954, a Registry title), but *Once Upon a Time...* unfolds in a completely different manner.

Given almost unlimited funding by Paramount, Leone had the luxury of fully exploring his theories of filmmaking, which included staging scenes to music. He had tried this in *The Good, the Bad, and the Ugly*, but ran out of time during shooting. For *Once Upon a Time...* he turned again to composer Ennio Morricone, a school friend who had scored the earlier Western trilogy.

"I always give him all the indications he needs to create, with in-depth descriptions and comparisons," Leone said of the composer. "I also ask him to think in linear terms, as I want to be free to do some permutations and associations when I use his themes." Morricone drew on a variety of musical influences: a fuzz-tone guitar from rock, trumpets from mariachi music, even an orchestral motif built around "vocalise," a style of wordless singing popular at the turn of the twentieth century.

Morricone wrote separate musical themes for each of the main characters and recorded them with an orchestra and chorus before filming started. During shooting Leone would play the music through loudspeakers to help the actors time their movements. Tied to Tonino Delli Colli's majestic cinematography,

Morricone's score, both lush and spare, with sweeping orchestral passages and stark pieces in small combo settings, adds complex emotional colors to Leone's material, from terror to grandeur, from humorous to macabre.

The ten minutes of opening credits, on the other hand, unfurled with no music at all. Inspired by a piece of music performed with a metal ladder he had seen in Rome, Morricone told Leone to use natural sound instead: the creak of a rotor on a water tower, water dripping from a roof.

Since he was working on such a large scale, the director needed iconic figures to play his leads. Claudia Cardinale was a popular Italian actress who chose her roles carefully, resisting typecasting. Charles Bronson had been a strong supporting character in films for almost two decades, and had played a similar killer with morals in *The Magnificent Seven* (1960). Leone saw him as an immovable object, with a face like granite that he captured in extreme close-ups. Jason Robards had been known for his challenging stage roles, and for his sometimes challenging personality. Leone cast him as Cheyenne, a bandit whose allegiances are always in question. Robards had appeared in Westerns before, even playing Doc Holliday, a character similar to Cheyenne, in *Hour of the Gun* (1967). Gabriele Ferzetti, who plays the railroad tycoon Morton, was a matinee idol in the 1940s. According to biographer Christopher Frayling, choosing Ferzetti was "like casting Laurence Olivier in a Western."

The real casting coup was Henry Fonda, Abe Lincoln and Wyatt Earp rolled into one. Eli Wallach (the "Ugly" in *The Good, the Bad, and the Ugly*) persuaded a reluctant Fonda to meet with Leone. After screening his movies, Fonda agreed to play "Frank," a ruthless killer. At first he tried to disguise himself with contacts and a moustache. "Sergio says, 'Off!'" the actor remembered later. "He was buying the baby blues, and I didn't know why." Fonda realized what the director was trying to do during the staging of his first shot, a meticulous track around the actor's body as he walks toward a killing. "The camera comes and people would say, 'Jesus Christ, that's Henry Fonda!'"

Leone directed the actors in Italian with a translator by his side, but as Argento pointed out, "Sergio mimed. He's a big mime." According to Ferzetti, "He loved working with actors. His method of working resembles a kind of inverted pyramid: rehearse, repeat the scene adding some of his ideas, and after that it was my turn again." Cardinale for one was impressed with Fonda. "I watched the way he was moving," she said. "It was like slow motion." Bronson, staying in character, "was always in a corner, he wasn't speaking to anyone, he was a very mysterious man."

Most of the film was shot in Almería, a desolate area in the Spanish interior. Leone worked with several long-time collaborators, including set designer Carlo Simi and cinematographer Delli Colli. Paramount's money gave them the luxury to take their time building sets and shooting scenes. Simi built a complete frontier town called Flagstone. The set cost more than the entire budget for *A Fistful of Dollars*.

121

Delli Colli remembered taking half a day to choreograph one shot with Cardinale. A close-up of water dropping onto a hat, something Delli Colli thought would require fifteen minutes, took another half-day. "It had to happen exactly the way he imagined it," the cameraman said. (He also remembered Leone fidgeting with props on the set, repositioning objects that wouldn't even show up in shots.) Delli Colli accompanied Leone, Cardinale, and a skeleton crew to shoot in Monument Valley, the site of so many memorable John Ford landscapes.

Leone quickly discovered that shooting to music slowed the pace of the film more than anyone expected. He sent for screenwriter Sergio Donati to help him trim the story. Several scenes were discarded, and Donati rewrote the remaining material, trying to compress it.

Filming took four months, followed by six months of editing. Leone took more scenes out, including one in which Bronson is beaten up. (Snippets of the scene made it into the film's trailer.) Even so, Paramount executives were bewildered by Leone's cut, which ran over 170 minutes. Soon after the initial release, they cut twenty minutes from the film.

With five story lines and several competing subplots, *Once Upon a Time...* can be difficult to follow—especially since Leone hides the meaning of several scenes until the final moments of the film. Taking out transitional scenes and entire roles made *Once Upon a Time...* even harder to understand. But Leone was working with stereotypes, and with the fundamental story lines of the genre. A widow tries to make sense of her husband's estate, a bandit on the run wants revenge, a killer on a mission searches the empty landscapes, a hired assassin sets his own agenda, a robber baron tries to put off death.

Like opera, the scenes themselves don't matter as much as how they're played. It makes no sense for Jill, the widow played by Cardinale, to ride through Monument Valley on the way to her husband's ranch. But when Delli Colli pans across the landscape, and Edda and the Modern Singers of Alessandroni perform Jill's theme on the soundtrack, the effect is magical. This is cinema on such a high level of accomplishment that it almost doesn't matter what the story is.

The film did not do well in the United States, where Spaghetti Westerns were still regarded with derision by critics, but it was a significant hit in Europe, playing at one theater in Paris for 48 consecutive months.

It took seventeen years for Leone to film *Once Upon a Time in America*; during that period, he filmed *A Fistful of Dynamite* (1972), or *Duck! You Sucker*, as it's also known. Along with *Once Upon a Time in the West*, they form a sort of American trilogy.

Over the years repertory theaters scheduled screenings of different edits of *Once Upon a Time in the West*. (One I attended in the 1980s switched from 35mm to 16mm in unsubtitled Italian.) In a 1971 interview, author Graham Greene referred to its "almost balletic quality," but the film is also the most operatic of Westerns (especially considering there is no one, definitive version).

More than any film of its time, *Once Upon a Time...* revels in its scenes of breathtaking photography, backed by one of the best scores of the decade, and edited with an eye to detail and a weakness for digression. It is a summation of the Western form, set during the "boom that would make it disappear," as Leone put it. Despite the post-dubbed dialogue, the Spanish landscapes, and the occasional misogynist moment, it is as persuasive a vision of the West as anyone working at that time could deliver. Leone gives us images that had never been seen in film before: a traveling shot through scores of workers laying track, a crane up to reveal an entire vista created out of nothing but his imagination, riveting close-ups, wide shots teeming with action, a world lost to time, and one that would be next to impossible to recreate on film today.

A bandit known as "Harmonica," played by the "very mysterious" Charles Bronson.

I Am Joaquin

Luiz Valdez used a variety of graphic resources in compiling *I Am Joaquin*.

El Centra Campesino Cultural, 1967. Sound, color, 1.37. 16mm. 20 minutes.

Credits: Based on a poem by Rodolfo Corky Gonzales. Produced by El Teatro Campesino. Music: Daniel Valdez. Musicians: Felipe Rodriguez, Teresita Armenta, Santiago Ramirez, Lydia Reyna, Lupe Valdez, Alfredo Flores. Narration: Luis Valdez. Photography: George Ballis.

Additional credits: Directed by Luis Valdez.

Available: Online at the University of California, Santa Barbara, *ImaginArte* site: http://cemaweb.library.ucsb. edu/ETCList.html

Produced by Teatro Campesino, *I Am Joaquin* helped crystallize the goals of what some have called the Chicano Movement of the 1960s. Both an educational tool and an expression of ethnic pride, the widely seen film also helped bring Teatro Campesino to a mainstream audience.

With some notable exceptions, Hollywood filmmakers tended to reduce Mexican-Americans to easy stereotypes. Numerous films in the early 1900s featured Mexicans as villains, like *Broncho Billy and the Greaser* or *The Greaser's Revenge* (both 1914). Later Westerns like *The Wild Bunch* (1969, a Registry title) still depicted Mexican-Americans with ugly clichés. Even allegedly sympathetic portrayals—*Viva Villa!* in 1934, or *Viva Zapata!* in 1952—fell back on stereotypes: lazy peons, buffoonish soldiers, etc.

I Am Joaquin was an attempt to redefine the Chicano's place in culture, to take back stereotypes and misconceptions and replace them with a truer record of Chicano accomplishments. The source poem was written by Rodolfo Gonzales, a Denver political activist and former professional boxer who was the son of migrant farm laborers.

Gonzales founded the Crusade for Justice, which became a national voice for the movement, and embraced the idea of Aztlan, the concept that the American Southwest was a national homeland for Chicanos. His epic poem was first printed as *I Am Joaquin/Yo Soy Joaquin* in 1967. It cited the progress of Chicanos from the Aztec empire through Spanish colonialism to the Mexican Revolution of the early twentieth century, and then to the setbacks caused by wars, urban problems, and social segregation.

The approach Gonzales took may have been derived from that used by José Vasconcelos, a Mexican nationalist and education minister who turned to the arts to unite social and racial classes after the revolution. Vasconcelos commissioned the great muralists Diego Rivera, David Siqueiros, Jose Clemente Orozco, and others to create works that embraced Mexico's pre-Hispanic heritage, equating it with the accomplishments of other ancient civilizations like Greece.

This sense of empowerment was key to the Chicano Movement of the 1960s. From fighting for basic rights (in an early case, a Mexican veteran of WWII was denied funeral services in his hometown of Three Rivers, Texas), the movement expanded to seeking better housing, education, and working conditions. In California, community organizer César Chávez helped form what became the United Farm Workers Association, which at one point was the bargaining agent for some 50,000 migrant laborers. With its boycott of grapes, the UFWAC brought the Chicano Movement to a national platform.

Born in 1940 in Delano, California, Luiz Valdez was also the son of migrant workers. While attending San Jose State University, he won a writing contest for his play, *The Theft*. During a stint with the San Francisco Mime Troupe, he learned the fundamentals of agitprop and street theater. In 1965, Valdez joined Chávez in organizing migrant grape pickers near his hometown of Delano. Here he brought farm workers and students together in *actos*, theatrical scenes that presented and debated issues in the bold, bright style of *commedia dell'arte*.

Huelga, a 1965 documentary short directed by Robert Merchasin and David Holden, shows a segment of one of Valdez's early "programs" for what was now called El Teatro Campesino. In Chavez's words, the theater was "a very good way to get the message across." The film shows the director instructing and exhorting his troupe. "We can get very angry about this," he says, "but there's a way to get back at them, and that's to make fun of them."

El Teatro Campesino began performing in union halls and from the backs of pickup trucks. In 1967, Valdez expanded the scope of the theater beyond the immediate concerns of the United Farm Workers. He drew from vaudeville, *corridos*, Bertolt Brecht, and religious pageants for inspiration. In a collection of Teatro Campesino *actos*, Valdez set out a manifesto of sorts in his preface. He wrote that *teatros* must promote nationalism based on an Amerindian past. "*Teatros* must never get away from La Raza [or the People]," he continued. " If the Raza will not come to the theater, then the theater must go to the Raza. This, in the long run, will determine the shape, style, content, spirit and form of *el teatro chicano.*"

Like the poem, the film version of *I Am Joaquin* presents a sort of collage of Chicano history, from the Aztecs to the present, using photographs and music as a backdrop to Gonzales's verse. The sources are wide-ranging, from sculpture, painting, and prints to news photographs, and the references are equally diverse. The film cites everyone from Benito Juarez and Father Miguel Hidalgo to Janis Joplin and Carlos Santana, with a nod to Gonzales himself in a montage of boxing photos. Valdez pays particular attention to demonstrators against the Vietnam War, in effect equating their struggles with those of Chicanos.

By intercutting archival material with contemporary photographs, Valdez could draw connections that were more difficult to achieve in Gonzales's essentially linear and chronological poem. The freedom to cut between a proud past and a degraded present, and to use Gonzales's text to form allusions the poet may not have originally intended, gave Valdez the opportunity to bring into sharp relief any aspect of Chicano life he wanted. At the same time, the director felt a responsibility to remain true to the poem, and to keep his audience's interest in mind. As a result, *I Am Joaquin* can seem dated today. The stentorian narration, the manipulative editing, even the selection of artwork are all indicative of a style that seems too forced and hectoring.

Finding a balance between delivering a message and entertaining a mass audience has proven difficult for Valdez. He mounted a number of plays through El Teatro Campesino and also wrote for movies and television. *Zoot Suit*, based on the Zoot Suit Riots in Los Angeles in 1943, opened in Los Angeles, later transferred to Broadway, and was eventually released as a feature film in 1981. In 1987 he wrote and directed *La Bamba*, a film about the Hispanic musician Richie Valens. "Everyone knows me for *La Bamba*," he complained to an interviewer in 2000. "It got me a lot of development deals and that was it."

"My problem was always that my projects were too esoteric," he said in the same interview. "I was never much interested in writing for sitcoms." But in the years since *I Am Joaquin*, Mr. Valdez and his Teatro Campesino have won Obies, Emmys, and Peabody awards, as well as grants from the Rockefeller Foundation and the National Endowment for the Arts. Valdez also received the prestigious Aguila Azteca Award from Mexico. In 1970, Valdez purchased land in San Juan Bautista for El Teatro Campesino. The theater continues to perform in that location.

The Chicano culture in the meantime has drawn closer to the mainstream. The poetry of Gary Soto, books like *The House on Mango Street* by Sandra Cisneros, and punk comics like *Love and Rockets* by Los Bros Hernandez (Gilbert and Jaime Hernandez) make no excuses for their backgrounds. Actors like George Lopez have made their Mexican-American heritage central to their performances. As for Valdez, he has announced plans for a film about César Chávez.

Our Lady of the Sphere

Larry Jordan, 1969. Sound, color, 1.33. 16mm. 10 minutes.

Credits: Filmmaker: Larry Jordan.

Available: The London-based Lux gallery offers rentals: http://www.lux.org.uk/collection/works/our-lady-sphere. Facets DVD (2008), *The Lawrence Jordan Album*. ISBN: 156580760X. UPC: 736899117429.

Some have traced the use of collage in art to scrapbooks assembled by hobbyists in the nineteenth century. The Oxford University Press attributes the "first deliberate and innovative use in fine art" to Pablo Picasso, who used it in two pieces in the spring of 1912, followed quickly by his Cubist colleagues. Collage became an important technique for Dadaists, Futurists, Constructivists, and other schools of modern art.

In film, collage is almost always used in conjunction with stop-motion animation. In his *Early Abstraction No.10* (included in the Registry under the title *Early Abstractions*, 1939–56), Harry Smith moved cut-out images across a background, building them up on top of each other until they swirled into outer space. As Smith described the film, "The final scene shows Aquatic mushrooms (not in *No. 11*) growing on the moon while the Hero and Heroine row by on a cerebrum." *Our Lady of the Sphere*, one of several dozen films made by Lawrence Jordan in a career spanning fifty years, also takes place in part on the moon.

Born in Denver, Colorado, in 1934, Jordan went to school with Stan Brakhage (whose *Dog Star Man*, 1964, is in the Registry). According to film historian Jackie Leger, the two explored "psychodrama" films, assembling dream imagery into narratives driven by free association. While attending Harvard, Jordan discovered the collage novels by surrealist painter Max Ernst and films by Jean Cocteau. Jordan began to collect engravings, filming them in his first experiments with collage. He also dropped out of Harvard. Returning to Colorado, he started a movie theater with Brakhage. Moving to San Francisco, he joined the merchant marine.

Jordan made several films by this point, but used animation infrequently. Like Brakhage, he was drawn to the work of artist and filmmaker Joseph Cornell (his *Rose Hobart*, 1936, is in the Registry), in particular his boxes of collage. While both filmmakers collaborated with Cornell, Jordan took the step of becoming his assistant, spending the summer of 1965 with him and filming the artist at work.

By this time Jordan had a substantial body of work, but according to historian P. Adams Sitney, the artist revisited his pieces so much that "the distinction between a finished film and a work-in-progress seems to have dissolved for him." What's clear is that he began to turn away from the psychodramas he experimented with earlier for a style that relied on collages animated by stop motion.

Hamfat Asar (1965), for example, used a period engraving of waves striking a shore ringed with mountains as a backdrop for a series of cutouts he maneuvered along a tightrope that bisects the frame. To a soundtrack of bongos, Jordan enacts jokes, puns, and non sequiturs. A man on stilts dissolves into a bird, tears fall onto a compass, a schematic of human musculature metamorphoses into a moth, etc.

Our Lady of the Sphere, completed in 1969, uses similar techniques toward more ambitious goals. Jordan employs color filters and tints, for example, drenching frames in primary reds and greens, or highlighting scenes with pale blues and silvery tints. By adopting a generally darker palette, he makes his dissolves and animations seem smoother, less abrupt. A soundtrack of electronic tones, insect noises, and other sounds provides an aural collage that mimics his visual one.

The film also has a more obvious narrative than Jordan's earlier works. Jordan never explicitly states what this narrative "means," preferring that viewers draw their own conclusions about his work. In interviews, he has spoken about "predispositions" that influence what viewers think about what they are seeing. (Jordan was reportedly delighted when a reviewer cited images in *Hamfat Asar* that weren't actually in the film.)

Leger wrote that the film's theme came from the *Tibetan Book of the Dead*. Sitney, on the other hand, avoided drawing any narrative conclusions. He felt that *Our Lady of the Sphere* allowed Jordan to "break through the conventions of continuity he had created and then thoroughly explored in his earlier collage films." (Sitney also complained that Jordan had to sacrifice "crucial tension" when his work became more complex.)

Jordan's sounds and images are specific enough that viewers inevitably try to form a story from them. Whether *Our Lady of the Sphere* takes place chronologically, or is split into separate story lines, is up to the viewer to decide. (Sitney, for example, believes that a scene involving a horse and easel leads into a "film within a film," something Jordan has toyed with repeatedly.) As with *Abstraction No. 10*, it's up to the viewer to determine why some scenes take place on the moon, or why Victorian engravings have science fiction elements. A sequence set in a circus evokes Winsor McCay's animations, but the tolling bells and alarm clock buzzers on the soundtrack add an ominous, even menacing mood.

Jordan's later films elaborated on the collage technique in *Our Lady of the Sphere*, by using color graphics, for example. The artist also returned to live-action filmmaking. After receiving a John Simon Guggenheim Memorial Foundation Fellowship in 1970, Jordan made *The Sacred Art of Tibet* (1972), featuring his friend, the actor Dean Stockwell. Orson Welles narrated Jordan's version of *Rime of the Ancient Mariner*, based on the Coleridge poem. The feature-length *Sophie's Place* came out in 1984. About *The Visible Compendium* (1991), Jordan wrote, "Photography is, to me, not about things, but about light. Light is our primary reality when we are at the movies — light which suggests things, the secondary reality, a construct by the mind. *The Visible Compendium* attempts to engage the mind, and particularly what is unknown in the mind, rather than what has been seen and known a thousand times over." *Cornell, 1965* (1978) and *Candy Colors* (2007) are short documentaries about filmmakers. *Enid's Idyll* (2004) uses illustrations by Dore for *Idylls of a King* to provide a new narrative for the Tennyson poem. *Blue Skies Beyond the Looking Glass* (2006) sets clips of silent film stars to Tibetan sound effects. *Beyond Enchantment* (2010), "where light and music become one," adds splashes of color to black-and-white cutout animation.

After teaching for many years at the San Francisco Art Institute, Jordan retired to Petaluma. He remains an important influence on filmmakers and animators, perhaps most obviously to mainstream viewers in the interstitial collages director Terry Gilliam animated for the television series *Monty Python's Flying Circus*.

McCabe & Mrs. Miller

A pensive Mrs. Miller (Julie Christie).

Warner Bros., 1971. Sound, color, 2.35. 35mm. 121 minutes.

Cast: Warren Beatty (John McCabe), Julie Christie (Constance Miller), Rene Auberjonois ([Patrick] Sheehan), William Devane (The Lawyer), John Schuck (Smalley), Corey Fischer (Mr. Elliott), Bert Remsen (Bart Coyle), Shelley Duvall (Ida Coyle), Keith Carradine (Cowboy), Michael Murphy ([Eugene] Sears), Antony Holland ([Ernest] Hollander). The killers: Hugh Millais (Butler), Manfred Schulz (Kid), Jace Vander Veen (Breed). Bearpaw whores: Jackie Crossland (Lily), Elizabeth Murphy (Kate), Carey Lee McKenzie (Alma), Tom Hill (Archer). Seattle whores: Linda Sorensen (Blanche), Elisabeth Knight (Birdie), Janet Wright (Eunice), Maysie Hoy (Maisie), Linda Kupecek (Ruth). McCabe's people: Jeremy Newsom (Jeremy Berg), Wayne Robson (Bartender), Jack Riley (Riley Quinn). Sheehan's people: Robert Fortier (Town drunk), Wayne Grace (Bartender), Wesley Taylor (Shorty Dunn), Anne Cameron (Mrs. Dunn), Graeme Campbell (Bill Cubbs), J. S. Johnson (J. J.), Joe Clarke (Joe Shortreed), Harry Frazier (Andy Anderson), Edwin Collier (Gilchrist), Terence Kelly (Quigley), Brantley F. Kearns (Fiddler), Don Francks (Buffalo), Rodney Gage (Sumner Washington), Lili Francks (Mrs. Washington). Townspeople: Joan McGuire, Harvey Lowe, Eric Schneider, Milos Zatovic, Claudine Melgrave, Derek Deurvorst, Alexander Diakun, Gordon Robertson.

Credits: Directed by Robert Altman. Screenplay by Robert Altman and Brian McKay. Based on the novel *McCabe* by Edmund Naughton. Produced by David Foster and Mitchell Brower. Director of photography: Vilmos Zsigmond. Production designed by Leon Eriksen. Art directors: Philip Thomas, Al Locatelli. Film editor and 2nd unit director: Louis Lombardo. Sound mixer: Barry P. Jones. Sound by John W. Gusselle and William A. Thompson. Wardrobe: Ilse Richter. Makeup: Robert Jiras, Ed Butterworth, Phyllis Newman. Assistant director: Tommy Thompson. Songs by Leonard Cohen. Associate producer: Robert Eggenweiler. A Robert Altman & David Foster production.

Available: Warner Home Video DVD (2002). ISBN: 0–7907–6522–5. UPC: 0–85391–10552–7.

Among his contemporaries, Robert Altman was unusually well qualified to direct a Western. Having broken into episodic television through Alfred Hitchcock, Altman worked on several Western series: *Maverick, Sugarfoot, Bronco, Sheriff of Cochise/U.S. Marshal,* and the landmark *Bonanza.* It was for this last series that he directed "Bank Run" in 1960. In it, the Harrison Bank, Mine, Mill Investment, and Steamship Company tries to take control of a Virginia City area silver mine, as well as the Cartwright family's Ponderosa ranch.

Altman's follow-up to *MASH* (1970, a Registry title) was the labored fantasy *Brewster McCloud*, a troubled production and a box-office failure. Five weeks before it was released, its screenwriter, Brian McKay, finished a draft for a script called *The Presbyterian Church Wager*. It was adapted from *McCabe*, a literary Western by Edmund Naughton that was published in 1959. Rights to the novel were controlled by producer David Foster, who had already rejected a version by screenwriter Ben Maddow.

By the spring of 1970, Altman had a 120-page script which he said would "destroy all the myths of heroism." With Altman "stripping away a lot of plotty things," very little of McKay's fairly straightforward adaptation remained. (Joseph Calvelli, screenwriter for *Death of a Gunfighter*, 1969, contributed to the script.) Altman considered the story "an easy clothesline for me to hang my own essays on." Since viewers were so familiar with the traditions of the Western, "I did not have to dwell on them. Instead, I was able to say, 'You think you know this story, but you don't know this story, because the most interesting part of it is all these little sidebars.'"

The end result looked like an anti-Western, especially to critics and viewers of the time, although today it falls more easily into how we think of the genre. *McCabe & Mrs. Miller* repeats the Western's creation myth in the same way that *My Darling Clementine* (1946) and *Once Upon a Time in the West* (1968, both Registry titles) do, with a different setting and atmosphere, it's true, but with the same conclusions about how the frontier world developed.

Warner Bros., where Foster had set up the production, wanted a star like George C. Scott to play John McCabe, a two-bit entrepreneur who gets in over his head in the mining town of Presbyterian Church. Julie Christie had already been cast as Mrs. Miller, a prostitute trying to promote herself to madam, when Warren Beatty read the script. (According to biographer Patrick McGilligan, Beatty, his friend Robert Towne, and Christie all contributed to the screenplay.) Arguably one of the biggest stars of the 1970s, Beatty was not the kind of actor Altman could push around. Indeed, the director complained later about Beatty's nitpicking. "He bugged me," Altman said, but then he also "kept me honest."

Altman filled the other parts with members of what would become his own acting troupe: Bert Remsen, John Schuck, Shelley Duvall, Keith Carradine, and others would work with the director on several more projects. So would the crew, notably editor and second unit director Lou Lombardo and cinematographer Vilmos Zsigmond. In fact, *McCabe* and Altman's subsequent four films—*Images*, 1972; *The Long Goodbye* and *Thieves Like Us*, both 1973; *California Split*, 1974—have a unity of style and purpose that is unparalleled in cinema of the time.

Since the dawn of film, directors have relished going on location to shoot Westerns, free of studio oversight and meddling executives. Altman was no different, escaping to West Vancouver, where he had art director Leon

Erickson construct an actual town, with real buildings and roads, and even its own restaurant and cocktail lounge for the cast and crew. Altman felt that having the crew live on location helped make the sets look more realistic. Like he did on *MASH*, he was building a community of eccentrics and outsiders who were banding together against the mainstream.

The locations on *McCabe & Mrs. Miller* look so remarkable in part because Altman and his assistant director Tommy Thompson were scouting camera angles while they were being built. Another reason was cinematographer Vilmos Zsigmond, who told the director about flashing and fogging the negative. "It makes it sort of grayish, very grainy, especially if you underexpose it and push the film, and you are going to get this old look that way," Zsigmond explained. "We decided fifteen percent of flashing would be just perfect for the movie."

In the 1970s, no one could dolly and zoom as expertly as Zsigmond, and *McCabe...* is filled with breathtaking shots that draw the viewer into the action. (Occasionally Zsigmond can be too pointed, zooming in on a gun, for example, to drive home a point too forcefully.) The combination of sets, cinematography, and Vancouver's mountain weather gave the film a look like no other Western of its time.

McCabe is also distinguished by Altman's preoccupation with overlapping dialogue and layered sound. He was among the first film directors to work with sixteen tracks, and in this film he began developing his concept of a "sound zoom," in which viewers would pick up dialogue from different characters as the camera passed by them. When Zsigmond complained, "I can't understand what they're saying," Altman replied, "Have you ever been in a bar where there's so much noise, so many people talking, do you hear everything that they say three tables away?"

On the other hand, editor Lou Lombardo felt that the original sound had "a dirty track, a muddy track. It was like trying to get an out-of-focus picture in focus." In Beatty's opinion, "Sometimes extreme relaxation can bite you in the tail. In the sound mix of the first two reels, it bit."

Much of *McCabe & Mrs. Miller* feels overdetermined. The heroics, the shootouts, the romance, even the weather are all too obviously anti-Western, tinged with Altman's characteristic misanthropy, his juvenile sense of irony, his tendency to push points that viewers have already perceived. Religion is empty, hollow, literally in the case of the town's namesake; capitalism is just a form of prostitution, albeit more violent; the good-natured young cowboys are the first to die, although the elderly suffer heavy-handed accidents as well. In a few brief lines, Altman can build an entirely persuasive backstory for a mining representative who will casually destroy everything McCabe has worked for, but then can find nothing to say about a minister except that he's a hypocrite.

And yet Presbyterian Church is a remarkable creation, perhaps Altman's best. Like *MASH*, it's an ad hoc, haphazard community, filled with outcasts who gradually build relationships. It's a town growing out of mud, and in each scene we can see the upgrades: new lamps, new walls, new curtains, glass windows. Like *The Long Goodbye*, it's filled with amiable whores, twisty, narrow passageways, and moments of inexplicable violence.

For once the worn, dirty clothes and long hair seem real and not costume. And for once Beatty, so content to play a heroic martyr in films like *Mickey One*, *All Fall Down*, and *Splendor in the Grass*, is just a character with believable failings, an overmatched Bret Maverick gone wrong, full of cheap patter and not nearly as smart as he thinks he is. Tied to Leonard Cohen's melancholy soundtrack, to Zsigmond's elegiac cinematography, and to Christie's hard-bitten performance, McCabe is some of the best work Beatty has ever put on screen.

In many ways *McCabe & Mrs. Miller* is one of Altman's most accomplished works, even though his usually reliable technique deserted him in the opening reel's muffled sound mix and the closing reel's optically printed snowfall. Every subsequent Western has shown its influence, from its lantern-lit interiors to its harsh assessment of frontier economics. But as producer David Foster said, "It didn't do much business. It was so disappointing." Altman later called it a cult film: "To me, a cult means not enough people to make a minority."

Hot Dogs for Gauguin

Adrian (Danny DeVito) gives his views on the ethics of photojournalism.

Martin Brest, Jacques Haitkin, 1972. Sound, B&W, 1.33. 16mm. 22 minutes.

Cast: Danny DeVito (Adrian), William Duff-Griffin (Fletcher); Rhea Perlman, Martin Brest (Couple on ferry).

Credits: Written, directed, and edited by Martin Brest. Cinematography: Jacques Haitkin. Sound recording: Rob Lindsay, Irv Kass, Bob Kates. Sound mix: Clayton Rawson, Lee Osborne. Special effects: Randolph Herr, Martin Brest. Post-production assistant: Jim McCalmont. Titles: Nick Tanis. With thanks to Steve Peck, Ezra Sacks, Joe Weiss, Alan Herr, Chandra Huang, Janice Houston. Special thanks to Haig P. Manoogian, Tim Curnan, Lee Osborne. Thanks to Lee Kingsley, without whose kindness and generosity this film would not have been possible. Produced in association with New York University and UGF/TV.

Available: NYU Digital Media Library.

Few student films of the 1970s could boast as star-studded a cast as *Hot Dogs for Gauguin*. Made under the auspices of NYU's Film School, it featured performances by Danny DeVito, at the time a stage and screen veteran, and his future wife Rhea Perlman. They agreed to work on a student film for a number of reasons, not the least being the strength of Martin Brest's script.

Brest was born in the Bronx in 1951. He attended Stuyvesant High School and then studied film under Haig Manoogian at New York University's School of the Arts. At NYU, students started out by rotating positions on films, from cinematographer to editor to director, for example. During the course of a semester cliques would form which a director might capitalize on in order to form a crew. Students got access to 16mm cameras and editing equipment and some rudimentary lighting, but not much else. They had to pay for film stock, performers, locations, and props themselves.

These limitations had a heavy impact on the kinds of films students could make. Action scenes and chases were complicated and time-consuming. Road movies soaked up money. So did special effects. Most students focused on small-scale, low-key character sketches, generally set in locations like student housing because filming there was free. Most films ended up being dramas, because comedy has its owns difficulties. The films also tended to be autobiographical, because students generally had little to draw on when writing other than themselves.

Hot Dogs for Gauguin operates on an entirely different level from most student films. For one thing, it's an extremely well-written comedy with engaging characters. For another, it creates a believable world far removed from the personal concerns of typical film students. Third, it moves beyond production and acting problems that plague beginner filmmakers to develop a specific style of comedy.

Some student directors see their first films as an opportunity to explore cinematic devices, or to make statements about their taste and talent. Brest, on the other hand, is remarkably assured and confident in *Hot Dogs for Gauguin*. There are no bravura passages, no long, tricky takes or demanding soliloquies, no gasp-inducing sets, nothing in fact that calls attention to himself. Instead, there is a meticulous attention to detail, in props, camera movement, and editing. Brest also displays an almost preternatural understanding of the filmgoing audience. He knows what viewers want to see and, just as important, when they want to see it. *Hot Dogs* has pauses, digressions, moments for viewers to catch their breath, but it also has the pacing and momentum of professional Hollywood product.

Brest accomplishes all this with technique that seems anonymous. In *Hot Dogs* the camera moves not for effect but because it has to—to keep action in frame, to draw attention to a character or detail, to punctuate a scene. Brest edits in the same manner, not to call attention to his visuals or to make viewers aware of his aesthetics, but to advance the story. Brest's material is so strong, and his vision so precise, that it almost doesn't matter whether his shots look pretty or not. He doesn't have to rely on lighting or extraordinary camerawork to make his points.

What Brest does rely on is his attention to detail. *Hot Dogs* is filled with grace notes that viewers may or may not appreciate, like the accordion-tinged version of "I Surrender, Dear" that provides a backdrop to one character's lowest emotional point. Brest's range of references, from Bing Crosby to Giovanni Ruffini, are as impressive, and as accurate, as the enlarger in the background of a photographer's studio or the bystanders hanging around outside a Lower East Side bodega or the glare from a boyfriend watching his date flirt with another man. These ideas build a world that viewers can accept without question. Instead of worrying about what sets are supposed to represent or why the camera is moving the way it is, they can concentrate on the characters and their stories.

Anchored by solid performances, *Hot Dogs* is structured in a three-act style, with scenes that modulate from euphoric comedy to cleverly staged suspense to despair. The premise finds starving photographer Adrian (DeVito) trying to stage an incident that will draw the world's attention, much like the Hindenburg disaster did in 1937, in order to cash in on a picture only he will be able to take. It's not hard to see DeVito and Brest in the same boat as Adrian, with perhaps only one chance to establish themselves as viable filmmakers.

The plot to *Hot Dogs* is so audacious that it's hard to imagine the film being made today; it's also so clever that it would be unfair to reveal. Unfortunately, *Hot Dogs for Gauguin* is not an especially easy film to screen, although New York University has copies.

Hot Dogs for Gauguin offers hints to subsequent work by DeVito and Brest. DeVito, for example, would made a career playing smart, sour curmudgeons who hover on the edge of sanity—in *One Flew Over the Cuckoo's Nest* (1975, a Registry title), for example, where he played a sexually obsessed mental patient; or in the long-running television series *Taxi*, where his misanthropic, amoral dispatcher Louis De Palma became the most popular character on the show. DeVito parlayed his experience on *Hot Dogs* into producing and cowriting his own short, *The Sound Sleeper* (1973), which in turn led to a stint at the American Film Institute in Los Angeles.

While still pursuing acting, DeVito started directing professionally. Episodes of *Taxi* led to TV movies and then features. *Throw Momma from the Train* (1987) was the first of more than a half-dozen features DeVito has directed. Through Jersey Films, DeVito has helped produce features as varied as *Pulp Fiction* (1994) and *Erin Brockovich* (2000).

Rhea Perlman has continued acting, both with and without her husband. She is also the author of a best-selling series of books for children based on the "Otto Undercover" character.

Brest also participated in the AFI directing program, where he wrote, produced, directed, and edited the comedy *Hot Tomorrows* (1977). This in turn led to a contract at Warner Bros. to direct the comedy/drama *Going in Style* (1979). Brest began directing *WarGames* (1983), but became so insistent on his vision that its producers fired him. The shooting of *Beverly Hills Cop* (1984) was equally troubled, but the film was an unqualified hit at the box office, establishing a new franchise for Warner Bros. and cementing Eddie Murphy's career as a movie star.

In some ways, Brest's *Midnight Run* (1988), an action/buddy blockbuster starring Robert De Niro and Charles Grodin, played off the dynamic between Adrian and Fletcher (William Duff-Griffin) in *Hot Dogs*. Brest's next film, *Scent of a Woman* (1992), earned an Oscar for its star, Al Pacino. The director's last feature to date, *Gigli* (2003), received some of the harshest reviews of the decade; the production was marked by disputes between Brest and studio executives, but also by intense media coverage of its stars, Ben Affleck and Jennifer Lopez.

The Exorcist

Chris MacNeil (Ellen Burstyn) learns that a homicide detective has unraveled a murder.

Warner Bros., 1973. Color, Sound, 1.85. 35mm. 121 minutes.

Cast: Ellen Burstyn (Chris MacNeil), Max von Sydow (Father Merrin), Lee J. Cobb (Lt. Kinderman), Kitty Winn (Sharon), Jack MacGowran (Burke Dennings), Jason Miller (Father Karras), Linda Blair (Regan [MacNeil]), Reverend William O'Malley, S.J., Barton Heyman, Pete Masterson, Rudolf Schündler, Gina Petrushka, Mercedes McCambridge.

Credits: Directed by William Friedkin. Written for the screen and produced by William Peter Blatty. Based on his novel. Executive producer: Noel Marshall. Associate producer: David Salven. Director of photography: Owen Roizman. Makeup artist: Dick Smith. Special effects: Marcel Vercoutere. Production design: Bill Malley. First assistant director: Terence A. Donnelly. Set decorator: Jerry Wunderlich. Music: Krzystztof Penderecki, Hans Werner Henze, George Crumb, Anton Webern, Beginnings, Mike Oldfield, David Borden. Additional music composed by Jack Nitzsche. Supervising film editor: Jordan Leondopoulos. Film editors: Evan Lottman, Norman Gay. Sound: Chris Newman. Dubbing mixer: Buzz Knudson. Sound effects editors: Fred Brown, Ross Taylor. Special sound effects: Ron Nagle, Doc Siegel, Gonzalo Gavira, Bob Fine. Sound consultant: Hal Landaker. Music editor: Gene Marks. Casting: Nessa Hyams, Juliet Taylor, Louis DiGiamo. Technical advisors: Reverend John Nicola, S.J., Reverend Thomas Bermingham, S.J., Reverend William O'Malley, S.J. Technical advisors: Norman E. Chase, M.D., Herbert E. Walker, M.D., Arthur I. Snyder, M.D. Optical effects: Marv Ystrom. Title design: Dan Perri. Color: Metrocolor. A Hoya production.

Iraq sequence: Director of photography: Billy Williams. Production manager: William Kaplan. Sound: Jean-Louis Ducarme. Film editor: Bud Smith. Assistant film editor: Ross Levy.

Additional credits: Stunt double (for Regan's "spider-walk" scene): Linda R. Hager. Premiered December 26, 1973. Later rated R.

Awards: Oscars for Writing – Adapted Screenplay; Sound.

Other versions: *The Exorcist: The Complete Anthology* (box set) was released in October, 2006. This DVD collection includes the original theatrical release version *The Exorcist*; the extended version, *The Exorcist: The Version You've Never Seen*; the sequel with Linda Blair, *Exorcist II: The Heretic*; the end of the trilogy, *The Exorcist III*; and two different prequels: *Exorcist: The Beginning* and *Dominion: A Prequel to The Exorcist*.

Available: Warner Home Video (2000). ISBN: 0–7907–5167–4. UPC: 0–85391–86322–9.

One of the least successful (or most amusing, depending on your point of view) elements of horror or suspense films is the explanation: the reason for the zombie plague or alien attack, the steps the criminal took to evade detection, the scientific process behind becoming invisible. The banks of phony equipment in Dr. Frankenstein's lab, the learned professors discussing the ins and outs of vampirism, the physicists charting a radioactive outburst: here is where filmmakers butt heads with their viewers, where rationalism takes over from imagination, where serious movies become unintentionally funny. A film like *Jaws* (1975) is awash with marine details and nautical anecdotes so viewers will accept the actions of its great white shark. The scientists in *The Thing from Another World* (1951) spew out their mumbo-jumbo about carnivorous vegetables too quickly for most to follow.

The Exorcist takes refuge in religion, hoping that centuries of church doctrine will justify the events that occur in the story. Based on a novel by William Peter Blatty, the film details the demonic possession of a twelve-year-old girl in horrific detail, with some attention also paid to the ritual steps to exorcise her. It was such a big box-office hit that it brought horror back into the mainstream, spawned sequels and imitators, and changed the boundaries of what was acceptable on screen. Its influence persists in everything from Japanese horror (*Ringu*, 1998) to *The Da Vinci Code* (2006).

A successful novelist and screenwriter prior to *The Exorcist*, Blatty based the book on one 1949 incident in Maryland and another in Iowa in 1929. It remained on bestseller lists for over a year, which gave the author some leverage over its inevitable screen adaptation. (The fact that Blatty had worked with Blake Edwards on films like *A Shot in the Dark*, 1964, also helped him in dealing with studios.) When Warner Bros. optioned the screen rights to the novel, Blatty insisted on William Friedkin, who had just won an Oscar for *The French Connection* (1971), as director.

Friedkin, who started out in television directing documentaries, had both a specific vision for the adaptation and the determination to see it through to the finish. "We're not surprised," he once complained at an AFI seminar. "Often, the viewer is ahead of the filmmaker. You know where the next shot's going to come from...You know this guy's never going to die. So, in a few films I made, I said, 'Well, I'm going to kill the hero.' You know why? That's life. People die."

Several elements in *The Exorcist* bear out the director's theory of filmmaking—"You must try to surprise the audience in every way." Friedkin shot at an archeological dig in Iraq to introduce one character, had a bedroom set refrigerated to achieve a condensation effect, and was verbally and physically abusive to the cast. Both Ellen Burstyn and Linda Blair suffered painful back injuries when stunts went awry.

"Friedkin's a lunatic," Jason Miller, who played Father Damien Karras, said almost thirty years later. "He's not very respectful to actors. He's afraid of them. He doesn't understand the process." The director did know enough to cast Miller over the more bankable stars Warner Bros. suggested. "The story was the star," Miller said. Blatty and Friedkin wanted "someone like me with no face at all to lend a sense of honesty and truth to the character."

In terms of technique and style, Friedkin was an expert. He may have wanted to surprise viewers, but he also wanted to direct them, to control their responses to his material through production design, cinematography, editing, and music. He assigned visual motifs to characters—Karras is often seen ascending into or out of the frame, for example—and spoke about using scenes to plant "seeds" that would emerge later in the story.

Friedkin was especially careful about angles within a scene: characters in effect direct the viewer's gaze by where they are looking. In an early scene, Burstyn looks to her left, and Friedkin cuts to a close-up of a doorknob taken from her point-of-view. When she passes through the door and walks down a hallway, Friedkin continues to alternate between shots in which she looks in specific directions and shots from her point-of-view.

The director preferred his actors to move and project rather than react. Combine this with Owen Roizman's precise camera movements and the film's editing scheme, and it's possible to follow the action in *The Exorcist* without hearing the dialogue. Simply by watching the characters' expressions and their positions in the frame, you can determine pretty accurately what they are thinking and what is about to happen to them.

This is true even during scenes that seem to be entirely dialogue-driven. Friedkin has said that his favorite scene is a confrontation between a homicide detective played by Lee J. Cobb and Burstyn, the possessed child's mother. The cop suspects that the daughter committed a murder, and presents the logic behind his reasoning. The mother's own suspicions are confirmed, but to protect her daughter she can't let on to the detective that she knows. Friedkin pulls the camera in subtly on both actors, punctuating lines of dialogue with incidental close-ups, like a spoon stirring a coffee cup. It doesn't matter what Cobb is actually saying: viewers know that he is suspicious, and that Burstyn is worried about it.

All of this expertise was expended on a pretty simple horror plot, albeit one updated with profanity and cutting-edge special effects. Production dragged on for months, from the scheduled 85 days to over 200. The efforts taken to transform Blair from innocent schoolgirl to superpowered thrall to the devil included dummies, prostheses, blood packs, contact lenses, and tubes of green pea soup glued to the side of her face. The effects were so lurid, and her lines of profanity so vile, that they had the paradoxical effect of pulling viewers out of the reality of the moment. They became gross-out points to discuss with friends later, something that made the story and the characters easier to take less seriously.

As a novelist, Blatty's smartest strategy was to insist that the story was real, which he did by propping up the narrative with "facts"—about church rituals, medical procedures, the history of Georgetown, meteorological phenomena, etc.—as if the weight of data could overcome the plot's clichés. It was a lesson taken to heart by novelists like Peter Benchley (*Jaws*) and Dan Brown (*The Da Vinci Code*).

But as a screenwriter, Blatty did not appreciate how Friedkin was handling his material. (Friedkin eventually prohibited him from working on the film's post-production.) Blatty was not alone. Friedkin fired veteran composer Lalo Schifrin just as he was completing his score, replacing him with Jack Nitzsche. Musician Ken Nordine, hired to contribute sound effects, had to sue Friedkin to get paid. So did Mercedes McCambridge, who was originally denied credit for supplying the voice of the demon.

On its release, *The Exorcist*—for a brief period the highest-grossing film of all time—became the film to beat, something for other directors to copy and best. A long line of demonic possession movies followed, including two *Exorcist* sequels, *Beyond the Door*, *Abby* (both 1974), *The Omen* (1976, remade in 2006) and its ilk, and tangentially titles like *Carrie* (1976). *The Exorcist* can also be seen as inspiring a wave of horror films set in "normal" locations, like *Poltergeist* (1982) and *Halloween* (1978, a Registry title). And a character similar to Blair's surfaces in *Ringu* (1998), a film that helped lead to a cycle of movies sometimes referred to as "J-horror."

At one point the *Ringu* demon scuttles across the floor like a crab, echoing a moment in *The Exorcist* when Blair's character descends a flight of stairs by walking upside down on her fingers and toes. But Friedkin actually deleted the scene from *The Exorcist* before it opened, worried that the effects were too obvious. The scene showed up in a BBC documentary years later, and a digitally remastered version with additional effects was added to the film for its 2000 theatrical release.

This rerelease boasted several other changes as well, including a different opening and ending, dialogue added and cut, new music, and new scenes. The changes point out the difficulty in preserving even blockbuster titles. Which version is authentic? The original release? The 1979 release reformatted for 70mm? The edit billed as the "Version You've Never Seen"?

Dog Day Afternoon

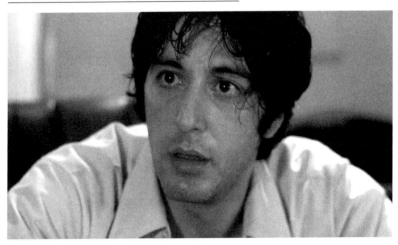

Al Pacino as Sonny Wortzik.

Warner Bros., 1975. Color, sound, 2.35. 35mm. 124 minutes.

Cast: (in alphabetical groups) The Bank: Penelope Allen (Sylvia), Sully Boyar (Mulvaney), John Cazale ([Salvatore] Sal [Naturale]), Beulah Garrick (Margaret), Carol Kane (Jenny), Sandra Kazan (Deborah), Marcia Jean Kurtz (Miriam), Amy Levitt (Maria), John Marriott, (Howard), Estelle Omens (Edna), Al Pacino (Sonny [Wortzik]), Gary Springer (Stevie). The Law: James Broderick (Sheldon), Charles Durning ([Detective Sgt.] Moretti), Carmine Foresta (Carmine), Lance Henriksen (Murphy), Floyd Levine (Phone cop), Dick Anthony Williams (Limo driver). The Family: Dominic Chianese (Father), Marcia Haufrecht (Neighbor), Judith Malina (Mother [Vi]), Susan Peretz (Angie), Chris Sarandon (Leon [Shermer]). The Street: William Bogert (TV anchorman), Ron Cummins (TV reporter), Jay Gerber (Sam), Philip Charles MacKenzie (Doctor), Chu Chu Malave (Maria's boyfriend), Lionel Pina (Pizza boy).

Credits: Directed by Sidney Lumet. Screenplay by Frank Pierson. Based on a magazine article by P.F. Kluge and Thomas Moore. Produced by Martin Bregman and Martin Elfand. Director of photography: Victor J. Kemper. Film editor: Dede Allen. Production designer: Charles Bailey. Costume designer: Anna Hill Johnstone. Associate producer: Robert Greenhut. Assistant director: Burtt Harris. Sound mixer: James Sabat. Rerecording supervisor: Richard Vorisek.

Awards: Oscar for Best Writing, Original Screenplay.

Available: Warner Home Video DVD (2003). ISBN: 0–7907–9304–0. UPC: 0–85393–37373–9.

Since making his feature film debut as a director with *12 Angry Men* (1957, a Registry title), Sidney Lumet worked with some of the leading actors of the period, including Marlon Brando, Anna Magnani, Sophia Loren, Katharine Hepburn, Jason Robards, and three films apiece with Sean Connery and James Mason. Lumet directed screen adaptations of plays by Eugene O'Neill, Anton Chekhov, Arthur Miller, and Tennessee Williams, and of novels by Mary McCarthy, Lawrence Sanders, John le Carré, and Wallace Markfield. He also contributed to the Oscar-winning documentary *King: A Filmed Record* ...

143

Montgomery to Memphis (1969, a Registry title). To industry insiders, Lumet was viewed as an expert in dealing with actors. By 1974, with the release of *Serpico*, an adaptation of Peter Maas's book about police corruption, he was also considered first among directors dealing with New York City.

The story behind *Dog Day Afternoon* first came to the attention of producer Martin Bregman when an assistant showed him a *Life* magazine article by P.F. Kluge and Thomas Moore about a botched bank robbery in Brooklyn on August 22, 1973. John Wojtowicz, one of the robbers, had a close physical resemblance to actor Al Pacino. That, and the peculiarities of the robbery, were reasons enough for Bregman and producer Martin Elfand to pursue a screen adaptation.

After obtaining rights from Wojtowicz (who had yet to be tried for the robbery) and his family, the producers contacted screenwriter Frank Pierson. (More about Pierson's career can be found in *Cool Hand Luke*, 1967.) Given cartons of printed material and videotapes, Pierson found himself struggling to define a story and point of view for a screenplay. He never had the opportunity to meet with Wojtowicz, who was in a dispute over finances with Warner Bros., but felt that the robber was the core of the story.

Pierson did interview Wojtowicz's wife and mother, as well as the bank employees involved in the robbery. "It was all so contradictory," he said later. "Everyone knew a different person and described a different person." Pierson decided to try to capture these different characteristics. He also honed in on the robber's sense of compassion. "Basically he would look at you and say he'd take care of you," the writer decided. Pierson finished a draft after Christmas, 1973.

Pacino, who had worked with Bregman and Lumet on *Serpico*, was hesitant about the part at first. Once he committed to the role, he was active in casting the film. Several parts were filled with theatrical colleagues, such as John Cazale. Although Cazale was twice the age of Sal, Wojtowicz's cohort in the robbery, he is one of the crucial elements to the film's success. "We thought of these two people not knowing each other," Pacino said about how he and Cazale approached their parts. The robbers were "finding out about each other under this pressure."

Other Pacino choices included Judith Malina for Sonny's overprotective mother and Charles Durning, who played a police detective who establishes a relationship with Sonny (the name chosen for Wojtowicz's character in the film) after the robbery turns into a hostage situation. "Sidney didn't know who I was," Durning remembered. Lumet thought he was auditioning for the bank manager, but Pacino got the director to change his mind, even though Durning would be shooting Robert Wise's disaster epic *The Hindenburg* (1975) at the same time.

"This was my first film," Lance Henriksen remembered later. He auditioned for the role of Leon, Sonny's boyfriend, but was cast as an FBI agent instead.

Chris Sarandon, the eventual Leon, had also never worked in film. "We got lucky with Chris," Pacino recalled. "He was just there." Sarandon said he found the key to his role after Lumet told him, "A little less Blanche DuBois, a little more Queens housewife."

"Shooting on location was essential," Bregman said later. Lumet agreed, in part because the front wall of the bank was a large window. Trying to match the light and street scenes through the window in a studio would have been too difficult. Furthermore, working on location helped the cast develop a connection to their surroundings.

After building a version of the bank in a former automotive repair shop in Brooklyn, Lumet settled in for three weeks of rehearsals. He was so impressed by the rapport of the cast, and the level of improvisation, that he recorded their sessions. Together with Pierson and Bregman, Lumet composed a script based on the improvised dialogue. "Structurally, nothing was changed," Lumet said. "It was his [Pierson's] structure scene by scene."

Although it may not seem as noteworthy today, the script's use of homosexuality was unnerving to some at the time, in part because Pierson treated it so casually. Still, a scene in which Sonny and Leon kiss almost caused Pacino to drop out of the project. The actor confronted Pierson, saying the real point of the scene should be about "these two people who love each other but can't find a way to live together." Forced to agree, Pierson came up with a telephone call between the two characters that is among the most heartfelt and moving passages in the film. "It wasn't a relationship between a drag queen and his boyfriend, it was a relationship between two people," Sarandon explained.

Lumet, his cinematographer Victor J. Kemper, and editor Dede Allen still faced several problems during production. A city bus line had to be rerouted during production. Lumet had to keep control over extras that swelled from 300 to over a thousand. He also had to simulate a hot summer day during a fairly brisk autumn shooting schedule.

Kemper remembered struggling to maintain the illusion that all the action was taking place during one day. The cinematographer also fashioned several tracking shots that hurtle through the length of the bank, following characters in moments of panic. During the story, police cut electricity to the bank, so Kemper would need another source of lighting for the night scenes. He added emergency lights in the bank's interior during preproduction.

Allen, who also cut *Serpico*, found the rapport the director encouraged among the cast an aid to her editing. She also appreciated the fact that Lumet usually had at least two cameras running during the street scenes. *12 Angry Men* proved that Lumet could stage action within a limited set, but it was up to Allen to maintain a mood of tension and immediacy throughout the film. Sonny and Sal share a moment of panic at one point in the story, scurrying for safety behind a wall of tellers' windows. Allen builds a seamless montage out of several tracking shots, cutting in one nine-frame shot of Cazale to sustain the illusion of movement.

It was Lumet's willingness to trust his material that may have had the greatest impact on *Dog Day Afternoon*. When he set out to film the opening, he said, "The important thing about that opening montage was not to do the colorful things." When choosing the bank employees: "You do not cast them 'colorful' because then you'll have a bunch of disjointed vignettes going on having nothing to do with the movie. I didn't want 'characters.'" He didn't want artificial light, either, using the fluorescent lights inside the bank and police spotlights for the streets at night.

Lumet didn't push the storyline, by making the homosexual aspect more melodramatic, for example, or by portraying the police as stereotypes. While he shaped the performances, he clearly gave the actors the room they needed to achieve remarkable results.

Dog Day Afternoon delighted viewers at the time, won significant awards (including Academy Award nominations for Best Picture and Director), and cemented Lumet's reputation as a director of New York movies. His next film, *Network* (1976), is also on the Registry.

Quasi at the Quackadero

Inside Quasi's pleasure dome. Courtesy of Sally Cruikshank.

Sally Cruikshank, 1975. Sound, color, 1.33. 16mm. 10 minutes.

Credits: Written, animated, and directed by Sally Cruikshank. Music by Bob Armstrong and Al Dodge. Recorded at Sierra Sound Labs. Ink and paint: Kathryn Lenihan. Special art assistant: Kim Deitch. Sound engineer: Steve Halbert. Special thanks to: E.E. Gregg Snazelle, Rose S. Cruikshank, Diana Pellegrini.

Available: *Sally Cruikshank* DVD, http://www.funonmars.com/

A favorite with midnight audiences when it was released in 1975, *Quasi at the Quackadero* was one of the first counterculture cartoons to reach a wide audience. It helped introduce a new generation of animators to filmgoers, as well as to popularize trends in alternative comics and music.

Born in New Jersey in 1949, Sally Cruikshank attended Smith College, where she won a scholarship to a summer term at Yale Art School. A classmate persuaded her to pursue animation. Back at Smith she completed her first film, *Ducky*, a three-minute cartoon featuring an early version of her Quasi character, a duck-like figure who wears a hat and cape.

Cruikshank enrolled in the San Francisco Art Institute, where she was taught by Larry Jordan (his *Our Lady of the Sphere*, 1969, is on the Registry). Cruikshank's *Fun on Mars* (1971) shows the influence of Jordan's style of collage, but also retained her duck creatures. (The animator has said that her ducks were derived from Donald Duck drawings by animator Carl Banks.)

147

Cruikshank found a patron of sorts in E.E. Gregg Snazelle, head of Snazelle Films, one of the first large film production companies in San Francisco. Snazelle Films rented out studio space and equipment, made industrial films and commercials, and provided production services for other film companies. Cruikshank rented a Moviola there to complete *Chow Fun*. "Gregg saw the film and offered me a job," she wrote later, "to experiment with animation, and do commercials for him when the jobs came in. He also hoped I'd figure out how to solve 3D without glasses!" She was employed there for ten years, spending most of that time working on her own films, a situation she describes as unimaginable today.

Cruikshank expanded her animating repertory over her next films. *Chow Fun*'s influences ranged from firecracker packaging to the 1930s cartoons by the Fleischer brothers and the Van Buren Studio. Not coincidentally, 1930s animation was a big influence on underground comics as well. Cruikshank said that when she first saw Robert Crumb's work, "It was so good I almost couldn't stand it." Cruikshank reworked many of the ideas used in 1930s cartoons, notably the way animators brought objects like furniture and buildings to life. In the opening shots of *Quasi at the Quackadero*, an easy chair dances in time to the music, just like manhole covers and lamps dance in Fleischer cartoons like *Bimbo's Initiation* (1931).

Crumb and fellow artists and musicians Bob Armstrong, and Al Dodge took this fascination with the thirties further, forming the Cheap Suit Serenaders, an acoustic band that specialized in string versions of period tunes. Armstrong and Dodge provided the "strange, gallopy" music for *Quasi*, and for Cruikshank's *Make Me Psychic* (1978) as well.

It took Cruikshank two years to create all the artwork for *Quasi*, and another four months to shoot and edit it. She screened it at the Los Angeles Film Exposition and commercially at theaters around the Bay Area. Later, the film was distributed by Serious Business, a Berkeley company, and also by Picture Start.

Viewers who watched *Quasi* when it first came out may have found it easier to connect the film to underground comics, as well as to the Fleischers, whose Betty Boop was undergoing a rediscovery. Out of necessity, *Quasi* abandoned the qualities and restrictions of classical animation. Like many underground comic artists, Cruikshank adopted a "do it yourself" attitude that existed outside the corporate boundaries of a Hanna–Barbera cartoon. Initially, animation festivals shunned the film.

Quasi's story line and characters share with the early Fleischer films the same propensity to change shapes, to distort, evolve, and revert in time to music. "Animation is sort of this open door to fantasy land," Cruikshank said in an interview. "You're only limited by what you can draw."

She admitted that her characters could "look really weird on individual frames." "I take a lot of liberties," she added. "You can get the personality of the character expressed through distortion…instead of just opening and shutting their mouths."

Technique can't salvage a poor script; fortunately, *Quasi* is overflowing with ideas, from a character with wheels named Rollo to a punning shot of an angry Anita (a sort of upright female dog who acts as an antagonist in Quasi's films) shooting real daggers from her eyes. Cruikshank introduces a succession of carnival sideshow rides and exhibits, including a segment with fun-house mirrors that echoes Winsor McCay's *Little Nemo* (1911). But Cruikshank goes a step further by suggesting that some changes are irrevocable, like a peepshow that moves time backwards.

The success of *Quasi at the Quackadero* enabled Cruikshank to raise the budget of her next film, *Make Me Psychic* (1978). This film received an even wider distribution than *Quasi*, opening in San Francisco with the feature *The China Syndrome*. As she put it, "The future seemed wide open." With a grant from the National Endowment for the Arts, she began work on a proposed feature, *Quasi's Cabaret*. Cruikshank also spent years trying to finance *Love That Makes You Crawl*, a feature that in collaboration with director Joe Dante that would combine live action and animation. Neither project moved forward.

After making *Face Like a Frog* (1987), Cruikshank animated and produced almost twenty pieces for *Sesame Street*. Animated to songs by Fats Waller, Betty Carter, and others, these function as the equivalent of music videos for kids. *I'm Curious*, for example, follows a walking lizard who shifts sizes while exploring the world. *Island of Emotion* uses reggae music to help show feelings like sadness and love. Cruikshank's use of surrealism and free-form fantasy turns out to be wonderfully appropriate for children.

Cruikshank has also contributed animated sequences to feature films like *Twilight Zone: The Movie* (1982), *Ruthless People* (1986), and *Mannequin* (1987). Her influence is unmistakable in the work of performers like Pee-wee Herman (Paul Reubens), who employs a dancing easy chair in his act reminiscent of the one in *Quasi*. *Futurama*, the cartoon sitcom by Matt Groening and David X. Cohen, featured a clip from *Quasi* in an opening credit sequence.

Grey Gardens

"Little Edie" Beale waves the flag during a routine in *Grey Gardens*.

Maysles Films, 1975. Sound, color, 1.33. 16mm. 95 minutes.

Featuring: Edith Beale, "Little Edie" Beale, Jack Helmuth, Brooks Hires, Jerry Torre, Lois Wright.

Credits: Directed by David Maysles, Albert Maysles, Ellen Hovde, Muffie Meyer. Filmed by Albert Maysles and David Maysles. Edited by Ellen Hovde, Muffie Meyer, Susan Froemke. Sound mixer: Lee Dichter/Photo-Mag.

Other versions: Albert Maysles assembled outtakes into *The Beales of Grey Gardens* (2006). A musical adaptation, *Grey Gardens*, starring Christine Ebersole and Lois Wilson, with a book by Doug Wright, music by Scott Frankel, and lyrics by Michael Korie, opened in New York in February, 2006. Jessica Lange and Drew Barrymore starred in a made-for-cable feature, *Grey Gardens*, directed by Michael Sucsy and written by Sucsy and Patricia Rozema. It aired on HBO in 2009.

Available: Criterion Collection DVD (2006). UPC: 7–15515–01792–3.

Despite the critical success of *Salesman* (1969, a Registry title), funding was a constant issue for Albert and David Maysles. The cost of mounting a feature documentary was a huge risk for independent filmmakers, especially the Maysles, who used cinema verite methods. Without narrative short-cuts like voice-overs or directed interviews, filmmakers like the Maysles had to commit time as well as money to their features. To decide on a subject for a feature, they first had to anticipate an audience for their film.

A documentarian like Frederick Wiseman relied on grants from public television and other philanthropic organizations to finance his films. The Maysles instead offered themselves out for hire, shooting television commercials for Citibank, filming a "making of" background short for the John Ford production *Young Cassidy* (1965). The brothers also made short films, such as *Running Fence*, about an art project by Christo and Jeanne-Claude.

Hired by the Rolling Stones to cover their 1969 tour of the United States, the brothers, in conjunction with Charlotte Zwerin, came up with *Gimme Shelter*, one of the most harrowing of rock concert documentaries. A hit both with critics and moviegoers, *Gimme Shelter* gave the Maysles enough of a financial cushion to consider another feature project. The brothers must have been delighted when the opportunity arose to make a real-life version of *Whatever Happened to Baby Jane?*

Inspiration for the film came from a *New York* magazine article by Gail Sheehy, "The Secret of Grey Gardens." In it, Sheehy described how she and her daughter met Edith Beale outside her home in East Hampton. "Little Edie" lived with her mother "Big Edie" in a decaying Long Island mansion that had been built near the turn of the twentieth century. Big Edie's husband Phelan Beale purchased the mansion in 1924.

As the article related, Phelan deserted Big Edie. Her father cut her out of his will except for a small trust fund, which her brother Jack Bouvier managed. One son had a successful business career and moved to another part of Long Island; the second son moved to Oklahoma. Born in 1917, Little Edie pursued modeling, acting, and dance in New York City, but returned to Grey Gardens to care for her mother in 1952.

For the next twenty years, mother and daughter lived on the proceeds from the trust fund, and by selling off their belongings. On October 22, 1971, inspectors from the Suffolk County Health Department warned the Beales that their house was in danger of being condemned. The story made national headlines in part because the Beales were related to Jacqueline Kennedy Onassis and to Lee Radziwell. Onassis and Radziwell helped pay to bring Grey Gardens up to code.

Sheehy wrote "The Secret of Grey Gardens" in breathless prose that highlighted the gothic aspects of the Beale's lives, from a "haunted house" tour of the grounds to Little Edie's rambling, frightening monologues. The article blamed the Beales' problems in part on a shady conspiracy by the Bouvier men to cheat the women out of their home, but Sheehy also found time to fault "the infinite self-confidence of the indomitably rich." The author knew she had a fascinating subject in Little Edie, who cooperated with the author and who posed for photographs that made her look like Morticia Addams from Charles Addams' ghoulish cartoons. In effect Edie was delivering a performance. Sheehy made sure to include in her article dialogue and behavior from Edie that bordered on unbalanced.

Sheehy sidestepped a different issue: whether the Beales' story had any intrinsic value, or was of interest to *New York* readers because of the connection to Jacqueline Onassis. Even in East Hampton the author could have found people living in similar poverty and filth. Would they have earned a feature article in *New York*?

"The Secret of Grey Gardens" provided a blueprint for the Maysles' film, which they shot over an extended period in the mansion and its surroundings. (They even incorporated Big Edie's off-screen shrieks, used by Sheehy as the equivalent of a punchline or rim shot.) The Maysles were still following the tenets of cinema verite, which eschewed voice-over narrations, question-and-answer interviews, and supplementary materials in order to provide a more "objective" version of reality. At the same time, the Maysles were breaking all the "rules" of the style. In *Gimme Shelter*, their previous film, they appeared on camera, questioned musicians as they screened footage in an editing room, and in general acted as more than just observers.

For *Grey Gardens*, the Maysles went further, encouraging the Beales to perform, setting up situations in the hopes of capturing material on film, interacting with their subjects on camera. Albert Maysles adjusted his camera techniques to emphasize the gothic elements of the story, stopping down exposures in hallways to make them appear dark and dingy, using harsh, flat lighting in bedrooms to make Big Edie look more garish.

How the Maysles chose to portray the Beales, and what incidents they decided to film, raise serious questions about the role and responsibilities of documentary filmmakers. Like characters in a Tennessee Williams play, the Beales clearly fed off each other, amplifying their fears and neuroses. When the Maysles manipulate their subjects into revealing painful memories, or goad them into arguments, are they documenting the Beales or exploiting them? When the brothers follow Little Edie into the attic and film her leaving loaves of bread for wild raccoons to eat, are they exacerbating her illness?

Finally, how much did editing alter how viewers perceive the footage? In a 2005 interview with Matthew Hays, Albert Maysles spoke about removing a ten-minute sequence in which Little Edie debated whether she was schizophrenic because "It just didn't work for the film." He criticized documentarians like Frederick Wiseman who tried not to involve themselves emotionally with their subjects. "Whatever intimacy we had with the women in *Grey Gardens* only helped to create a rapport. We wouldn't have gotten the access we did without that," Maysles answered. "If Fred Wiseman had that idea then he never would have gone as far as we did with those women."

Grey Gardens was shown at the New York Film Festival in September, 1975, and received a theatrical release the following February, garnering the Beales more attention in the press. "Big Edie" died in 1977; "Little Edie" sold Grey Gardens to *Washington Post* managing editor Ben Bradlee two years later. Over the years the film became a cult favorite for the gay community, in Maysles' words because, "Outsiders often want desperately to be insiders. The women in *Grey Gardens* got both. I suppose that's true of homosexuals: they would like to be accepted for who they are, but maintain their individuality."

David Maysles died in 1987. Since his death, Albert Maysles has collaborated on almost twenty additional documentaries, including *Sally Gross—The Pleasure of Stillness* (2007), about the famed choreographer, and *The Gates* (2008), about a project in Central Park by Christo and Jeanne-Claude. In 2006, Maysles released *The Beales of Grey Gardens*, outtakes from the original shooting sessions.

All the President's Men

Robert Redford and Dustin Hoffman as reporters Bob Woodward and Carl Bernstein.

Warner Bros., 1976. Sound, color, 1.85. 35mm. 138 minutes.

Cast: Dustin Hoffman (Carl Bernstein), Robert Redford (Bob Woodward), Jack Warden (Harry Rosenfeld), Martin Balsam (Howard Simons), Hal Holbrook (Deep Throat), Jason Robards (Ben Bradlee), Jane Alexander (Bookkeeper [Judy Hoback]), Meredith Baxter (Debbie Sloan), Ned Beatty (Dardis), Stephen Collins (Hugh Sloan), Penny Fuller (Sally Aiken), John McMartin (Foreign Editor), Robert Walden (Donald Segretti), Franks Wills (Frank Wills).

Credits: Directed by Alan J. Pakula. Screenplay by William Goldman. Based on the book by Carl Bernstein and Bob Woodward. Produced by Walter Coblenz. Director of photography: Gordon Willis. Film editor: Robert L. Wolfe. Production designer: George Jenkins. Music by David Shire. Associate producers: Michael Britton, Jon Boorstin. Casting: Alan Shayne. 1st Assistant Directors: Bill Green, Art Levinson. Production sound mixers: Jim Webb, Les Fresholtz. Supervising sound editor: Milton C. Burrow. Costume supervisor: Bernie Pollack. Title design: Dan Perri. Prints by Technicolor. A Wildwood Enterprises production. A Robert Redford–Alan J. Pakula film.

Additional cast includes: F. Murray Abraham, Lindsay Ann Crouse, Valerie Curtin.

Additional credits: Screenwriting by Alan J. Pakula, Robert Redford, Alvin Sargent. Art direction: George Gaines. Premiered Washington, DC, April 4, 1976. Opened New York City April 5, 1976.

Awards: Oscars for Best Supporting Actor (Robards); Screenplay adaptation; Art Direction (George Jenkins, George Gaines); Sound (Arthur Piantadosi, Les Fresholtz, Dick Alexander, Jim Webb).

Available: Warner Home Video DVD (2004). ISBN: 1–4198–1706–X. UPC: 0–12569–73401–2.

One of the threads running through *All the President's Men*, the nonfiction book written by *Washington Post* reporters Carl Bernstein and Bob Woodward, is their fear of getting the facts wrong, making an error that would call their research into question. The filmmakers behind the screen version felt that same pressure: one false detail would make it easy for critics to dismiss the entire picture.

The best-selling account of the Watergate break-in and its aftermath was in a way written for the movies. Actor Robert Redford was on a publicity tour for his film *The Candidate* (1972) when the Watergate story broke. He pursued Bernstein and Woodward for the screen rights. Learning that they were planning a book about the Watergate burglars, he advised them to concentrate on their own investigative work instead. "It was helpful for me to hear him say that," Woodward admitted later. "He planted the seed."

Redford wound up paying $400,000 for the rights, dashing his initial plans to film a small, black-and-white drama. Now he was committed to a big budget, and ultimately had to star in the film to get studio backing. Dustin Hoffman agreed to play Bernstein after talking with Redford at a New York Knicks basketball game. Screenwriter William Goldman, who worked with Redford on *The Great Waldo Pepper* (1975), accompanied the actor to Washington to meet the reporters before starting an adaptation.

Even with the two stars and Goldman, arguably among the most coveted screenwriters of his time, attached, the only studio that agreed to the project was Warner Bros. Redford approached directors like Elia Kazan and William Friedkin unsuccessfully before contacting Alan Pakula.

Pakula was attached to another project and couldn't start work on *President's* until December 1974. By then Goldman had turned in a script that Redford found disappointing "because Goldman writes for cleverness." The writer did solve some structural problems, notably discarding the second half of the book.

"You can't do a whole historical overview of Watergate and all the ramifications," as Pakula said later. "The film we're making is, 'What was it like to have been these two young men who broke through this cover-up?'" As the start of shooting approached, he and Redford holed up in a Washington hotel room rewriting, "Ruthlessly boiling it down; discarding, discarding, discarding." They even took out scenes Alvin Sargent had written of the reporters and their girlfriends, keeping the focus exclusively on the investigation. (Apart from the break-in itself and *Post* editorial meetings, the reporters are in almost every scene.)

The filmmakers faced daunting obstacles. The Watergate hearings had already been televised, President Richard Nixon had resigned, and the film was opening in a charged political climate. What's more, *President's* had to present a dramatic story in which most of the narrative incidents concerned failure and rejection. And it had to win over a potentially hostile audience of journalists, politicians, and insiders. "Our fears, or certainly mine, was that it would become a Hollywood production number," Bernstein said later, "and it wouldn't be the truth."

Pakula, Hoffman, and Redford had a lot to prove as well. All three had faced recent commercial setbacks, and had expressed their dissatisfaction with how the Hollywood hierarchy operated. In a way their struggle with *President's* mirrored that of Bernstein and Woodward, relatively upstart reporters intent on pushing a story that most journalists considered played out. The filmmakers knew that many would be expecting them to fail, and that one of their key defenses would be accuracy.

"I had to be extra diligent on being authentic, very careful on research," Redford said. "I spent so much time focusing on detail." As Pakula put it, "His fascination with detail went in to outer space." Since they couldn't film inside the *Post* newsroom, a replica had to be constructed on two soundstages in Los Angeles. Production designer George Jenkins famously had trash imported from the *Post* to fill the wastebaskets on the set.

All the attention to research makes *President's* seem overly cautious at times. When Pakula and his crew do find time to express their creativity, it's with elaborate stunts that call attention to themselves, like a $90,000 crane shot that ends with a camera dangling from the Library of Congress rotunda. Helicopter shots meant to show the enormity of the task facing Bernstein and Woodward are confusing instead because Pakula doesn't take the time to explain or locate the reporters within them.

On the other hand, several of Pakula's decisions were more rewarding. A courtroom scene in which Woodward can barely hear the proceedings, a montage of the reporter struggling through a series of dead-end phone calls, a jet flying overhead that drowns out an interview at an outdoor restaurant — moments like these capture the drudgery and hard work journalists face daily. The director used television sets and radio broadcasts to remind viewers of the story's villains, and cast expert actors like Jane Alexander and Robert Warden to fill key roles.

Gordon Willis, a cinematographer famed for his dark palette and uncompromising artistic choices, provided some of the most effective moments in the film. "One look had to be a thousand words," he said later. "You were delivering information all the time." He keyed the colors of the film to poster art, what Pakula called "hard electric blues, hard oranges and reds, hard greens."

Wide-angle lenses and a sliding diopter system allowed Willis and Pakula to construct "counterpointed" scenes, in which action took place on several planes deep into the background of the newsroom. (The sliding diopter let Willis keep both Hoffman in the foreground and reporters in the distance in focus.) Pakula said, "I wanted a world without shadows; I wanted a world where nothing is hidden." Willis responded with a complicated lighting scheme that Redford spoke of appreciatively: "The only time you really saw light was in the newsroom. Once they left there, you're in the dark."

Pakula wanted very little camera movement until Jason Robards, playing editor Ben Bradlee, entered the story. Willis devised a remarkable tracking shot that followed the actor through the newsroom set, perhaps subconsciously echoing similar shots in *The Front Page* (1931, a Registry film). The shot explains Bradlee's status, his command of his surroundings, in visual terms. As the story progresses, and Bernstein and Woodward become more confident of their work, they too figure in detailed tracking shots.

Redford had worked with Robards on a television production of *The Iceman Cometh*. Pakula liked the idea of casting Robards because, "Bradlee is the star personality in the newsroom. They're not. He is." What's more, the veteran actor could make Redford and Hoffman "feel insecure."

Bradlee, meanwhile, worried that he would be portrayed as a Walter Burns. "We didn't have any choice about this movie—it would be made regardless—and I could see that," he was quoted during the filming. "Lacking that choice, it seemed to make more sense to try to influence it factually than to just stick our heads in the sand."

President's has its gaps and omissions. Although Geraldine Page had been cast as Katherine Graham, the publisher of the *Post* refused to allow her character to appear in the film. Some characters, like city editor Barry Sussman (known to his colleagues as the "Watergate editor"), were written out of the script entirely. Bradlee said his relationship with *Post* managing editor Howard Simons—who felt that his role in the film was "fatally shortchanged"— "was never the same after the film." In 2005, Woodward's background source Deep Throat, played by Hal Holbrook, was revealed to be W. Mark Felt, deputy director of the FBI. (Holbrook gets the film's most famous line, "Follow the money.")

Pakula credited Goldman with the film's ending, which occurs immediately after Bradlee and the *Post* are singled out for criticism by the White House. Woodward and Bernstein "were right but their story was wrong," Pakula said. "That was Bill Goldman's concept before I came on the film and the more I worked on the film the more I came to trust it. The two of them and Bradlee against the world."

President's had two preview screenings, a generally positive one in Denver and a more negative one in Louisville. After the Denver showing, Pakula added the film's current ending, a montage of headlines seen on a teletype machine, because the "audience needed a reminder" of just how significant the Pulitzer Prize-winning series of Watergate articles was. "Thank God they had the twenty-one-gun salute, because it set up the typewriter keys as weapons," the director said, referring to Nixon's resignation ceremony.

Saturday Night Fever

John Travolta as frustrated dancer Tony Manero.

Paramount, 1977. Color, sound, 1.85. 35mm. 119 minutes. Rated R.

Cast: John Travolta (Tony Manero), Karen Lynn Gorney (Stephanie), Barry Miller (Bobby C.), Joseph Cali (Joey), Paul Pape (Double J.), Donna Pescow (Annette), Bruce Ornstein (Gus), Julie Bovasso (Flo), Martin Shakar (Frank, Jr.), Sam J. Coppola (Fusco), Nina Hansen (Grandmother), Lisa Peluso (Linda), Denny Dillon (Doreen), Bert Michaels (Pete), Robert Costanza (Paint store customer), Robert Weil (Becker), Shelly Batt (Girl in disco), Fran Drescher (Connie), Donald Gantry (Jay Langhart), Murray Moston (Haberdashery salesman), William Andrews (Detective), Ann Travolta (Pizza girl), Helen Travolta (Lady in paint store), Ellen March (Bartender), Monti Rock III (The Deejay), Val Bisoglio (Frank, Sr.)

Credits: Directed by John Badham. Screenplay by Norman Wexler. Based upon a story by Nik Cohn. Produced by Robert Stigwood. Executive producer: Kevin McCormick. Director of Photography: Ralf D. Bode. Production designer: Charles Bailey. Editor: David Rawlins. Original music by Barry, Robin and Maurice Gibb. "How Deep Is Your Love," "Night Fever," "Staying Alive," "More Than a Woman" performed by the Bee Gees. Additional music and adaptation by David Shire. Musical numbers staged and choreographed by Lester Wilson. Associate producer: Milt Felsen. Costume designer: Patrizia von Brandenstein. Hair designs by Joe Tubens. Make-up by Henriquez. Sound mixer: Les Lazarowitz. Sound Editor: Michael Colgan. Assistant choreographer: Lorraine Fields. Dance consultant: Jo-Jo Smith. Dolby sound system. A Paramount Pictures presentation of a Robert Stigwood production.

Additional credits: Premiered in Los Angeles and New York December 16, 1977.

Other versions: Sequel *Staying Alive* (1983).

Available: Paramount DVD (2002). ISBN: 0–7921–8016–X. UPC: 0–97360–11134–7.

Designed to cash in on a fad that was already expiring, *Saturday Night Fever* instead became a world-wide phenomenon. It established John Travolta as a movie star, boosted the record sales of the Bee Gees, and introduced a new generation of moviegoers to the musical genre.

Impetus for the film came from producer Robert Stigwood and his assistant Kevin McCormick, who saw an advance copy of a *New York* magazine article by Nik Cohn called "Tribal Rites of the New Saturday Night." Stigwood purchased the article—purportedly an inside look at the disco phenomenon in Bay Ridge, Brooklyn, but actually a piece of fiction modeled after Britain's mods—for $90,000.

Born in Australia, Stigwood moved to England in the late 1950s. He formed a theatrical agency, and then moved into promoting and booking musical acts and tours. By the late 1960s he was managing groups like Cream and the Bee Gees, a brother act from Australia. Stigwood produced the London version of the musical *Hair* and the Tim Rice/Andrew Lloyd Webber musical *Evita*, which later won seven Tonys on Broadway. He also began developing television shows.

Stigwood's first involvement in movies came with *Jesus Christ Superstar* (1973), an adaptation of the stage musical directed for film by Norman Jewison. *Tommy*, a feature-length film adaptation of the rock opera by The Who, followed in 1975. Stigwood saw the potential in the Cohn article to capitalize on the disco phenomenon, a genre of music and dance that was moving from underground status into the mainstream.

When director John Avildsen was assigned to the project, he brought with him screenwriter Norman Wexler. The two had collaborated on the anti-hippie hit *Joe* (1970); Wexler had gone on to write the screenplay for *Serpico* (1973), while Avildsen had recently directed the music-themed *W.W. and the Dixie Dance Kings* (1975). Stigwood also began assembling musical talent for the film from his stable of performers. In particular, he appropriated a half-dozen songs planned for an upcoming Bee Gees album. The group, which had made its mark with lugubrious ballads tinged with psychedelia (like "New York Mining Disaster 1941"), had been moving successfully into dance music, notably with the disco hit "You Should Be Dancing."

By this point Stigwood had cast John Travolta in the lead role as Tony Manero. Travolta had developed a huge following as Vinnie Barbarino on the TV sitcom *Welcome Back, Kotter*. "I knew this was my opportunity," Travolta said years later. He spent months rehearsing dance routines with Deney Terrio.

Travolta was attracted to the harsh qualities of Wexler's script. Manero was crude, uneducated, and emotionally detached from both his dysfunctional family and his boorish friends. The script included extensive profanity, drug and alcohol abuse, gang fights, and rape. The star did not agree with Avildsen's interpretation of the story, however. "He wanted me to be this kind of guy who did all the favors in the neighborhood." Stigwood fired Avildsen and hired John Badham to replace him just days before shooting was scheduled to start. (Avildsen could comfort himself with the knowledge that his latest film, the Registry title *Rocky*, had become a phenomenon of its own. The director would release his own take on youth aspiring for success, *Slow Dancing in the Big City*, in 1978.)

Born in England, Badham grew up in Alabama, where his sister Mary was cast as Scout in *To Kill a Mockingbird* (1962, a Registry title). Moving to Los Angeles, he followed a classic career path, working his way from the mailroom to assisting Steve Spielberg on the TV series *Night Gallery*. Badham began directing television episodes, graduating to features with a period sports comedy, *The Bingo Long Traveling All-Stars and Motor Kings* in 1976.

Badham found that his first job during shooting was to work around the thousands of Travolta fans who gathered at every location. The director resorted to handing out fake call sheets to keep onlookers away.

Travolta said he cried when he saw a rough cut in the spring. "I thought the acting scenes were fabulous," he remembered, "but my solo dance that I had worked for nine months had been cut in close-up." After complaining to Stigwood, Travolta was allowed to re-cut the scene. He told Badham and editor David Rawlins, "It's very simple. Stay in the master until you go to the midshot right where I go across there," where the actor swept his arm across a crowd of onlookers. "'That's all you do. That's all I want.' It took two minutes," said the actor later.

In reality, the sequence is made up of several different takes, including a circular, hand-held shot to follow Travolta when he drops to the floor. Even the "masters" were filmed from different angles, which meant that the sequence was never really intended to be seen "close-up." Notable for its athleticism and precision, the piece is very much of its time. Mostly strutting and posing, with knee drops and a split for punctuation, the dance lacks the narrative form and integrity of solo choreography from an earlier age.

But Travolta had an electric presence, something Lester Wilson, the film's choreographer, did not want to change. He encouraged the actor to incorporate moves from his earlier rehearsals with Terrio, in effect to improvise his dances.

Since none of its characters actually sang or played music, *Saturday Night Fever* couldn't be considered a musical per se. In fact, the dance sequences take up a very brief portion of the film, about ten minutes. Structurally the film is really a coming-of-age story, one with the gritty milieu and harsh details of a *Marty* (1955) updated to the 1970s.

The filmmakers get the details right, even if the plot is by turns mawkish and predictable. But Travolta's desperate, naked ambition powers the film through its most melodramatic moments. As Badham put it, "The brilliant thing about John Travolta is that he is able to make you like a character who is basically unlikable." The actor did this despite the loss of his girlfriend Diana Hyland to breast cancer during shooting.

The locations, clothes, hair and make-up, cars, and especially the social attitudes pinpoint the film and its characters to a very specific time and place. What worried Stigwood and Badham was the fear that this time had already passed. Even by the end of 1976, a backlash to disco had set in, tinged with racism and homophobia. "Disco sucks" became a rallying cry for teens who felt that their musical preferences were being overshadowed. Badham tried to fend off disco detractors by including a scene in which a middle-aged dance class practices to Rick Dees' parody number "Disco Duck."

Badham needn't have worried. The soundtrack to the film stayed on the *Billboard* charts for almost three years, selling millions of copies and not incidentally causing a surge in sales for the entire dance music market. The film itself eventually grossed $285 million.

Saturday Night Fever made Travolta a bona fide movie star. He had a similar impact in films which addressed other musical genres: 1950s rock'n'roll in *Grease* (1978) and country music in another film based on a *New York* article, *Urban Cowboy* (1980). His subsequent career has included some head-scratching decisions, like an ill-advised *Saturday Night Fever* sequel directed by Sylvester Stallone, *Staying Alive* (1983). Stigwood continued to work with Travolta, notably *Grease* and *Staying Alive*. Badham directed a number of popular films in the 1980s, including *WarGames* (1983) and *Stakeout* (1987).

The Muppet Movie

ITC, 1979. Sound, color, 1.85. 95 minutes. 35mm. Rated G.

Cast: Muppet performers: Jim Henson (Kermit the Frog, Rowlf, Dr. Teeth, Waldorf), Frank Oz (Miss Piggy, Fozzie Bear, Animal, Sam the Eagle), Jerry Nelson (Floyd Pepper, Crazy Harry, Robin the Frog, Lew Zealand), Richard Hunt (Scooter, Statler, Janice, Sweetums, Beaker), Dave Goelz (The Great Gonzo, Zoot, Dr. Bunsen Honeydew).

Actors: Charles Durning (Doc Hopper), Austin Pendleton (Max).

Special guest stars: Edgar Bergen, Milton Berle, Mel Brooks, James Coburn, Dom DeLuise, Elliott Gould, Bob Hope, Madeline Kahn, Carol Kane, Cloris Leachman, Steve Martin, Richard Pryor, Telly Savalas, Orson Welles, Paul Williams.

Featuring: Scott Walker (Frog Killer), Lawrence Gabriel, Jr. (Sailor), Ira F. Grubman (Bartender), H.B. Haggerty (Lumberjack), Bruce Kirby (Gate Guard), Tommy Madden (One-eyed midget), James Frawley (Waiter), Arnold Roberts (Cowboy).

With Muppet performers: Steve Whitmire, Kathryn Mullen, Bob Payne, Eren Ozker, Caroly Wilcox, Olga Felgemacher, Bruce Schwartz, Michael Davis, Buz Suraci, Tony Basilicato, Adam Hunt, and Carroll Spinney (as Big Bird).

Credits: Directed by James Frawley. Written by Jerry Juhl and Jack Burns. Producer: Jim Henson. Executive producer: Martin Starger. Director of photography: Isidore Mankofsky. Production designer: Joel Schiller. Film editor: Chris Greenbury. Music and lyrics by Paul Williams and Kenny Ascher. Music scored and adapted by Paul Williams. Co-producer: David Lazer. Creative consultant: Frank Oz. Arranged and conducted by Ian Freebairn-Smith. Executive in charge of production: Richard L. O'Connor. Production manager: Kurt Neumann. Casting: Gus Schirmer. Camera operator: Richard Edesa. Art director: Les Gobruegge. Set designers: Julia Harmount, Julius King. Special effects: Robbie Knott. Sound mixer: Charles Lewis. Makeup: Ben Nye II. Costume designer: Gwen Capetanos. Titles by Wayne Fitzgerald. Special thanks to David Odell. Big Bird courtesy of Children's Television Workshop. Dolby Stereo. A Sir Lew Grade and Martin Starger presentation of a Jim Henson production.

Additional cast: John Landis (as Grover), Jerry Juhl.

Additional credits: "This film is dedicated to the memory and magic of Edgar Bergen." Released June 22, 1979.

Other Versions: Sequels: *The Great Muppet Caper* (1981), *The Muppets Take Manhattan* (1984), *The Muppet Christmas Carol* (1992), *Muppet Treasure Island* (1996), *Muppets from Space* (1999), *The Muppets* (2011).

Available: Walt Disney Pictures DVD (2005). ISBN: 0–7888–6011–9. UPC: 7–86936–28776–9.

The Muppets began as one-off joke puppets pulled together in the 1950s before evolving into some of the more significant cultural figures of the last forty years. *The Muppet Movie*, their first big-screen appearance, was a sensation that prompted awards, sequels, and an avalanche of commercial tie-ins. But like many film debuts, the history behind its stars was a long and complicated one.

Born in Mississippi in 1936, Jim Henson became a fan of puppeteers like Burr Tillstrom (whose TV show *Kukla, Fran and Ollie* began airing in 1948) and Bil Baird. He was also drawn to the dry, ironic humor exemplified by Stan Freberg, Walt Kelly, and Ernie Kovacs. He was eighteen when he began performing with his puppets on television, first on WTOP's *Junior Good Morning Show*, then for seven years on WRC, the NBC affiliate in Washington, DC. At first Henson used hand-and-rod puppets: hands moved the puppets' heads, rods their arms. He called them "Muppets"—a combination of marionettes and puppets—right from the start.

By 1955, Henson had his own five-minute daily show, *Sam and Friends*, for which he would win a local Emmy. Kermit (at that stage not yet a frog) showed up that year, fashioned from one of his mother's coats and two halves of a ping-pong ball. Commercials were an important source of income and inspiration for Henson. Just as many future movie stars relied on advertising early in their careers, Cookie Monster and Rowlf the Dog first worked in ads, Rowlf for a Purina Dog Chow piece.

Henson had been working on sets with his wife Jane; in 1961 Jerry Juhl stepped in for her in the studio. Henson met Frank Oz on a trip to California; Oz, Juhl, and designer Don Sahlin joined Henson when he opened a studio in New York in 1963. Henson, who had purchased a 16mm Bolex camera and animation stand in the late 1950s, began concentrating on filmmaking. He wrote, produced, directed, and starred in *Timepiece*, an experimental short that received an Academy Award nomination in 1965; made sponsored films for the USIA; worked on performance art that incorporated special effects into sound and screen pieces; developed "counterculture" television shows like *Youth '68*; and had the ultimate responsibility for Muppet growth and branding.

Rowlf was by now a national star as a result of his work on ABC's *The Jimmy Dean Show*. Kermit went from a vaguely defined reptile to a frog in *Tales from Muppetland—The Frog Prince*. Miss Piggy, who first appeared on a Herb Albert variety special, would soon become one of the most popular performers in the troupe. An expert judge of talent, Henson nurtured his characters carefully, waiting for years to fully unleash Miss Piggy's ego, reducing screen time for appealing but limited stars like Rowlf, and assigning slapstick and dialect bits to character actors in an effort to make Kermit a more sophisticated presence.

The turning point for Henson and the Muppets came as a result of a 1966 Carnegie Institute study on children's television, whose bleak conclusions led to the formation of the Children's Television Workshop in 1968. CTW's team included producer Jon Stone and musical director Joe Raposo, and its mission was to broadcast a higher quality of programming for youngsters. According to writer Christopher Finch, *Sesame Street*, the first CTW show, was designed to exploit how children loved television commercials, especially their quick cuts and jingles. It premiered on November 10, 1969, and is almost universally regarded as the most important children's show in the history of television.

According to Finch, "*Sesame Street* was the training ground that prepared Kermit for the rigors of *The Muppet Show*." (A lesser-known area for the Muppets characters to develop were industrial films Henson made for clients like IBM.) Once the equivalent of a stand-up comedian, Kermit became a sort of host or emcee, a voice of reason and the central character in Muppet narratives.

The Muppets appeared on *Saturday Night Live* in 1975, and on an ABC special that same year, but Henson couldn't find funding for a series until he turned to Lord Lew Grade of ITC (a British company founded in 1954 as Incorporated Television Company). *The Muppet Show*, usually broadcast at 7:30 p.m., took advantage of a campaign for family-oriented primetime programming. Even so, it had to win over viewers, which it did through its combination of proven stars, creative techniques, and intelligent scripting and songwriting.

The Muppet Show was a variety show, a form with antecedents in vaudeville. A collection of tunes, skits, and novelty routines, the variety show had its heyday on television in the 1950s, but by the 1970s had largely disappeared from the tube. Henson's masterstroke was to add his own ironic commentary to the proceedings, usually delivered by grouchy customers as they watched from a theater box, but also through scenes set in dressing rooms where stars could comment on their roles. The show was a global success, eventually shown in 120 countries and attracting guest stars like Bob Hope, Julie Andrews, and the puppets from *Star Wars*.

So by the time Henson and his performers were ready to make *The Muppet Movie*, they had been working and maturing together in a variety of formats. Feature films called for a different approach than television or shorts. Like the great slapstick clowns before him, Henson realized the importance of story over jokes. *The Muppet Show* format allowed writers to develop skits for specific jokes or punchlines. Length wasn't an issue, and if a routine threatened to flag, writers could pull the plug as it were by cutting to onlookers for a quick laugh before proceeding to the next skit.

But *The Muppet Movie* would have to be played relatively straight. Aside from brief cameos (including everyone from Edgar Bergen and Charlie McCarthy to *Sesame Street*'s Big Bird), the script focuses on advancing the plot, not on the digressions and tangents. As Buster Keaton did in *The Cameraman* (1929), and Preston Sturges in *Sullivan's Travels* (1941, both Registry titles), Henson made moviemaking itself the subject of *The Muppet Movie*.

Henson felt he had to justify the project as a "movie," not simply a glorified television special. That meant expanded effects, as in an opening scene set in a swamp. Kermit, perched on a log, sings the Oscar-nominated "Rainbow Connection," as the camera circles around him—at the time a shot next-to-impossible to achieve on TV. Later, Kermit will pedal a bike down a lane, face down a villain in a Western-style shoot-out, and otherwise act as a character, not as a puppet.

As a filmmaker, Henson held onto his early innovations, like performing to a TV monitor, but kept adding new ideas. *Emmet Otter's Jug-Band Christmas* had platformed sets so the puppeteers could stand upright, and one scene took place on a boat rowed across an artificial river. Puppeteers expanded on both strategies for *The Muppet Movie*.

"The way we shoot is very technical," Henson said in an interview. "We will shoot a master as long as we can, but that usually means maybe twenty seconds because the limitations of puppetry dictate the edits. Often there is no choice. We have to go to a given shot because that's the only way you can get from the first shot to the third shot."

Of course technique can be a crutch, a means of impressing or bewildering your audience at the expense telling an involving story. What kept the Muppets so vital for so many years was the insistence by Henson and his colleagues on treating their characters and stories, and by extension their audience, with respect. And what Henson did better than just about anyone of his time was make sense, in ways children could believe, of a confusing and frightening world. The blustering characters, the devices that didn't operate as expected, the sudden arguments, the outbreaks of silliness showed youngsters that the world was a manageable place, even if it often didn't work the way they or adults wanted it to.

The Muppet Movie was filmed in Los Angeles during the third season of the television series, and released a year later. It was so successful that Henson could begin a sequel, *The Great Muppet Caper*, in London in 1980. The Muppets were used to sell records, dolls, shampoo, cars, mugs, sippee cups, clothes, clocks, phones, lunchboxes, sheets, puzzles, games, cake mixes, and books. Kermit got his own float for the Macy's Thanksgiving Day Parade in New York City. Henson expanded his projects to a wider audience, with adult-oriented films like *The Dark Crystal* and *Labyrinth* and TV shows like *Jim Henson's Muppet Babies* for even younger viewers.

Henson died in May, 1990. The Muppets, through Jim Henson's Creature Shop, continued on in film and television. But without Henson's guidance, they gradually lost their hold on the public, replaced in part by a proliferation of cable programming targeted towards kids. An acrimonious dispute with Walt Disney Studios didn't help. (Disney purchased rights to Henson's characters in 2004 and assumed distribution of Muppets films. The studio produced its own feature-film version, *The Muppets*, as of this writing scheduled for a November 20011 release.)

The Empire Strikes Back

Princess Leia (Carrie Fisher) and Han Solo (Harrison Ford) at a moment of truth.

Twentieth Century Fox, 1980. Sound, color, 2.35. 35mm. 124 minutes.

Cast: Mark Hamill (Luke Skywalker), Harrison Ford (Han Solo), Carrie Fisher (Princess Leia), Billy Dee Williams (Lando Calrissian), Anthony Daniels (C-3PO), David Prowse (Darth Vader), Peter Mayhew (Chewbacca), Kenny Baker (R2–D2), Frank Oz (Yoda), Alec Guinness (Ben (Obi-wan) Kenobi), Jeremy Bulloch (Boba Fett), John Hollis (Lando's Aide), Jack Purvis (Chief Ugnaught), Des Webb (Snow Creature), Kathryn Mullen (Performing Assistant for Yoda), Clive Revill (Voice of Emperor). Imperial Forces: Kenneth Colley (Admiral Piett), Julian Glover (General Veers), Michael Sheard (Admiral Ozzel), Captain Needa (Michael Culver); John Dicks, Milton Johns, Mark Jones, Oliver Maguire, Robin Scobey (Other Officers). Rebel Forces: Bruce Boa (General Rieekan), Christopher Malcolm (Zev–Rogue 2), Denis Lawson (Wedge–Rogue 3), Richard Oldfield (Hobbie–Rogue 4), John Morton (Dak [Luke's Gunner]), Ian Liston (Janson [Wedge's Gunner]), John Ratzenberger (Major Derlin), Jack McKenzie (Deck Lieutenant), Jerry Harte (Head Controller); Norman Chancer, Norwich Duff, Ray Hassett, Brigitte Kahn, Burnell Tucker (Other Officers).

Credits: Directed by Irvin Kershner. Screenplay by Leigh Brackett and Lawrence Kasdan. Story by George Lucas. Produced by Gary Kurtz. Executive producer: George Lucas. Production designer: Norman Reynolds. Director of photography: Peter Suschitzky. Edited by Paul Hirsch. Special Visual Effects: Brian Johnson, Richard Edlund. Music by John Williams. Performed by the London Symphony Orchestra. Associate Producers: Robert Watts, James Bloom. Design Consultant and Conceptual Artist: Ralph McQuarrie. Make-up and Special Creature Design: Stuart Freeborn. Costume designer: John Mollo. Sound Design and Supervising Sound Effects Editor: Ben Burtt. Production Sound: Peter Sutton. Panavision. Dolby Stereo. Color by Rank Film Laboratories. Prints by Deluxe. A Lucasfilm Ltd. Production. A Twentieth Century-Fox Release. Novelization from Ballantine Books.

Additional cast: James Earl Jones (voice of Darth Vader).

Additional credits: Premiered Washington, DC, May 17, 1980.

Other versions: Sequel to *Star Wars* (1977). Followed by *Return of the Jedi* (1983).

Awards: Academy Award for Best Sound (Brian Johnson, Richard Edlund, Dennis Muren, and Bruce Nicholson)

Available: 20th Century Fox Home Video DVD (2006) UPC: 0–24543–26383–8–20.

The unprecedented box-office success of *Star Wars* (1977, a Registry title) vindicated George Lucas's approach to filmmaking, but saddled him with the pressure of trying to top himself. First he had to fulfill contractual obligations to Universal by overseeing the sequel to *American Graffiti* (1973, also on the

Registry). *More American Graffiti* (1979) was a critical and financial disappointment, leaving Lucas even more apprehensive about a film that would necessarily be darker in tone than *Star Wars*.

Lucas had always envisioned *Star Wars* as a trilogy (later he announced plans to turn the series into nine separate episodes grouped within three trilogies), and even signed stars Mark Hamill (who played Luke Skywalker) and Carrie Fisher (Princess Leia) for three films. Harrison Ford, who was in the key role of Han Solo, only agreed to one film. When Lucas negotiated with Ford over the new film in early 1979, the actor won a higher salary and a share of the profits. Lucas also prepared a special cliffhanger ending for Solo in case Ford balked at a third film.

By design, *The Empire Strikes Back* would offer more plot and action, less romance and character development, than *Star Wars*. Lucas first turned to pulp writer Leigh Brackett, author of sword-and-sorcery novels like *The Sword of Rhiannon*, but also a veteran screenwriter who had contributed to *The Big Sleep* (1946, a Registry title). Working from Lucas's notes, Brackett turned in a draft in March, 1978. She died of cancer two weeks later.

Lucas tinkered with Brackett's script, discarding most of the material. Director Steven Spielberg showed him a script by Lawrence Kasdan called *Continental Divide* (later filmed with John Belushi and released in 1981). Kasdan was hired to write *Raiders of the Lost Ark* (1981, a Registry title); afterwards, Lucas used him to rewrite the *Empire* script. Lucas kept Brackett's name in the credits so her estate would receive a portion of *Empire*'s profits.

Kasdan saw *Star Wars* as "jaunty, wise-ass fast, very modern," and tried to duplicate its feel in *Empire*. Lucas kept tight control over the story, eliminating background material and exposition. "The trick is to know what you can leave to the audience's imagination," he said. "If they start getting lost, you're in trouble. Sometimes you have to be crude and just say what's going on, because if you don't, people get puzzled."

In another interview, Lucas admitted, "I'm not that interested in narrative. The dialogue doesn't have much meaning in any of my movies. I'm very much of a visual filmmaker, and very much of a filmmaker who is going for emotions over ideas." One result of this approach is the almost complete lack of context for the events in *Empire*. The film has no time to explain the battle between rebels and the empire, to reintroduce characters, to dwell on the rivalry between Luke and Han, or on the romance between Han and Leia. "Nothing is more boring than two people acting lovey-dovey all the time," as Lucas put it. "There's no conflict." In narrative terms, conflict is about all *Empire* has to offer.

Lucas showed a draft of the *Empire* script to Fox producer Alan Ladd, Jr., in November, 1978. After all the desert material in *Star Wars*, *The Empire Strikes Back* started on an ice planet, Hoth, and immediately introduced a new animal, the camel-like Tauntaun. The story had a cameo for Obi-Wan Kenobi;

introduced new characters like Yoda, a diminutive Jedi master, and Lando Calrissian (Billy Dee Williams), a trader seen by some as an attempt to appease criticism that *Star Wars* was overwhelmingly white; and added a floating Cloud City to show off special effects.

But essentially the *Empire* script boiled down to a tight, action-filled story that broke easily into three acts. In it, the evil Darth Vader used Han, Leia, and Chewbacca as bait to trap Luke, destroying civilizations and entire planets in his quest to pervert the future Jedi knight.

Lucas eventually signed an unprecedented deal with Fox executive Tom Pollock in which Lucasfilm would receive 50% of gross profits, rising to 77% over time. Fox would pay all distribution costs (for prints and advertising), advance Lucasfilm $10 million, and return all rights to the film to Lucas after seven years. It was such a punitive arrangement that the Fox board objected. Ladd ended up leaving Fox for his own production company at Warners.

However, Lucas had to deliver the film within two years, or all rights to it and future *Star Wars* films would revert to Fox. Just as he had with *Star Wars*, Lucas was tying himself to deadlines that would have been impossible for most filmmakers to meet.

The experience of directing *Star Wars* was so dispiriting that Lucas and his producer Gary Kurtz began looking for another director to helm *Empire*. They settled on Irvin Kershner. A World War II veteran who had worked in television and documentaries, Kershner was known for modest, eccentric, character-driven films like *The Flim-Flam Man* (1967) and *Loving* (1970). Lucas told reporters that he could "trust" Kershner, as he knew that the director had already made one sequel, *The Return of a Man Called Horse* (1976). Kershner had also shown that he could handle "difficult" actors like George C. Scott and Barbra Streisand.

Kershner admitted that he was nervous about taking on *Empire* until he saw how committed Lucas was to completing his Skywalker Ranch complex in Northern California, perhaps drawing his attention away from the production. A classically trained musician, Kershner saw *Empire* as the middle passage of a symphony: "It has to be slower and more lyrical. The themes have to be more interior, and you don't have a grand climax. That became the challenge."

Shooting began on March 5, 1979, near Finse, Norway, and ran into trouble right away. When the cast and crew left for soundstages at Elstree in England, they had shot less than half of the expected footage. The filming schedule stretched to 175 days (*Star Wars* had taken 82) and went $10 million over budget, forcing Lucas to renegotiate his deal with Fox. Lucas blamed Kurtz ("He was in over his head.") and never worked with the producer again.

Kurtz in turn felt that Kershner was taking too much time; the producer also worried that *Empire* wouldn't make sense until viewers saw the third part of the trilogy, *Revenge of the Jedi*. "Well, if we have enough action, nobody will notice," Lucas replied. As for Kershner, he recalled having to battle his cast over scenes that he couldn't judge properly because they lacked special effects.

About Harrison Ford, Kershner remembered: "If we did just two takes and I'd say, 'That's great,' he would say, 'Wait a minute, wait a minute. What's so great? Was it great for the special effects or for me?'" Ford said later that some of his scenes were "too much on the nose," Fisher thought that Leia was "a cartoon character," and Hamill said he felt "helpless."

Lucas flew to London in March, 1979, to visit the set. After seeing an eighty-minute rough cut, he reportedly said, "You're ruining my movie." Lucas later admitted that Kershner suggested changes that worked "beautifully."

The details and logistics behind *The Empire Strikes Back* were staggering. The film had 605 special effects shots (twice that of *Star Wars*), 64 sets, 250 scenes. The effects ranged from stop-motion animation for the Imperial Walkers to a 26–inch-high puppet of Yoda built by Jim Henson and Stuart Freeborn. (It was voiced and operated by Muppet mainstay Frank Oz.)

The Imperial Walkers sequence showed some of the problems Lucas and his workers at Industrial Light and Magic faced. They were shot using a travelling matte system so they could be superimposed making their way over the icy Hoth landscape. But the mattes left a blue or black halo around the image. This halo wouldn't show up in a nighttime image, but was too obvious on top of snow. According to author John Baxter, "Technicians reduced the contrast by overexposing the layers, but at the cost of the lower images showing through. After weeks of futile experiment, ILM resigned itself to battle scenes in which the ground was faintly visible through a supposedly solid snowspeeder."

Other scenes had to be inserted due to unexpected problems. Hamill required plastic surgery after an automobile accident left scars on his face. Lucas added a sequence in which Luke Skywalker is abducted and mauled by a snow monster to explain the changes in his appearance.

But on the whole, *The Empire Strikes Back* moves with admirable speed and focus. "The way you can get an audience going is to make them believe that you as a filmmaker are going to do some really rotten thing," Lucas said. Consequently, *Empire* is filled with reversals, cliffhangers, and a general sense that any one of the heroic leads is at risk.

When it was released in May, 1980, *Empire* was an immediate box-office success. Although it had cost $33 million to make (the most expensive independent film yet), it grossed almost ten times that amount in the United States alone. Sales for the novelization tie-in, soundtrack album, a special book-and-record set for children, and video games added to Lucasfilm's profits.

"When I looked at it creatively in the beginning, I was very upset," Lucas said later. While granting that the film "looks pretty," he added, "It was just a lot better than I wanted to make it. And I was paying for it."

Airplane!

Julie Haggerty and Robert Hays face another catastrophe.

Paramount, 1980. Sound, color, 1.85. 35mm. 88 minutes. Rated PG.

Cast: Robert Hays (Ted Striker), Julie Hagerty (Elaine [Dickinson]), Kareem Abdul-Jabaar (Murdock), Lloyd Bridges (McCroskey), Peter Graves (Captain Oveur), Leslie Nielsen (Dr. Rumack), Lorna Patterson (Randy), Robert Stack ([Rex] Kramer), Stephen Stucker (Johnny), and introducing Otto as himself. Also Jim Abrahams (Religious zealot #6), Frank Ashmore (Victor Basta), Jonathan Banks (Gunderson), Craig Berenson (Paul Carey), Barbara Billingsley (Jive lady), Lee Bryant (Mrs. Hammen), Joyce Bulifant (Mrs. Davis), Mae E. Campbell (Security lady), Ted Chapman (Airport steward), Jesse Emmett (Man from India), Norman Alexander Gibbs (First jive dude), Amy Gibson (Soldier's girl), Marcy Goldman (Mrs. Geline), Bobby Gorman (Striped Controller), Rossie Harris (Joey), Maurice Hill (Reporter #3), David Hollander (Young boy with coffee), James Hong (Japanese general), Howard Hong (Jack), Gregory Itzin (Religious zealot #1), Howard Jarvis (Man in taxi), Michael Laurence (Newscaster), David Leisure (First Krishna), Zachary Lewis (Religious zealot #3), Barbara Mallory (Religious zealot #2), Maureen McGovern (Nun), Nora Meerbaum (Cocaine lady), Mary Mercier (Shirley), Ethel Merman (Lieutenant Hurwitz), Len Mooy (Reporter #1), Ann M. Nelson (Handing Lady), Laura Nix (Mrs. Hurwitz), John O'Leary (Reporter #2), Cyril O'Reilly (Soldier), Bill Porter (Hospital contortionist), Nicholas Pryor (Mr. Hammen), Conrad Palmisano (Religious zealot #4), Mallory Sandler (L.A. ticket agent), Michelle Stacy (Young girl with coffee), Robert Starr (Religious zealot #5), Lee Terri (Mrs. Oveur), Kenneth Tobey (Air controller Neubauer), William Tregoe (Jack Kirkpatrick), Hatsuo Uda (Japanese newscaster), Herb Voland (Air controller Macias), Jimmie Walker (Windshield wiper man), Jill Whelan (Lisa Davis), Al White (Second jive dude), John-David Wilder (Second Krishna), Windy (Horse), Jason Wingreen (Dr. Brody), Louise Yaffe (Mrs. Jaffe), Charlotte Zucker (Make-up lady), David Zucker (Ground crewman #2), Jerry Zucker (Ground crewman #1).

Credits: Written for the screen and directed by Jim Abrahams, David Zucker, Jerry Zucker. Produced by Jon Davison. Executive producers: Jim Abrahams, David Zucker, Jerry Zucker. Associate Producer: Hunt Lowry. Director of photography: Joseph Biroc. Production designer: Ward Preston. Film editor: Patrick Kennedy. Set decorator: Anne D. McCulley. Music by Elmer Bernstein. Special thanks to Kim Jorgensen, Pat Proft. Director of photography special effects: Bruce Logan. Recording mixer: Tom Overton. Sound editor: Sound FX Inc./Jim Troutman. Make-up artist: Edwin Butterworth. Costume supervisor: Aggie Lyon. Special effects: John Frazier. Generally in charge of a lot of things: Mike Finnell. A Paramount Pictures presentation of a Howard W. Koch production.

Additional credits: Opened New York City and Los Angeles, July 2, 1980

Other versions: *Airplane II: The Sequel* (1982)
Available: Paramount DVD (2005). ISBN: 1–4157–1387–1. UPC: 0–97360–30903–1.

Often looked upon as a lower form of comedy, parody has been one of the fundamental elements of cinema since the earliest public screenings. The first American blockbuster, *The Great Train Robbery* (1903, a Registry title), was mocked in a 1905 parody, *The Little Train Robbery*. Mack Sennett built his Keystone Studio largely around films that made fun of other films, like *A Burlesque on Carmen* (1915), which starred Charlie Chaplin. Stan Laurel followed suit, taking on titles like *Blood and Sand* (1922) with *Mud and Sand* (also 1922). In *The Frozen North* (1922), Buster Keaton took some affectionate stabs at Western star William S. Hart. The Hal Roach comedies and shorts from Educational Films and Columbia are filled with parodies and pastiches. Warner Bros. had a sort of mini-industry in making parodies. Through its cartoons and Vitaphone shorts, the studio could simultaneously publicize and make fun of both prestige titles like *I Am a Fugitive from a Chain Gang* (1932, a Registry title) and contract stars like James Cagney and Edward G. Robinson.

The popular Broadway revue *Hellzapoppin'* (filmed in 1941) took on a wide variety of topics, as did the films of Abbott and Costello and, later, Dean Martin and Jerry Lewis. Mel Brooks revitalized his career with the Western spoof *Blazing Saddles* (1974, a Registry title). Brooks in turn was a key influence on the comedy team of Jim Abrahams and the brothers David and Jerry Zucker.

The Zuckers began their comedy career in Milwaukee, performing skits in high school talent shows. At the University of Wisconsin at Madison, they teamed up with Jim Abrahams, also a Milwaukee native, and comedian Pat Proft to form the Kentucky Fried Theater, a comedy group specializing in short sketches that satirized popular culture. They were successful enough to move to Los Angeles in 1972, where they performed in an abandoned warehouse.

The Kentucky Fried group found material by videotaping late-night television commercials, movies, and shows and then reworking the content. Performing live taught them to strip away nonessential lines to concentrate on jokes—and also that no gag was too shameless or vulgar as long as it drew laughs. With $28,000, they filmed a sort of "greatest hits," a preview reel which they used to obtain $600,000 in financing to make a feature film.

Directed by John Landis, *The Kentucky Fried Movie* was a huge success financially, although it was largely dismissed by the mainstream. The equivalent of turning on a television and finding nothing but junk, no matter how many different channels you tried, *The Kentucky Fried Movie* taught the group a valuable lesson: without a narrative framework, it's hard to hold onto moviegoers for the length of a feature film.

One night the Zuckers and Abrahams accidentally recorded *Zero Hour!*, a 1957 precursor to a later cycle of disaster movies involving airplanes. Written by Arthur Hailey, the film took place aboard a plane whose pilots have been stricken with food poisoning. The Zuckers and Abrahams optioned the rights and then wrote a script which they showed to Paramount producer Howard Koch. He not only accepted the project, he assigned the trio to direct with a budget of $3.5 million.

The trio actually used some of the dialogue and many of the situations from *Zero Hour!*, adding to them jokes based on the *Airport* series of disaster films inspired by an Arthur Hailey novel. Kentucky Fried Theater jokes showed up as well, in particular a running gag involving religious panhandlers who at one time besieged airport passengers.

One unacknowledged inspiration was *Mad* magazine, a crucial source of comedy for boys growing up in the late 1960s. During that period, each issue of *Mad* contained a parody of a hit film. The best of these parodies pointed out the illogic in the film's own dialogue and situations, or pushed story ideas to bizarre lengths. The Zuckers and Abrahams did exactly the same thing, and like *Mad* they took care to play by the rules.

As the trio discovered in *The Kentucky Fried Movie*, parodies lose their impact if the target audience has no frame of reference. *Airplane!*, as their script was called, adhered to a strict narrative formula. Each scene advanced a clear, easy to follow storyline—granted, with time for gratuitous, irrelevant jokes.

The Zuckers and Abrahams had the additional advantage of following a plot that most of their viewers would not immediately recognize. Viewers could place the settings and even individual plot incidents in *Airplane!*, but on the whole would not have been familiar with *Zero Hour!* To them, *Airplane!*'s story would have seemed relatively new.

What the trio added to the story, and to the disaster genre in general, was a new set of cultural references. *Airplane!* is best appreciated by a specific audience who could connect to these references. Perhaps *Mad* magazine readers who were raised on television as much as movies, and who grew up with a relaxed sense of what was permissible to show in comedy.

In *Airplane!* as well as in *The Kentucky Fried Movie*, the trio had a tendency to spell out their jokes too carefully, to work out visual puns as if to make sure no viewer was left behind. In *Kentucky Fried Movie*, director John Landis had the luxury of cutting to another skit whenever inspiration ran dry. For *Airplane!*, the Zuckers and Abrahams were locked into material, no matter how strong or weak it was. When all else failed—when the story flagged or a scene went nowhere—they made fun of blacks, Asians, and homosexuals; put dirty words into the mouths of children; and flashed naked breasts across the screen.

Revue and sketch comedy always relied on sex for laughs. In vaudeville and later burlesque, sex became a running topic, and at times the sole point, to most skits. (There's a reason why Raquel Torres is in the cast of the 1933 Registry title *Duck Soup*, and it's not her comedic skills.) In *Airplane!*, as in *The Kentucky Fried Movie*, the Zuckers and Abrahams could explore the subject with a freedom unavailable to earlier filmmakers. In a sense the profanity, nudity, and suggestive situations in *Airplane!* became a dividing line between generations.

Airplane!'s audience also grew up believing that older art forms, and performers, were "square" and worthy of derision. "Old" was a relative term. The *Airport* franchise (which was still playing out in theaters: *The Concorde—Airport '79* opened the previous August) was a target. So was *Saturday Night Fever* (1977) and the entire disco phenomenon, mocked in a flashback sequence set on the tropical island of "Drambuie." Even in this scene, the Zuckers and Abrahams are careful to play by the rules, following the original film's choreography and camera movements and even using the original score, albeit slightly sped up.

The danger to *Airplane*'s approach to comedy is that viewers who don't understand the references can't get the jokes. If you haven't seen *Saturday Night Fever*, a scene that mocks a dance from it will not make much sense. When an elderly white woman tells a stewardess that she can speak "jive," and translates for two black passengers, it's just a minor (and racist) joke. You would have to know that the woman was played by Barbara Billingsley, and that she also played the mother on the television sitcom *Leave It to Beaver*, for the joke to have its full impact. (For that matter, you'd have to agree that *Leave It to Beaver*, a show admired more by parents than children, deserved scorn.) Will a younger generation watching *Airplane!* understand jokes about gas station attendants, Hare Krishna mendicants, and singing nuns?

Casting *Airplane!* proved more of a problem than it did for *The Kentucky Fried Movie*. Robert Hays, the lead, had had limited exposure on television series. Julie Hagerty had appeared in a few of her brother Michael's New York theater productions. The trio wrote the copilot's role for baseball star Pete Rose, but scheduling conflicts forced them to use basketball icon Kareem Abdul-Jabaar instead.

The heavy acting chores fell upon the supporting cast, in particular Robert Stack, Lloyd Bridges, Peter Graves, and Leslie Nielsen. Graves, star of the television series *Mission: Impossible* and the brother of actor James Arness, was reluctant to play a pedophile pilot. "Stack got it right away, though," Jerry Zucker remembered. (Stack had starred in his own airplane thriller, 1954's *The High and the Mighty*.) Bridges had a long career in movies, but the *Airplane!* audience would have known him from the television series *Sea Hunt* (just as they would always know Stack as Elliot Ness from TV's *The Untouchables*).

Leslie Nielsen was not known as a comedian, although he had shown a light touch as the romantic lead in *Tammy and the Bachelor* (1957). Born in

Canada, Nielsen followed a traditional path for actors of his time. Announcing on radio led to studying at the Neighborhood Playhouse in New York City and with Martha Graham. He accumulated bit parts and speaking roles in movies, larger responsibilities on television. He was in the science-fiction classic *Forbidden Planet* (1956) as well as the disaster film *The Poseidon Adventure* (1972). *Airplane!* revitalized his career. Nielsen took leading roles in several film comedies, continued to work on television and the stage, and even wrote books, like *Bad Golf My Way* (1996).

Airplane! grossed over $80 million, turning the Zuckers and Abrahams into bankable writers and directors. Often joined by comedian Pat Proft, they followed with films like *Top Secret!* (1984), *Ruthless People* (1986), and *The Naked Gun: From the Files of Police Squad* (1987). They have also worked individually. Jerry Zucker directed the popular hit *Ghost* (1990) and produced the Julia Roberts vehicle *My Best Friend's Wedding* (1997). Recently he produced *Fair Game* (2010), about Valerie Plame's exposure as a CIA agent. David Zucker produced *A Walk in the Clouds* (1995) and directed two of the entries in the *Scary Movie* series: *Scary Movie 3* (2003) and *Scary Movie 4* (2006).

The trio had an enormous influence on film comedies, in parodies like *Date Movie* (2006) and the *Scary Movie* series, but also in the films by Peter and Robert Farrelly (*Dumb & Dumber*, 1994, *There's Something About Mary*, 1998). Cartoon series like *The Simpsons* and animated features like *Shrek* and *A Shark's Tale* also use a similar scattershot approach to gags.

Thriller

Optimum Productions, 1983. Sound, color, 1.85. 35mm. 14 minutes.

Cast: Michael Jackson, Ola Ray.

Credits: Directed by John Landis. Written by John Landis & Michael Jackson. Produced by George Folsey, Jr., Michael Jackson, John Landis. Director of photography Robert Paynter. Special make-up effects Designed & Created by Rick Baker & EFX, Inc. Choreography by Michael Peters & Michael Jackson. Edited by Malcolm Campbell & George Folsey, Jr. Art director Charles Hughes. Costumes designed by Kelly Kimball & Deborah Nadoolman. Production manager: Dan Allingham. First Assistant director: David Sosna. Scary music by Elmer Bernstein. Song "Thriller" performed by Michael Jackson. Featuring "Rap" by Vincent Price. Produced by Quincy Jones & Michael Jackson. Written by Rod Temperton. Recorded & Mixed by Bruce Sweden. Available on Epic Records & Cassettes. 1983 Optimum Productions. Vestron Video.

Additional credits: Choreography: Vince Paterson. Premiered Los Angeles November 14 1983. First screened on MTV December 2, 1983.

Awards: Grammies for Best Video Album (1984), Best Video–Long Form (1985).

Available: Sony Home Video *Michael Jackson Number Ones* DVD (2003). UPC: 074645699998.

Regularly voted the best music video of all time, *Thriller* was originally conceived as a way to boost the flagging sales of musician Michael Jackson's sixth solo album, also called *Thriller*. For Jackson, the video would be a chance to recreate both the song-and-dance routines from classic musicals, and to indulge in the monster fantasies of drive-in films. Not incidentally, it would also promote the song "Thriller," which would be the seventh and last single released from the album.

Jackson had already finished two videos promoting other singles from the album, "Billie Jean" and "Beat It." The fact that the *Thriller* album had remained on the top of the charts since its release in November, 1982, gave him a sense of carte blanche about the new project. Having admired *An American Werewolf in London* (1981), he approached its director, John Landis, and asked him to helm the video. Both saw the possibility for fleshing out, as it were, a novelty song about monsters into a big musical number.

Landis and his producing partner George Folsey, Jr., first met with Jackson on August 20, 1983. The director offered to write a screenplay in which Jackson would act out the narrative of the song, and to film it as if it were part of a Hollywood musical, on 35mm stock, and with a professional crew—including special effects expert Rick Baker, who had worked with Landis on *American Werewolf*.

As Landis recalled, he went into the meeting concerned about the budget, which he estimated at $900,000. "Nobody would give us the money, because the album had already been so successful," he said. Reluctant to let Jackson finance it himself, Landis and Folsey offered to market the video as an hour-long featurette that also included a behind-the-scenes "making of" documentary.

The CBS/Epic label had given Jackson $250,000 for the "Billie Jean" video, but Jackson ended up spending $150,000 of his own money to film "Beat It." Landis cajoled an additional $100,000 from the label for the third video. Disney Studios agreed to release the video to Los Angeles theaters so it could be considered for the Academy Awards. But most of the production money came from cable TV, in particular, Showtime and MTV. Both networks optioned screening rights, Showtime for $300,000, MTV for $250,00. Landis said that these funds covered the production budget, although rumors have persisted that the video ended up costing significantly more.

A final crucial source of financing was Vestron, a video distributor. At the time, most videos were marketed for rentals, not "sell-through," and accordingly individual tapes were priced at close to $100. These would be purchased by video stores, who would make back their money by renting them to consumers. Vestron wanted to sell a tape of *Thriller* for $29.95, reasoning that volume would compensate for lower unit pricing.

Jackson rehearsed his dance routines with Michael Peters, who had worked on his "Beat It" video, and sat in on casting sessions with Landis. At the time, Jackson was in talks with director Steven Spielberg to star in a film version of *Peter Pan*. Landis told *Vanity Fair* reporter Nancy Griffin that he wanted to present a more virile Jackson: "The big thing was to give him a girl," he said. "That was the breakthrough." When Jennifer Beals declined the part, Landis chose Ola Ray, a twenty-three-year-old beauty who fortunately "was crazy for Michael." Landis had some qualms when he learned that Ray was a former *Playboy* Playmate, but Jackson ultimately agreed to the choice.

The script the director came up with used two time frames, one set in a generic 1950s, the other in the present. In the first, a takeoff on *I Was a Teenage Werewolf* (1957), Jackson warns his girlfriend that, "I'm not like other guys." When she demurs, he insists, "No, I mean I'm different." Landis cuts to a cloud crossing a full moon, then shows Jackson's transformation into a werewolf in the same excruciating detail that he used in *An American Werewolf in London*. (Devotees debate over whether Jackson becomes a werewolf or a werecat.)

Viewers see Jackson's eyes, teeth, ears, hands, fingernails change in what turns out to be an elaborate framing device that lasts some four minutes. Like Jackson himself, the *Thriller* video changes from one serio-comic horror film into another, this time a zombie story set in the present. The new setting not only introduces the "Thriller" song, but starts Jackson's carefully choreographed duet with Ray.

Landis builds the scene by having Ray and Jackson move in tandem down a street, from left to right in the frame (just as they do briefly in the opening scene), the camera tracking with them. Like the classic Fred Astaire routines, this is song and dance as seduction, with Ray gradually warming up to Jackson's entreaties because of the way he sings and moves. The director cuts to closer shots as the lyrics continue, switching to a crane as Ray and Jackson pass a cemetery. With Vincent Price rapping on the soundtrack, Landis has the crane pull in on the fog-shrouded tombstones as Rick Baker unleashes his zombies.

Thriller doesn't stint on special effects: one ground level shot has six figures, one emerging from a grave, all moving in different directions. Baker used latex bladders, foam latex appliances, hairpieces, rubber masks, grease-paint, and contact lenses on his creatures. Nor did Landis skimp on the cast. Peters wound up choreographing for eighteen professional dancers and four "pop dancers."

As much as he tried, Landis couldn't obtain a credible acting performance from Jackson. Nor did he pace the video's dialogue scenes very well, even if he intended them to parody old film styles. But the director clearly had fun with the details in the film, spotlighting Vincent Price on the theater marquee and in a poster for *House of Wax*; the director even gives a nod to his own film, *Schlock* (1973), seen briefly in a coming attractions window.

He also pushes the analogy between monster and rapist to a greater extent than he could in *American Werewolf*, partly because Jackson's persona still seemed so innocent. Subsequent music video directors continued to fetishize this sexual element, a trend echoed in computer games, which drew much of their visual style from music videos.

The *Thriller* video in various incarnations sold millions of units; at this writing, the album is the highest-selling of all time, with over 110 million copies sold. It was a career high point for Jackson, whose troubled personal life is the stuff of countless stories on the gossip circuit. The musician's chaotic finances led to both Landis and Ray suing him for royalties. Landis was also concerned when Jackson sold the theatrical rights for *Thriller* to the Nederlander Organization for some $400,000. Jackson's death in 2010 threw the financial obligations for *Thriller* into further disarray.

Purists fume when *The Jazz Singer* (1927, a Registry title) is described as "the first sound film" or "the first talkie." They react the same way when *Thriller* is called "the first music video" or the first to attach a narrative to a song. The real significance behind *Thriller* is its synergy, a now-obsolete term that was a sort of holy grail for media companies at the time. Just as *The Kiss* exploited newspapers, film, and theater in 1896, the *Thriller* video combined radio, consumer audio, cable, and home video into one marketing juggernaut, each stream feeding off and nurturing the other. In the process *Thriller* helped justify still-fledgling networks like MTV and new forms of distribution exemplified by Vestron.

Precious Images

Directors Guild of America, 1986. Sound, B&W and color, 1.37. 7 minutes.

Credits: Produced and directed by Chuck Workman. For the Directors Guild of America: Robert Wise, David Shepard. Assistant Editor: John Santos. Production assistance; Lois Anne Polan, Denise Marie Heffley, Victoria Stevenson. Production facilities: B/G/L Post, Calliope Films, Cinema Research, Consolidated Film Industries, Deluxe Laboratories, Dolby Laboratories, Inc., Sound West, Inc., Todd-AO.

Additional credits: Edited by Chuck Workman.

Awards: Oscar for Best Live Action Short.

Available: Directors Guild of America.

Compilation movies have a long and somewhat unsavory history in the film industry. They were among the first attempts at repurposing material, to trick the public into believing something old was new. The major studios routinely assembled clips from their greatest hits in promotional films, like Warner Brothers' 1931 Vitaphone short *The Movie Album*. Paramount did the same in *The House That Shadows Built* (1931) and a series called *Movie Milestones* later in the decade. Documentaries series like *The March of Time* and *Why We Fight* (1943–45, a Registry title) took clips from a variety of sources and juxtaposed them so that they were given added meaning, sometimes contradicting what the original filmmakers intended. Compilations were a favorite trick of animators pressed for new material. *Spinach-Packin' Popeye* (1944) used clips from the Registry title *Popeye the Sailor Meets Sindbad the Sailor* (1936) and *Popeye the Sailor Meets Ali Baba's Forty Thieves* (1937) as Popeye reminisced about his past exploits. In a sense, you could look at trailers as compilation films that extracted the best pieces of a feature for a similar but in some ways new mini-version.

Precious Images brought the compilation format to a new level of complexity. A collection of clips from 462 films, the short did more than just recognize significant moments in film, it provided a history of the industry itself: its stars, genres, themes, and filmmakers. Financed by the Directors' Guild of America to honor its fiftieth anniversary, it was produced and directed by Chuck Workman.

Founded in 1936 as the Screen Directors Guild, the Directors Guild of America currently represents over 10,000 members working in film and television. It bargains for directors, assistant directors, stage managers, and other professionals over working conditions, health care and pensions, as well as creative issues such as credits and editing. In 1976, the Guild established the Special Projects Committee under director Robert Wise with a mandate to protect and preserve the traditions of its members. That same year Wise hired David Shepard as the first Special Projects Officer. The Committee started an Oral Histories project, now the Visual History Program; organized tributes, retreats, and conferences; published books; and in 1986, to celebrate its golden jubilee, commissioned *The Television Makers* (produced and directed by Newton Meltzer) and *Precious Images*.

Born in Philadelphia, Workman began his career as an editor, cutting two features for Argentine director Leopoldo Torre Nilsson, *Monday's Child* and *Traitors of San Angel* (both 1967). By the early 1970s, Workman had established a reputation for editing trailers, and was responsible for the coming attractions pieces for *American Graffiti* (1973), the original *Star Wars* (1977), and *Close Encounters of the Third Kind* (1977), all Registry titles. He also directed award-winning commercials and behind-the-scenes "making of" shorts for features.

For this project, Workman had access to just about any feature (and short) produced by the major film studios, which donated prints and materials with the understanding that the resulting short would not be distributed for profit. First he had to winnow down thousands of film titles to the 500 or so he deemed significant. Viewers would already be familiar with many of the movies: *The Godfather* (1972), *Star Wars* (1977), *E.T. the Extra-Terrestrial* (1982). Workman added more obscure titles because they represented genres or time periods he wanted to include. The vigilante film *Death Wish* (1974), for example, or a cliffhanger moment from the silent film *Teddy at the Throttle* (1917).

Next Workman had to find a defining moment or image from each film, one vivid enough to register with viewers quickly. Some choices were easy: Paul Henreid lighting a pair of cigarettes in *Now, Voyager* (1942), or Vivien Leigh in silhouette against a flaming sunset in *Gone With the Wind* (1939), for example. *King Kong* (1933) and Superman (seen in a clip from *Superman III*, 1983) were instantly recognizable, but finding a moment that explained *Letter from an Unknown Woman* (1948), or that fit the film into Workman's narrative, took much more thought.

Workman then had to group the clips by theme and genre, thinking past simply cutting footage together to employ different theories of montage. Much as a museum presents works of art by schools and periods, Workman placed Westerns in one section, romances in another. He drew ingenious connections among the groups and individual films, using principles like vertical editing, cross-cutting, continuity editing, jump cuts, and reverse shots. Music and occasionally dialogue tied films together or contrasted them against each other.

Workman's sly sense of humor added another layer to the editing. He used the *William Tell* Overture, known to many viewers as "*The Lone Ranger* theme," to introduce the Western section, and in the midst of shots of horses thundering across landscapes threw in a startling but appropriate cut from the science-fiction film *Planet of the Apes* (1968). Three quick cuts, from *Mommie Dearest* (1981) to *Mildred Pierce* (1945) to *Whatever Happened to Baby Jane?* (1962) offer as concise an account as possible of Joan Crawford's career.

Workman's leaps across time and space—conflating the chariot race from *Ben-Hur* to a shoot-out from *The Wild Bunch* (1968)—show how broad and at the same time how self-contained the film universe is. For a dance segment, along with the expected examples (Astaire and Rogers, Gene Kelly, Busby Berkeley), Workman can fit in Charlie Chaplin's iconic "dance of the rolls" from *The Gold Rush* (1924) as well as Walter Huston's prospector's jig from *The Treasure of the Sierra Madre* (1948).

Genres and themes overlap. A shot of Esther Williams submerging into a swimming pool in *Million Dollar Mermaid* (1952) leads to an underwater shot of a swimmer in *Jaws* (1975), an example of both continuity and vertical editing. Disaster films intermingle with science fiction and horror, and then evolve into melodrama. Throughout it all, Workman keeps a tight rein on the structural integrity of *Precious Images*, even timing Bette Davis shooting a revolver in *The Letter* (1940) to Bernard Herrmann's theme from *Psycho* (1960).

About four minutes into the film, Workman speeds up the pace of the cutting, spinning through decades of film in seconds, slowing down again for some of the most iconic stars and images of our cinematic memory. Among these is Gloria Swanson, just after she has exclaimed, "We had faces then" in *Sunset Blvd.* (1950), and Workman proves her point without words. Characteristically, he tops the segment with an in-joke: Judy Garland accepts an award in *A Star Is Born* (1954) with the line, "This is Mrs. Norman Maine," and Workman cuts to two other versions of the film for the words "Norman" and "Maine."

Precious Images not only plumbs the history of movies, it connects films in ways viewers may not have considered. Judith Anderson darts her eyes in *Rebecca*, a gesture repeated by Greta Garbo in *Ninotchka*; a thumbs-up in *Easy Rider* is echoed by Clark Gable hitchhiking in *It Happened One Night*.

Precious Images is a film that rewards those who love movies. The more you know about stars, directors, and genres, the more you appreciate the scope and depth of the clips selected. They are a spur, a catalyst, unlocking memories and emotions, bringing back the viewers' pasts as well as the films themselves.

Precious Images was televised at the Academy Awards ceremony, where it won a well-deserved Oscar. Workman has since directed both fiction and nonfiction features, including *The Source* (2000) and *A House on a Hill* (2003). *Visionaries* (2010) is a combination of compilation film and documentary about experimental filmmakers. He has also made several additional compilation films, including *The Spirit of America* (2002), a response to the 9/11 attacks. *Director's Cut* (2011) celebrates the 75th anniversary of the Directors Guild of America. Workman is also responsible for the "In Memoriam" segments of Academy Awards ceremonies, invariably the emotional high point of the annual broadcast.

Malcolm X

A pensive Denzel Washington in *Malcolm X*.

Warner Bros., 1992. Sound, color, 2.35. 35mm. 201 minutes. Rated PG-13.

Cast: Denzel Washington (Malcolm X), Angela Bassett (Betty Shabazz), Albert Hall (Baines), Al Freeman, Jr. (Elijah Muhammad), Delroy Lindo (West Indian Archie), Spike Lee (Shorty), Theresa Randle (Laura), Kate Vernon (Sophia), Lonette McKee (Louise Little), Tommy Hollis (Earl Little), James McDaniel (Brother Earl), Ernest Thomas (Sidney), Jean LaMarre (Benjamin 2X), O.L. Duke (Pete), Larry McCoy (Sammy), Maurice Sneed (Cadillac), Debi Mazar (Peg), Phyllis Yvonne Stickney (Honey), Scot Anthony Robinson (Daniel), James E. Gaines (Cholly), Joe Seneca (Toomer), LaTanya Richardson (Lorraine), Wendell Pierce (Ben Thomas), Michael Guess (William X), Leland Gantt (Wilbur Kinley), Giancarlo Esposito (Thomas Hayer), Leonard Thomas (Leon Davis), Roger Guenveur Smith (Rudy), Craig Wasson (TV Host), Graham Brown (Dr. Payson), Gerica Cox (Eva Marie), Kristan Rai Segure (Saudi), Lauren Padick (Lisha), Danielle Fletcher (Attalah), Robinson Frank Adu (Chuck), Aleta Mitchell (Sister Robin), Curt Williams (Mr. Cooper), John Ottavino (Blades), John Reidy (Simmons), Frances Foster (Woman Outside Audubon Ballroom), Reggie Montgomery (Dick Jones), David Patrick Kelly (Mr. Ostrowski), Gary L. Catus (Doctor), Sharon Washington (Augusta), Shirley Stoler (Mrs. Swerlin), Oran "Juice" Jones (Hustler), Ricky Gordon (Lionel Hampton), George Lee Miles (Preacher), Raye Dowell (Sister Evelyn Williams), Veronica Webb (Sister Lucille Rosary), Abdul Salaam El Razaac (Fox), Keith Smith (Brother Gene), George Guidall (Mr. Holway), James L. Swain (Conductor), Pee Wee Love (Speedy), Lawrence James (Tully), Steve White (Brother Johnson), K. Smith (Roderick), Christopher Rubin (Sophia's Husband), Matthew Harris (Malcolm, 5 years old), Zakee Howze (Young Malcolm), Cytia Fontenette (Hilda, 3 years old), Marlaine Bass (Hilda, 8 years old), Benjamin Atwell (Philbert, 1 year old), Peter Dunn (Philbert, 6 years old), Dion Smack, Jr. (Reginald, 2 years old), Darnell Smith (Elijah Muhammad's Grandson), Tainesha Scott (Elijah Muhammad's Granddaughter), Chelsea and Chéla Counts (Yvonne, 6 months old), Natalie Clanton (Yvonne, 1 year old), Jessica Givens (Attalah), LaToyah Bigelow (Qubillah, 3 years old); Martaleah and Tamaraleah Jackson, Jasmine Smith (Ilyasah, 2 and 3 years old); Valentino Smith (Wilfred, 4 years old), David Thomas, Jr. (Wilfred, 8 years old), Simon Do-Ley (Son of Elijah Muhammad and Secretary Evelyn Williams), Bill Goldberg (The "John"), Jonathan Peck (Phone Voice), Leonard Parker (Jason), Lennis Washington (Mrs. Johnson), Dyan Humes (Maid at open air market), Lizbeth Mackay (White Woman in market); Terry Layman, Terry Sumter (CIA Agents); Jasper McGruder (Hotel Clerk), Mary Alice Smith (School Teacher), Rev. Wyatt T. Walker (Hospital Spokesperson), Hazel Medina (Cashier Person), Wendy E. Taylor (Numbers Woman), Ed Herlihy (Joe Louis Announcer), The Late and Great Ralph Cooper, Sr. (Radio Announcer), Christian J. Dacosta (Passerby), Karen T. Duffy (Sophia's Friend), Walter Jones (Barber's

Customer), Marc Phillips (Photographer), Showman Uneke (Hustler at Grand Central Station), Theara Ward (Moviegoer), Larry Cherry (Prison Barber); Clebert Ford, Grafton Trew, Rogers Simon, George T. Odom (Barbers); Vincent Moscaritola (Prison Guard, Larry Attile (Guard Baines), Brendan Kelly (Guard Cone), John Griesemer (Guard Wilkins), Fia Porter (Coed), Billy Mitchell (Man #1), Kent Jackman (Man #2), Beatrice Winde (Elderly Woman), Fracaswell Hyman (Bartender), Rion Johnson (Shoeshine Boy).

Special Guest Appearances: Bobby Seale (Speaker #1), Al Sharpton (Speaker #2), Christopher Plummer (Chaplain Gill), Karen Allen (Miss Dunne), Peter Boyle (Captain Green), William Kunstler (The Judge), Nelson Mandela (Soweto Teacher).

Credits: Directed by Spike Lee. Screenplay by Arnold Perl and Spike Lee. Based on the book *The Autobiography of Malcolm X* as told to Alex Haley. Produced by Marvin Worth and Spike Lee. Co-producers: Monty Ross, John Kilik, Preston Holmes. Associate producer: Fernando Sulichin. Photographed by Ernest Dickerson. Production design: Wynn Thomas. Editor: Barry Alexander Brown. Original music score: Terence Blanchard. Casting: Robi Reed. Costume design: Ruth Carter. Eulogy written and performed by Ossie Davis. Project Consultant: Dr. Betty Shabazz. Historical Consultant: Paul Lee. Sound recordist: Rolf Pardula. Supervising Sound Editor: Skip Lievsay. Music supervisor: Alex Steyermark. Stunt Coordinator: Jeff Ward. Choreographer: Otis Sallid. Special appearance by Branford Marsalis on tenor and soprano saxophones and The Boys Choir of Harlem. Dolby Stereo. A Warner Bros. presentation, in association with Largo International N.V., of a 40 Acres and a Mule Filmworks production and Marvin Worth production. A Spike Lee Joint. In memory of Alex Haley.

Additional cast includes: Michael Imperioli (Reporter at Fire Bombing); John Sayles, Martin Donovan (FBI Agents); Nick Turturro (Boston Cop), William Fichtner (Cop at Harlem Station), Rev. Al Sharpton (Street preacher), Vincent D'Onofrio (Bill Newman).

Additional credits: Principal shooting dates: September 16–December 20, 1991. Shooting completed January 26, 1992. Released November 18, 1992.

Available: Warner Bros. DVD (2005). UPC: 085393353124.

A crucial, if divisive, figure in the civil rights movement, Malcolm X was born Malcolm Little in Omaha, Nebraska, on May 19, 1925. His father Norton Little, a Baptist minister, was a follower of Marcus Garvey, which made his family the target of vigilantes in Nebraska, Wisconsin, and Michigan. When Reverend Little died in a suspicious accident, Malcolm and his brothers and sisters ended up in foster homes.

Discouraged from his dream of becoming a lawyer, Little drifted into crime in Boston and Harlem. Imprisoned for burglary in 1946, Little sought to remake himself through education. He dove into the teachings of Elijah Muhammad, leader of the Lost-Found Nation of Islam, and adopted the name Malcolm X upon his parole in 1952. Ordained a minister, he helped grow the Nation of Islam from 400 to over 10,000 members, in the process becoming one of the most provocative leaders of the civil rights movement.

Already controversial within the black community, Malcolm X provoked national outrage when he used the phrase "chickens coming home to roost" after the assassination of President John F. Kennedy. He was suspended by Elijah Muhammad, and eventually left the Nation of Islam in 1964. Later that year, Malcolm X returned from a pilgrimage to Mecca a convert to orthodox Islam, adopting the name El-Hajj Malik El-Shabazz.

In the following months, Malcolm X offered a more conciliatory message, playing down black separatism, admitting that he once held racist opinions, and reaching out to moderate blacks and whites while criticizing Muhammad and his confederates. A week after his house was firebombed, Malcolm X was assassinated on February 21, 1965, by three men with ties to the Nation of Islam.

Published at the end of 1965, *The Autobiography of Malcolm X*, a sort of oral history compiled with author Alex Haley, offered a multifaceted portrait of a man who struggled with the key racial issues of his time. An enduring best-seller, the book continues to speak to an audience searching for answers to intractable social problems. Its accuracy has been debated by scholars and critics.

Among the many artists influenced by Malcolm X is Spike Lee, who ended his *Do the Right Thing* (1989, a Registry title) with a quote from "The Ballot or the Bullet" speech: "By any means necessary." This became the rallying cry for Lee's 40 Acres and a Mule production company after the writer, director, and actor announced his intentions to film a biography of the civil rights leader.

A number of Malcolm X film projects had been announced through the years. Director Elia Kazan optioned the autobiography in April 1966, for a film to star James Earl Jones and to be written by actor Ossie Davis (who delivered Malcolm X's eulogy). Columbia, Twentieth Century-Fox, and CBS Theatrical Films took stabs at the autobiography, all ultimately frightened off by the subject matter and the difficulty in mounting what would necessarily be a costly, wide-ranging production.

In 1972, Warner Bros. released *Malcolm X*, an Oscar-nominated documentary produced by Marvin Worth and written by Arnold Perl. Made with the cooperation of Betty Shabazz, Malcolm X's widow, the film was Perl's last project (he died in December 1971, before its release).

Perl's script became the basis of Spike Lee's screenplay. Although director Norman Jewison had announced his own Malcolm X project, Lee campaigned for his version of the autobiography, wearing an "X" on his baseball cap as a preemptive branding strategy. Lee envisioned an epic biopic along the lines of earlier prestige biopics. (Perhaps *Wilson* or *Sunrise at Campobello*, stately, even stodgy, films that lionized US Presidents.) The only thing holding the director back: funding to mount the production he envisioned.

Lee's ace in the hole was actor Denzel Washington, who had just won an Oscar for *Glory*, where he played a slave who fought for the North in the Civil War. Born in 1954 in Mount Vernon, New York, Washington began acting in college, portraying Malcolm X on stage in 1980 and winning an Obie in 1981 for *A Soldier's Play* (he reprised his role in the film version, *A Soldier's Story*, 1984). Washington had the looks and the screen presence of an old-fashioned movie star, but he also had the technical skill and commitment to deliver a nuanced, persuasive impersonation of Malcolm X. And he had established a comfortable working relationship with Lee after starring in the director's film about the jazz industry, *Mo' Better Blues* (1990).

As he did on his earlier student films, Lee bulled his way past obstacles, using a steady stream of press releases and publicity stories to keep *Malcolm X* before the public while scrambling for financing behind the scenes. In later interviews he described how he got WBLS, a New York radio station, to appeal for extras to populate scenes set in a National Guard Armory. When the completion bond company fired his post-production staff, Lee turned to prominent black celebrities like Bill Cosby and Oprah Winfrey for additional funds. He also tried to work around budgetary restrictions from Warner Bros. by selling off foreign rights to the film. (Lee went into great detail about the *Malcolm X* production in the book *By Any Means Necessary: The Trials and Tribulations of the Making of Malcolm X*, written with Ralph Wiley and published in 1993.)

The strain of making *Malcolm X* may have contributed to the film's oddly restrained tone—that and its subject's intimidating stature. On the other hand, Lee is an unusually defensive director, willing to take uncomfortable positions but not to have his technique questioned. *Malcolm X* opens with an American flag filling the screen, just as it did in *Patton* (1970, a Registry title), but by the end of the credits Lee has set it on fire while mixing documentary footage of the Rodney King beating with "newsreel" recreations. On the soundtrack, Washington intones, "I charge the white man with being the greatest murderer on earth," and similarly incendiary statements. At the beginning of his most important project, Lee tests his audience, daring them to accept his approach to the story.

The story itself starts with a dazzling crane shot devised by Lee and his cinematographer Ernest Dickerson, one that leads from an elevated train station to a street scene teeming with crowds and cars. It's followed by a ninety-second shot that pulls back from a close-up of shoes being shined to show Lee himself, playing a zoot-suited dandy, swaggering down the street, crossing a four-way intersection and strutting into a barber shop. After testing his viewers, the director throws down the gauntlet, as if trying to prove he could pull off camera pyrotechnics just like Hitchcock or Scorsese.

Lee is at his loosest in the first hour of *Malcolm X*, which covers Malcolm Little's life as a wayward criminal. Like a DeMille epic before judgment is rendered, the movie revels in sin and decadence, with prolonged set pieces like a production number in the sort of nightclub only found in movies. You might argue with some of Lee's choices—did he really have to include all of Lionel Hampton's "Flying Home"? Why pull the camera ahead of his subjects during the tracking shots? Are his shock cuts and double exposures worth the effort?—but not with his filmmaking skills.

Watch how he depicts a scene in which Malcolm Little is sentenced to ten years' hard labor for burglary. A crane shot starts at the back of the courtroom as the judge speaks, his words obscured by a voice-over on the soundtrack. As the camera pulls in on the judge, Lee intercuts mug shots, close-ups of hands clasping, isolated features of faces, some only twelve frames long, in rhythm with the descending crane. It's a passage as focused as it is accomplished: everything works towards Lee's message, but so smoothly that you don't pay attention to how intricately it was assembled.

As the story proceeds, however, Lee finds himself hemmed in by facts. The real-life Malcolm X was a media celebrity whose actions and statements were covered by both mainstream and niche press. And as events in Malcolm X's life accelerated, Lee no longer has the luxury of inventing situations simply as digressions or to explore characters. His responsibility to the truth limits his creativity as a director.

The latter sections of the film are instead opportunities to admire Denzel Washington's performance. In recent years Washington has become one of Hollywood's few dependable stars, able to carry an action blockbuster as well as small-scale dramas. At the time of *Malcolm X*, he was still an unknown factor for a large part of the moviegoing audience. Washington imitates Malcolm X's mannerisms and cadences with such ease that he barely seems to be acting. An admiring Lee cites one long speech in which Washington went off script but remained in character, so immured in the role that he could extemporize words and gestures flawlessly.

Lee's production troubles became fodder for news items and gossip columns. The hooplah surrounding his projects tend to drown out the films themselves, and at times it has seemed that the director has encouraged controversy to avoid answering for his creative choices. Lee offered a number of explanations for the fact that *Malcolm X* was a box-office disappointment, including unenlightened critics and a cowardly audience.

On the other hand, if Lee is criticized for an opinion espoused in one of his films, he can reason that he doesn't necessarily share his characters' views. As he said in his autobiography *Spike Lee: That's My Story and I'm Sticking to It*, "I've never felt it was the filmmaker's job to have all the answers. I think, for the most part, if we choose to do so, we have more of a provocateur role, where we ask these questions and hopefully they will, by the way that they are asked, stimulate and generate some discussion and dialogue. But to find answers for racism and prejudice in film? You can't do that."

A director always makes choices, however. Preston Sturges didn't have to use black stereotypes for racist gags in *The Palm Beach Story*, for example, just as Lee didn't have to stir a feminist outcry in *Girl 6* or go to the racial extremes of a film like *Bamboozled*. Seen today, removed from the flurry of articles surrounding its release, *Malcolm X* is even more impressive for its even-handed, honest tone.

The Red Book

An example of the animation techniques used in *The Red Book*. Courtesy of Janie Geiser.

Janie Geiser, 1994. Sound, color, 1.37. 16mm. 11 minutes.

Credits: A film by Janie Geiser. Sound design: Beo Morales. Engineered at Harmonic Ranch. Funded in part by The Guggenheim Foundation and Alive T.V. Thanks to Scott Macauley, Neil Sieling, Millennium Film Workshop, A. Leroy, Laura McPhee, Mark Lapore, Cara Mertes, Mark McElhatten and Lewis Klahr. For Salley May. *The Red Book* video was produced by Twin Cities Public Television.

Available: Canyon Cinema, www.canyoncinema.com; The Film-Makers' Cooperative, http://www.film-maker-scoop.com.

Cryptic, elusive, menacing, *The Red Book* was the first stand-alone movie by puppetry artist Janie Geiser. Born in 1957 in Baton Rouge, Louisiana, Geiser studied art at the University of Georgia, specializing in painting and metalwork. One of her post-graduate pieces was a diorama with pop-up figures. After seeing a performance by Bruce Schwartz, she began investigating performance with puppets and objects, and, several years later, formed her own puppet company.

Geiser at first used film as a complement to her puppetry, then began exploring film as a separate medium. In the 1992 short *Babel Town*, she used traditional rod-marionette puppets to tell a story about a girl who runs away from home. Filming took place on a stage on which the puppets moved through constructed sets: a farmhouse, a city skyline, etc. But the film did more than capture a performance; in fact, Geiser used cinematic techniques to go beyond what a live audience could see. At one point the camera rack focuses (or changes what is in focus in the frame) over a barbed wire fence, showing viewers precisely what Geiser wanted. It was an effect impossible to achieve so accurately during a live performance.

Geiser abandoned puppets per se for her subsequent films, using cut-out or collage animation instead. Some films have dolls, wooden shapes, clocks, and other objects; these are moved through graphic spaces that Geiser draws or constructs. She often superimposes other visuals over objects, frequently words either printed or written out in script. At times her imagery is dense with collage, with different planes of visuals moving up or down.

For sound, Geiser uses a collage approach as well, building from snippets of noises and dialogue, layering industrial sounds over music and then mixing the results to achieve a murky, menacing mood. For *The Red Book* and her next film, *The Secret Story*, Geiser collaborated with Beo Morales, an engineer who has worked as a mixer and sound editor on several documentaries.

Geiser acknowledges Harry Smith (whose *Early Abstractions* is on the Registry) as inspiration, but her work shares similarities with other filmmakers as well. David Lynch used similar sound collages in *Eraserhead* (1977, a Registry title), for example. Experimental filmmaker Lewis Klahr, who receives thanks in the credits for *The Red Book* and who is Geiser's husband, is another influence, as are animator Suzan Pitt and experimental filmmakers such as Ernie Gehr, Maya Deren, and Ken Jacobs.

But Geiser is a more elusive filmmaker. Her works do not reveal their meanings easily, and it's possible that viewers may not understand her narratives at all. *The Secret Story* is just that, a story derived from Geiser's past, a past viewers could not be expected to know. As she told journalist Fred Camper, it's fine not to get all the details: "This is my own mythology—you may not know the players, but they may be recognizable archetypes. I want it to connect more on the emotional level."

The ideas behind *The Red Book* came to Geiser in the 1980s, when she read a book about a man suffering from amnesia. Through her writing and drawing, Geiser constructed a story about a woman with both amnesia and aphasia, or short-term memory loss. "You really lose a lot of your ability to communicate and to hold thoughts in your mind," she told artist Kathy High in an interview. "So there are a lot of images in the film, say, where she's writing and the writing disappears immediately."

Dreams played a part in forming the film. "I was watching these hands writing in the dirt and they were writing these hieroglyphs, and then the hieroglyphs turned into architect's plans. It made sense with the piece somehow—the architecture of the body, and images of home and body, and how women are so associated with those kinds of places."

Geiser started work on the film by constructing painted books, by painting cut-out figures and photographs, and gathering materials for about a year until she felt she had a "critical mass." She also experimented with creating double-exposures with a Bolex 16mm camera, a process that requires exposing film and then rewinding it to layer a second image over the first. It's a time-consuming technique that requires different calculations for exposures than normal photography. A mistake in the second or third exposure of course means starting from scratch.

As the title suggests, *The Red Book* is built around words, but language in the film is inconclusive when it can be comprehended at all. Phrases emerge, "never know," for example, or "time now so distant." But as Geiser told High, "With this piece I wasn't trying to make a literal narrative, but more what I call an emotional narrative. You're going through something, but I don't necessarily expect someone watching it to get the literal story that I'm starting out from."

Because she did not face a deadline for the project, and also received funding through a Guggenheim Fellowship, the director could spend as much time as she wanted both creating and editing the film. Early versions were constructed chronologically, but Geiser then began thinking in terms of an "elliptical structure of large circles becoming smaller and smaller as the film went on." She kept returning to specific images—a woman's body splitting apart, a key to a door—using them to re-edit the storyline.

If you don't already know that *The Red Book* is about an amnesiac woman, then what does the film "mean" to you? To Geiser, a viewer's subjective response is as valid as any other interpretation. But certain images and incidents in the film are unmistakable. A key opening a doorway, for example, or an ascending elevator. Geiser uses a limited color palette, primarily black, white, and red, providing emotional cues for viewers—the red suggesting blood, perhaps. Combine these elements with the tense, brooding soundtrack, and *The Red Book* builds a sense of unease. Not being able to decipher its meanings adds to its atmosphere.

Geiser's puppetry performances have been acclaimed throughout the world. *Invisible Glass* (2005, based on Edgar Allan Poe's *William Wilson*) combines actors, sets, projections, and music. Composed between 2004 and 2008, *Frankenstein (Mortal Toys)*, directed and designed with Susan Simpson, is a performance piece based on the traditions of 19th century toy theater. Geiser describes *The Reptile Under the Flowers* (2009) as "a multimedia peep show/diorama/performance with miniature puppetry and live video."

For her work, Geiser has received a Guggenheim Fellowship, a Rockefeller Media Arts Fellowship, and grants from the NEA and The Henson Foundation.

As an illustrator, she has contributed to *The New Yorker*, *The New York Times*, and *The Wall Street Journal*.

While continuing to teach at CalArts, Geiser is the Co-Artistic Director of Automata, which she founded with Susan Simpson in 2004. It is a non-profit organization based in Los Angeles and dedicated to experimental puppet theater, experimental film and "other contemporary art practices centered on ideas of artifice and performing objects." The director's latest films include *Ghost Algebra* (2009) and *The Floor of the World* (2010), both of which premiered in the United States at the 2010 New York International Film Festival's "Views from the Avant-Garde."

Scratch and Crow

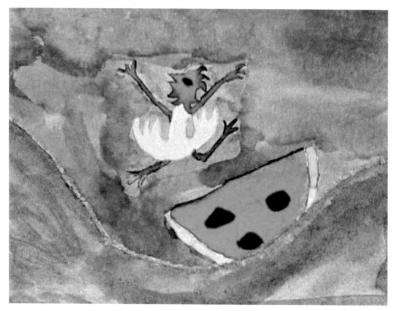

A typically exuberant moment from Helen Hill's film. Courtesy Paul Gailiunas.

Helen Hill, 1995. Sound, color, 1.33. 16mm. 10 minutes.
Credits: Directed by Helen Hill. Drawing and animation: Helen Hill. Produced at CalArts.
Available: The Harvard Film Archive, http://hcl.harvard.edu/hfa/collections/hill.html

By turns whimsical and troubling, stark and lyrical, *Scratch and Crow* is a work of promise as well as accomplishment. It was written and drawn by Helen Hill, a filmmaker who found solutions to obstacles that would have daunted others. Hill completed twenty-one shorts that explored all the possibilities of animation, from stop-motion with models to painting directly onto celluloid. In addition to filmmaking, she was a teacher, social activist, writer, wife and mother.

Hill was born in Columbia, South Carolina, in 1970. She began making movies on Super 8 at the age of eleven. *The House of Sweet Magic* (1981) featured stop-motion animation of a toy dinosaur; *Quacks* (also 1981) was a live-action comedy made in collaboration with classmates and teachers. Hill studied animation at Harvard's Visual Environmental Studies Program, where she drew *Rain Dance* (1990), based on a friend's poems, and used puppets for *Vessel* (1992), based on her own poem, "The Rag."

190

Hill's influences at this time included animators Suzan Pitt (*Asparagus*, 1979), for whom she interned for a summer, and Lotte Reiniger, a pioneer of cut-out animation, as well as painters like William Blake and Vincent van Gogh and writers like Flannery O'Connor. At Harvard she fell in love with Paul Gailiunas, a Canadian who was studying African history and medicine. After graduating, they moved to New Orleans, where Hill immersed herself in Southern culture.

While Gailiunas attended medical school in Nova Scotia, Hill studied graduate film at the California Institute for the Arts. Always a personal filmmaker, Hill used animation as a means to examine her beliefs and to pay tribute to figures in her life. *Mouseholes* (1999), for example, was about her grandfather Pop, who was dying in the summer of 1995.

For *Scratch and Crow*, Hill drew upon her memories of a cousin's farm in Fairview, North Carolina, but she also incorporated incidents in her present-day life. Gailiunas had become a vegan in medical school, and Hill eventually became one as well. (They married in June, 1995.) Scenes in *Scratch and Crow* of death and rebirth, of tableware and cutlery, seem to address vegan issues directly.

Hill's exuberant painting, with its visible brushstrokes and bright colors, gives *Scratch and Crow* a pulsing beat, rushing the narrative forward with the momentum of a dream. Her poetic intertitles and religious imagery evoke Blake, but her sense of humor adds a distinctive Southern touch. Watermelons rain from the sky; their seeds become portals to separate planes of life. A predominately black-and-white sequence suggests the influence of Len Lye (whose *Free Radicals*, 1979, is on the Registry), as well as the primitive woodcuts from the nineteenth century. Tombstones, plates, knives and forks, and "dusty angels" may be signals or warnings about what we eat.

After obtaining her masters from CalArts, Hill joined her husband in Halifax, where she taught animation at Nova Scotia College of Art and Design and contributed several shorts to the children's television series *Street Cents*.

Hill had a love for film as a medium, a taste shared by fewer and fewer artists, and she made it a goal to teach others about working with celluloid. She received funding from the Canadian Council for the Arts to study alternative filmmaking, learning about how to process film. From this came *Recipes for Disaster: A Handcrafted Film Cookbooklet*, a how-to guide that became a standard resource for alternative filmmakers. The animated *Madame Winger makes a film* (2001) discussed some of these issues, with Hill making a case for drawing directly onto film and hand-processing footage—treating celluloid like a canvas instead of something to be handed over to laboratory technicians. "Filmmakers! How will you survive the new century?" asks Madame Winger (actually the voice of Hill's godmother, Meredith Pogue), a question that would soon have unexpected relevance.

When Gailiunas received his medical degree, he and Hill moved back to New Orleans, finding a house in the Carrollton neighborhood. Gailiunas opened Little Doctors, a clinic for low-income patients, and played in a rock band, the Trouble Makers. Hill taught filmmaking and cofounded the New Orleans Film Collective while continuing to work on her own projects. One of these involved the chance discovery in 2001 of a hundred hand-sewn dresses that had been discarded on a sidewalk on Adams Street. Hill learned that they had been made by seamstress Florestine Kinchen, and thrown out by her family after her death at the age of ninety. In 2004, Hill received a $35,000 Rockefeller Foundation Fellowship to start work on what would become *The Florestine Collection*, a tribute to the seamstress.

In October, 2004, Hill gave birth to a son, Francis Pop Gailiunas. A year later, when Hurricane Katrina hit New Orleans, Hill and her family fled to Columbia. When they returned two months later to check on their house, Hill documented her neighborhood on Super 8 film. These home movies provided a devastating account of the hurricane's damage, told from the point-of-view of residents rather than visiting journalists.

Hill's home sustained extensive water damage. Some eighty reels of Super 8 footage had been completely submerged in the flood waters. She packaged what artwork and 16mm and 8mm films she could salvage and brought them back to Columbia. There she began work on restoring them, hand-washing the films with detergent and then using FilmRenew, a product marketed by Urbanski Film, to try to stop further deterioration by mold. Hill inadvertently became a textbook example of the problems faced in protecting and preserving independent art.

Although Gailiunas signed a contract to work in Columbia, Hill persuaded him to return to New Orleans in 2006. They rented a house on North Rampart Street in the Marginy neighborhood. On January 4, 2007, she was killed by an intruder, one of six murders that occurred in New Orleans during a twenty-four-hour period. Her case has not yet been solved.

In the aftermath of Hill's death, film archivists combined forces to ensure that her work would be preserved. The Film Preservation class of NYU's Moving Image Archiving and Preservation Program (MIAP) restored *Rain Dance* from original artwork and a VHS copy. Colorlab struck new preservation prints of her other films. Dwight Swanson of the Center for Home Movies and Kara Van Malssen, a Senior Research Scholar with MIAP, inventoried Hill's home movies. Funding from Harvard and the Women's Film Preservation Foundation helped pay for cleaning and restoring the Super 8 footage. Digital copies and 16mm blowups have been made.

The Harvard Film Archive offers new prints of ten of Hill's films, including *Scratch and Crow*. Several awards have been named in her honor: the Orphan Film Symposium's Helen Hill Award, Columbia's Indie Grits Film Fest Helen Hill Memorial Award, and the Halifax-based Linda Joy Media Arts Society Helen Hill Animated Award.

Paul Gailiunas has completed work on his wife's film *The Florestine Collection*, and has scheduled screenings in 2011.

Study of a River

View of the Hudson River. Courtesy of Peter Hutton

Peter Hutton, 1967. Silent, B&W, 1.33. 16mm. 15 minutes.

Credits: Photographed and edited by Peter Hutton.

Available: Canyon Cinema (http://canyoncinema.com/)

One of the more elusive titles on the Registry, *Study of a River* was filmed over a two-year period by Peter Hutton. Born in Detroit, Hutton shipped out as a merchant seaman when still a teenager. While stationed in the Pacific, he attended classes at the University of Hawaii. Drawn to the predominantly Eastern culture of the area, he took his first art class in Chinese brush painting. Later Hutton studied at the San Francisco Art Institute under experimental filmmaker Robert Nelson.

Hutton first used film to record performance art gatherings, then became intrigued with the idea of returning to the fundamentals of filmmaking. "Part of my cinematic influences came from those early formative art experiences, which were reductive and also contemplative," he said recently. In San Francisco, he turned away from the psychedelia that dominated experimental film at the time to focus on individual images, on the basic grammar of black-and-white film.

Moving to New York City, Hutton embarked on pieces modeled after actualities by the Lumières, also drawing from the pioneering urban films by Ralph Steiner, Jay Leyda, and Robert Flaherty.

In *Boston Fire* and *New York Portrait*, Hutton developed a style that returned to the earliest interests and techniques of film. Eschewing narrative and many of the theories of montage, Hutton presented viewers with pure imagery, meticulously composed landscapes with no explicit meaning beyond their beauty. The filmmaker would often dissolve to black between his shots, black leader helping to establish rhythm and pacing.

At first Hutton used a hand-wound Bolex 16mm camera, which limited his shots to about thirty seconds in length. Later, he purchased an Arriflex 16mm camera with a variable speed motor that enabled him to shoot 100- or 400-foot rolls without stopping. Hutton began by shooting almost exclusively in black-and-white reversal, a technically demanding process that gave his footage more contrast and crisper blacks than movies shot on negative. He also employed filters on his lenses—red to increase contrast, for example.

"There was a point in my life when I said I'm going to stay with black-and-white," he explained. "I just kept on going with it, twenty or thirty years. Black-and-white, particularly reversal, is much harder than color. Reversal is very unforgiving, it doesn't have the exposure latitude that negative has.

"But finally it became too difficult—labs were closing, I was having a harder time getting good prints. Also I thought it was time to open up. I mean the Hudson River School used color, and here I was in the same setting."

Study of a River feels personal, but paradoxically open. Hutton tries to recapture the experience of the first moviegoers, when everything filmed had a magical aura to it. At the same time, the filmmaker offers a sophisticated world view and a refined cinematic palette. The early cinema audience could be entranced by anything that moved, but Hutton does more than just prop a camera on a tripod and turn it on. His shots are the result of research, trial and error, of building an intimate knowledge of both location and technique.

Watching *Study of a River* is a luxurious experience: time is held in abeyance, content becomes paramount, meaning is equal to your appreciation of the images. "Not everyone gets it," Hutton admitted. "So much of Western culture is feeding us what we want. I think people are losing their ability to engage with things because they've become so passive. But when you allow the viewer the freedom to kind of sit and look, you're inviting them to bring their curiosity to the work."

Hutton's crisp compositions and unhurried pacing belie the effort behind his filmmaking. Like still photographer Henri Cartier-Bresson, Hutton is after a decisive moment, a perspective or insight that could define a landscape or situation. The only way to achieve that is to film relentlessly, in all seasons, at all times of day.

Hutton read a newspaper article about the Coast Guard Cutter *Sturgeon Bay*, for example, and rode along on one of its ice-breaking trips, obtaining several sweeping views of the Hudson shoreline. Years before a pedestrian walkway across the Poughkeepsie Bridge opened, Hutton had keys to the structure, enabling him to film overhead shots of the river. "It's like a 'seek and you shall find' philosophy," he said. "If you don't go out, you're not going to get it."

Other shots were more spontaneous, the result of having his camera with him during hikes through the Hudson Valley. That's how he came across an arresting image in which bolts of light dance across a pool of black. "I was shooting at four frames-per-second," he remembered. "There was a streetlight I framed just out of the puddle so it was catching the light. I was just experimenting, trying to see if I could get an exposure. When I got the image back, it made me start looking at the Hudson in that way, trying to get a more graphic feel to the light on the surface of the water."

In the completed film, the shot leads to a series of related images that evoke everything from Ralph Steiner's H_2O (1929, a Registry title) to video pixelation. Hutton describes his editing process as intuitive: he screens and rescreens his images until he finds relationships that form sequences. "It's not inordinately reconstructed," he said. "I usually take a year, something like that. I project, put it away, look at it again, project again until a sort of representational vocabulary forms. I don't want to disavow my responsibility to keep the viewer engaged. Even when you reduce film down to a very primary language of image, you still get caught up in the idea of, well, 'this is a film.' I work hard at what I do, I'm not just casual about it." (*Study of a River* took about six months to edit.)

As the original filmmakers did, Hutton uses motion to define his images and to punctuate his shots. What sets him apart from the actualities and travelogues of the past hundred years is his sense of humor. What appear to be projectiles in *Study of a River* are revealed as something entirely different with a ripple of water. A train suddenly changes the scale of a viewpoint.

Some of the best effects in *Study of a River* flow from Hutton's understanding of the frame. Many filmmakers treat the frame as if it contained all the information the viewer needs. To a Buster Keaton or Jacques Tati, the frame is an arbitrary dividing line that can be broken at will. Hutton remembered watching Tati's films with his father, who ran a film society in Detroit. "Tati was a really good influence for me, before I even thought about being a filmmaker," he said. "A lot of what I do is look beyond the frame, try to get into a mindset of anticipating what's going to happen."

The final shot of *Study of a River* sums up many of the qualities of Hutton's work, the serendipity of planning and chance. He filmed on a sub-zero day, capturing a rare phenomenon when snow blows across water like smoke. The reversal stock handles both the bright whites of the landscape and its black shadows. A shape breaks into the frame from the left, abstract, almost ominous, completely altering the meaning of the landscape.

Hutton's pieces work best as films, not as digital files, and for years he has resisted releasing them on DVD. He feels that digital is not as "warm" as film, but admits that in today's climate digital is inevitable. "If I were to make a high-def, good quality transfer, it might work, it would be closer to film," he said, "but I don't think many people care anymore about this stuff." (*Boston Fire* and *New York Portrait* appeared on a DVD release of *Wendy and Lucy*, a feature directed by a Bard teaching colleague, Kelly Reichardt.)

The size and weight of his equipment, the bulk and cost of stock, and the obstacles during travel have made filming more difficult. His latest project, *Three Landscapes*, includes footage from Detroit and from Ethiopia. On the first day of filming in Detroit, Homeland Security agents prohibited him from shooting an abandoned US Steel plant.

"I'm drawn to this industrial stuff, big structures, but now it's forbidden," he said. He encountered similar problems while filming in Budapest ("Why does he want to shoot that?" a Communist bureaucrat asked at an old industrial site. "We have a new textile factory.") and in Bangladesh, "the most stressful project I've ever worked on" and also his favorite.

Hutton continues to teach at Bard, where he is the Director of the Film and Electronic Arts Program. He has also worked as a cinematographer for other directors on features and documentaries.

Index of Films and Principal Filmmakers